4/09

D0085726

LIGHTING
the STAGE

Art and Practice

third edition

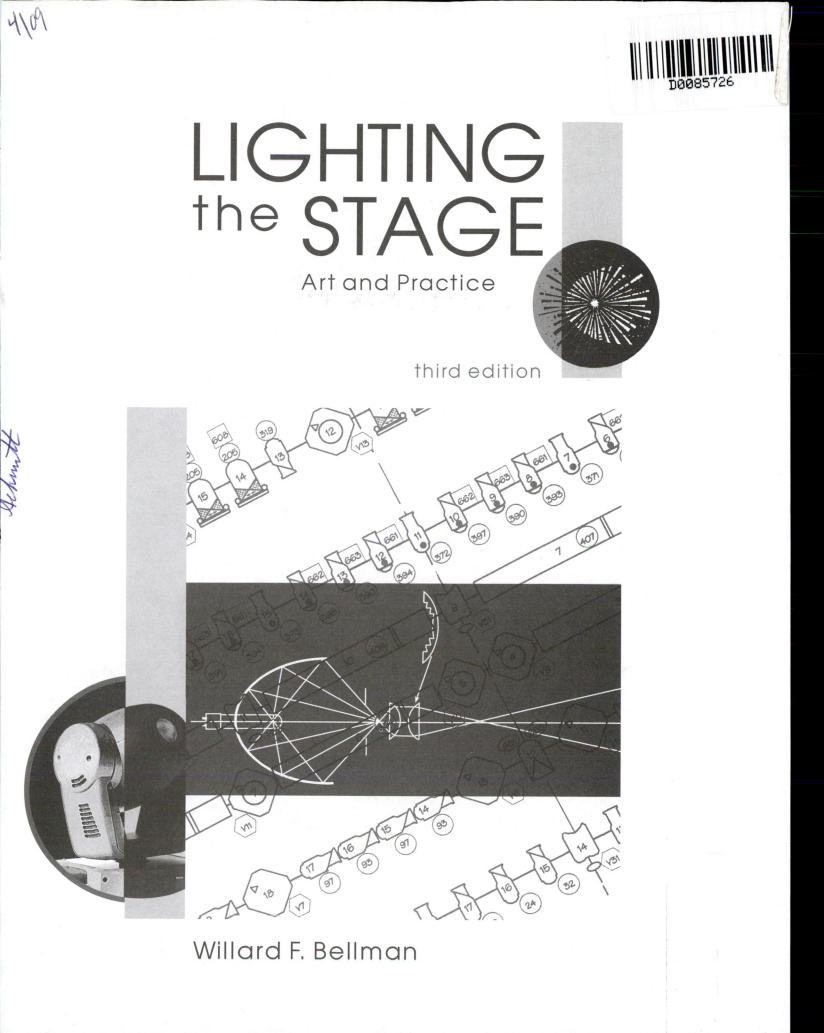

Willard F. Bellman

Copyright © 2001 by Willard F. Bellman.
All rights reserved.

The contents of this publication may not be
reproduced or duplicated in any way, either
in whole or in part, without the written
consent of the publisher.

ISBN: 0-911747-40-0

Second printing, May 2006.
Manufactured in the United States of America.

Broadway Press, Inc.
3001 Springcrest Dr.
Lousiville KY 40241

800-869-6372
www.broadwaypress.com

TABLE OF CONTENTS

PREFACE TO THIRD EDITION

This text is intended for the advanced student of stage lighting. It moves rapidly through basics and focuses on advanced concepts and technology. For example, there is no light plot illustrated here. A short summary reminds the reader of the purposes and lists the contents of a plot, but the details of making one are to be found in another text soon to be finished. In contrast, the artistic implications of the light plot are detailed.

Although many years have passed since the second edition appeared, the basic premise of this text remains the same: Lighting is an art, i.e., a part of one of the most human of all human endeavors. Within the limits of the legitimate theatre, lighting is a dependent art deriving its artistic unity via the import of the playscript as presented by the actors and the director. Other functions of lighting, while often of primary importance in its other many applications, remain secondary to its artistic raison d'être. Also, the ever growing technology of lighting remains in the role of "tool," always secondary to its art. To maintain this priority, the text evolves from philosophy to design to technology, generously interspersed with reminders of the purpose of those luminaires, complicated dimmers and computers—the creation of theatrical art.

A Note about Terminology

The first and second editions of this book sought with some success to urge the adoption the word "instrument" as generic for lighting equipment. However "instrument" carries implications of extreme precision, the engineer's micrometer or the surgeon's scalpel for instance, instruments which far exceed the precision of even the highest quality spotlight. Therefore this text joins the Illumination Engineering Society in its adoption of the word luminaire, for all manner of light producing equipment both in and out of the theatre. This term seems more appropriate, not being loaded with intimations of a high level of precision. Moreover, luminaire relates to the real purpose of these devices—the production and control of light.

Twenty-plus years is a vast time to survey in an effort to recall those who have contributed to this edition. However, one contributor stands out: Lou Erhardt, whose book, *Radiation Light and Illumination* served again and again to extricate me from blind forays into quantum theory and formulae too deep for my ancient math.

Acknowledgments

Special recognition is also due David Rodger for his role as editor/publisher. His knowledge of theatre and of the publishing world have made him the ideal person to guide this edition.

Below are listed a few of those who predominate in my memory although I am sure there are many more.

Robert Bell	Jarka Burian
Richard Devin	Charley Hulme
Ellen Jones	Cindy Limauro
Gordon Pearlman	Holly Sherman
Josef Svoboda	Joe Tawil
Anne Valentino	Ken Vannice

Many firms have also contributed:

A.C. Lighting	Altman
CASTLighting	Electronic Theatre Controls
Electronics Diversified	G.E. Lighting
GAM Products	High End/Flying Pig Systems Inc.
Laser Media	Lemieux Pilon Création inc.
Lycian	Martin
NSI Colortran	Oshio Theatre Magic
Osram Sylvania	Phase Four
Rosco	Strand Lighting
Strong International, Inc.	Vari-Lite
Wybron	

Chapter 1

LIGHTING AS ART

Writing About Design

Writers dealing with the various aspects of theatrical design have taken quite divergent courses:

1. Some assume that the process is so personal and varies so much from one artist to another that nothing useful can be said. This leaves the student wishing to develop his or her design talents entirely alone.

2. Some writers discuss the mechanics of the design process, organizing the studio, drafting, sculpting techniques, perspective drawing, etc., but leave the creative process out of the discussion. This does give the student designer valuable information about his/her studio and offers techniques for getting ideas expressed on paper or in three dimensions but the question, "How do I develop my designs?" remains unanswered.

3. Some discuss and illustrate past design successes, either theirs or the works of others, offering these as inspirational material for the student. Although two-dimensional illustrations of three dimensional design are often less than satisfactory, such discussions can be helpful, particularly in giving the student a vision of what can be accomplished. Unfortunately this approach is more helpful to the student designer of scenery or costumes than the designer of lighting because there is presently no effective way to display the artistic intricacies of lighting design except on the stage during a production. This approach is most helpful when adopted by a successful designer who can speak from vast experience and who is sufficiently skilled at writing to make word pictures of the lighting. Alas, such writers are rare indeed.

4. Yet other writers take a poetic/mystical approach to design. This too takes a high level of writing skill. Such writings can be found in the literature of theatre, for example, the works of Adolphe

Mechanics of the design process

Poetic/mystical approach to design

Appia, Edward Gordon Craig and Robert Edmund Jones. They are both inspirational and informative if read by those who are able to deal with the mysticism without either rejecting it out of hand or falling so deeply under the spell of its emotional qualities that they miss the core of useful information about designing.

Modern aesthetics explains artistic expression.

5. Another approach makes use of modern aesthetic writings which, unlike earlier writings in aesthetics, attempt to deal with how art expresses its "content" and, because these subjects are inextricably entwined, how artists achieve their artistic expression. This approach requires the development of a special vocabulary without which the discussion will have little meaning.

The approach of this text will follow the path through modern aesthetics but with frequent reference to the poetic/mystical approach. It will involve a short foray into the world of aesthetics to develop the necessary vocabulary.

Figure 1.1. *Nicholas Nickleby*. Dickens' story is centered on two contrasting worlds, the cruel world of the Yorkshire schools and the world of the social climbing self-absorbed upper crust. The general style of the visual production determined that abstract spaces would be made specific by acting and lighting—realism was not a consideration.

This photo illustrate how the lighting designer was able to establish contrast between these worlds, and to control the degree of attention each received, moment by moment. Note particularly how the highlighted figure in the background, while a secondary focus, still demands attention. This arrangement of lighting gives the designer precise control over the relative attention-getting power of each group of characters. Indeed, the lighting designer has the power of a director!

Scenes lit by Cindy Limauro. Produced at Carnegie Mellon Kresge Theatre. Directors, Gregory Lehane and Jed Allen Harris; set designer, Tony Mileto; costume designer, Cletus Anderson; lighting designers, Part I– Lauren Crasco, Part II– Cindy Limauro. Photo by Harold Corsini. Photos courtesy Cindy Limauro.

How Specific Can We Get?

Any discussion of a creative process, whether lighting design or musical composition, can only move so far without referring to a specific art work. Generalizations can only point the way. It comes down to this: Any aesthetic discussion of creative activity must stop at the point where the specifics of the show (or other art work) at hand begin. From that point forward, the concepts developed by the artist, or team of artists in the case of theatre, take over and can only be usefully discussed in their own terms. For example, we cannot discuss the specifics of a production of *Hamlet* unless we are thinking about a specific production done by a particular production team in a specific theatre situation. Thus this text cannot go beyond generalizations. It cannot tell you how to design your next production, only how to approach the problem. From there on, the chips are down; you must depend on your talent, skills, and past experience.

Generalizations about art are limited—we can only be specific about a particular production.

Figure 1.2. Lighting design by Cindy Limauro for a production of *Nicholas Nickleby*.

Figure 1.3 *Taming of the Shrew* (Shakespeare). Produced at the Telluride Repertory Theatre, Telluride Colorado on the Fred Shellman Memorial Stage. Producer, Suzan Beraza; director, James B. Nicola; setting and costumes, Jim Prodger; lighting, James Moody. Note the use of floor projections and the arrangement of lighting to focus on the actress. Photo by James Moody.

Defining the Art of Lighting

The art of painting creates images in paint on surfaces; music creates patterns in sound; sculpture creates three-dimensional forms, but what is the art of lighting? Much of the remainder of this text will be devoted to answering this question. For starters, here are some statements about lighting design which collectively suggest its nature:

Preliminary definition of lighting design

- Lighting art exists in time and space.
- Rhythm is of its essence.
- It, like all art, is about human emotions; whether it actually evokes them or not depends on the situation.
- It has its original artists (designers) and its interpreters (console operators)
- It is ephemeral—its notation and its technology tell you almost nothing about it as art.
- In live theatre, it is collaborative and depends on the moving, speaking actor for its artistic clarity.
- It can be an independent art.

If you set out to create the art of lighting, you are suggesting that you know what art is. This is a large, often erroneous, assumption. Here are some statements about art in general:

- Art is about "the beautiful."
- "Beauty is truth, truth beauty,"—that is all Ye know on earth, and all ye need to know. (John Keats, Ode On A Grecian Urn)
- Art is about human feelings.
- Art has no practical value.
- Artists are the last hope of civilization. (Peter Sellers)

Collaboration demands communication about art.

But, one might ask, "Why concern oneself about the definition of art? Why not just decide what art is for yourself and then do it?" One might well start out this way and make progress and, in some arts, one might succeed. But lighting is usually a collaborative art. That means you must share your developing creative thoughts with other artists; try to put into sentences and/or images what you and the other artists are trying to create. Without some knowledge of how communication about art gets accomplished, this gets frustrating. You will soon be forced to seek help from others who have tried to "explain" art in general and lighting in particular. In that moment, you have entered the field of *aesthetics*.

Aesthetics

Aesthetics is that branch of philosophy which deals with the human concept of "the beautiful," including art. Keats' quote above is a typical example of a poet's attempt to compress the philosophers' efforts into a single line. Philosophers, not famous for their brevity, have over past centuries, written voluminous tomes on this subject. They make interesting reading, but most of them are of little value to the would-be lighting artist.

More recently, philosophy has taken a different turn, one more useful to the artist. After at least two thousand years of posing the same philosophical questions and trying to answer them with diminishing results, twentieth century philosophers came to the conclusion that there was a need for some new questions. Instead of asking for the umpteenth time What is beauty? How is it related to truth or to morality?, Susanne Langer[1] asked "*How does art achieve its expressive quality? How does it mean?*"

With this, a philosophy of art that is useful to artists came into being. Langer's discussions make the jump from "How does art express itself?" to "How is art created in the first place?"—The very job you, the lighting artist, are trying to do. Even better, Langer and her cohorts have provided us with a useful vocabulary for talking and writing about art—just what we need for our collaborative sessions with other artists.

New vocabulary for talking and writing about art

Ms. Langer, like all other philosophers who try to explain "meaning" as it relates to art, found herself dealing not only with *how art means* but also *what it means*. At that point she encountered the ages-old problem of the relationship between art and human emotions. We commonly hear in the theatre, for example, that theatrical art "evokes human emotions" or that good acting "makes the audience feel what the character is feeling." Yet we almost instinctively know that there is a vast difference between, say, experiencing sorrow at a play and experiencing it in life. Mrs. Langer went straight to the heart of this conundrum by making a clear distinction: art is *about* human feelings as opposed to *expressing* them. One learns about sorrow at the theatre, one experiences it in life—a distinction with important implications for both actors and designers.

Art is about *human emotions.*

Having clarified the difference between considering art to be an *expression* of human emotions and seeing it as being *about* them, Langer was ready to move on to a more fundamental question: How do art and life relate? Is art part of life? Outside of the normal stream of life? Irrelevant?

All of these views have been argued by philosophers who found each to be apt in some situations and useless in others. However it seems clear that *art is a way of dealing with life*.

Art is a way of dealing with life.

In the next few pages we will seek to build up a background of concepts and terms that will enable us to phrase answers to such questions as:

- How does theatre, as art, relate to life?
- How does lighting relate to theatre?
- How does lighting "mean?"
- Where does one begin a lighting design?
- How can the lighting interrelate with the rest of theatrical art?
- How can I know I am on the right artistic track?
- What are the various approaches to lighting design? How do they relate to the nature of the production?

Just a warning: We are going to find that many of these questions are far more complex than they first appear and that they and their answers—if answers turn out to be possible— are based on assumptions that may turn out to be only partly true. They will not all apply to every design job, nor will a knowledge of their "answers," guarantee the success of any design.

Also, the following discussion is theoretical with only a few practical examples. However, the next chapter, "The Designer's Variables," will illustrate the application of many of these aesthetic concepts in some detail and with special emphasis on the art of stage lighting.

---

[1] Susanne Langer, *Philosophy in a New Key* (Cambridge, MA: Harvard University Press, 1942) and Susanne Langer, *Feeling and Form* (New York: Charles Schribner's Sons, 1953).

We begin with a somewhat deeper investigation of the relationship between art and life using Langer's thoughts as our guide:

Two Ways of Dealing with Experience

What we learn about life we first learn through our senses. We learn that bees can sting and cats can scratch most emphatically by experiencing stings and scratches. Having had the experience, we can recall it and avoid the unpleasantness a second time because we have made it into a *symbol*, a mental record that allows us to think about the experience without experiencing it again and again. Fortunately there are other ways of gaining many of life's experiences without going through the dangers of direct experience and these methods are the very heart of our discussion to come. Nevertheless most of the vast fund of human experience had its start in someone's sensory experience.

We go through life converting sensory data into symbols and then combining these symbols into more complex symbolic structures which are the material of thoughts. According to Ms. Langer, the process of *symbolic transformation*—making thoughts from sensory experiences—is what enables us to think. But humans are not merely creatures that cre-

Figure 1.4. Projected scenery for *Lucia di Lammermoor* (Donizetti). Design by Annaliese Corrodi.

ate and interrelate symbols; they are also somehow compelled to share the results of these activities. Sometimes we share the results of thoughts that examine the parts of an idea or object. This is called *analytical*. At other times we share experiences without taking them apart because we cannot do so without ruining the experience. This is called *experiential*.

The way we do the sharing depends on the nature of what is to be shared: Sharing analytical activities results in *discursive* expression; sharing experiential activities produces *nondiscursive* communications. Note that this is a special definition of the word discursive. It refers to the practice of dealing with data sequentially instead of presenting it as a whole. For example, most expressions in words are discursive: the ideas flow out in a sequence. However the use of words in poetry is usually nondiscursive—one must absorb the entire poem to perceive its meaning.

Discursive and non-discursive communication

Figure 1.5. *Candide* (musical adaptation by Leonard Bernstein, music and Richard Wilbur, lyrics). Produced by the Southern Illinois Theatre Department and the School of Music at Southern Illinois University, Carbondale, Illinois in the McLeod Theatre. Director, Timothy Fink; scenery, Christopher DePriest; costumes, Laura Thudium; lighting, James Moody. Note the use of directional light to produce a full-stage spectacle with the emphasis down stage. Background projections fill in the picture. Photo by James Moody.

Figure 1.6. *Brother to Dragons* by Robert Penn Warren as produced at Trinity Square Repertory. Director, Adrian Hall; scenery, Eugene Lee; costumes, Laura Crow; lighting Richard Devin. This is a single-source lighting design which the blocking has utilized to focus the characters down center. Photo by Richard Devin.

Discursive Discourse

When we discuss what we have discovered by *analysis*—i.e., we take the object of our study apart mentally, if not actually, and express our findings about the parts—it is called discursive discourse. For example, a salesman might hand you a sample of a new type of spotlight hoping you will like it and order a number of them. As you examine the new toy, you might make some notes, mental or actual. Finally, you might write the whole thing up to support your request that the business office purchase of some of the spotlights. As you prepare your notes, you would organize them in some logical manner for the reader, perhaps beginning at the front of the light and working your way back, comparing the new equipment with the antiques you are presently using.

Note what has been done: You have, in an organized manner, looked at the object one part at a time and reported your findings. The emphasis of your report will be on the parts and how they work together. The report itself will be organized sequentially.

This is the essence of analysis and its resulting discursive communication. It is sequential and focuses on parts and their relationship to each other; *it explains things*.

Discursive discourse is a powerful tool. It can explain things of the greatest complexity giving the recipient a clear picture of the arrangement of the parts and how they relate to each other. It can, for example explain the intricacies of a complicated machine like the Space Shuttle, or explain the principles of quantum mechanics. Discursive discourse can take place using language, using symbols such as in mathematics or chemistry, or using the form of drawings such as working plans for a stage setting.

Nondiscursive Discourse

But we all know that there are things in life that do not willingly submit to analysis. We can take them apart but having done so, we are left with the feeling that more has been lost than gained. Analyzing a butterfly comes to mind, or a sunset, or the feeling of being in love. Entomologists may dissect butterflies, physicists explain the optical phenomena of sunsets, and psychologists write tomes on love but none of these will have the same impact on us as the work of an artist.

Yet we do experience these things in life and share them with each other. But not by analysis—not by explanation but by experiencing them as symbols which present the experience *as a whole* instead of subjecting it to analysis. This is the world of the arts, of poets, dramatists, painters—and of lighting designers—along with, of course, people in love. Philosophers call this mode of communication *presentational*.

The reason we feel compelled to place quotes around "explain" and "meaning" when applying them to art is that "explanation" belongs in the world of the discursive. "Meaning" suggests discursive or analytical activity. While it is relatively easy to separate the meaning of discursive expression from its style or form, this is not the case with art. An attempt to separate form from "content" of an artistically successful poem will lead to frustration; its "meaning" or "content" is inextricably fused into its form. In the next chapter as we attempt to understand how lighting design affects the audience we will find that "meaning" and "content" are words we may wish to avoid using in this context. *The better term is import which does not suggest that the art work and what it seeks to express are separable or that analysis will clarify it.* Import does however effectively refer to that nondiscursive core which the art work seeks to communicate by allowing the recipient to experience it.

The term *import* does a better job of helping us understand a work of art than do words like *meaning* and *content*.

We now move to an examination of how art works present their import and from there to the specifics—how the art of lighting functions as a presentational symbol.

Virtual Worlds

"Virtual" has several meanings. The one we are concerned with might be best compared to the now-common concept of "virtual reality." This is a "reality" created inside a computer and displayed to the observer by means of special headgear that shuts out most of the person's perception of the real world around him or her and replaces it with what the computer displays—a non-real set of stimuli accepted voluntarily by the person wearing the headpiece. The viewer knows that what is seen and heard is not part of the real world, and that it has been specially created for his or her reception.

In a different and not quite so all-inclusive way, artists have been doing this for centuries. They create *virtual* worlds—worlds of metaphors—worlds where the audience is invited to make comparisons, to infer similarities and differences, thereby to discover the import of the scene. Like all arts, but even more conspicuously than most, the theatre deals in virtuality:

Theatre creates virtual worlds.

Consider Shakespeare's *Macbeth*: As he moves toward certain defeat and death, he utters:

Tomorrow and tomorrow and tomorrow…

During this soliloquy the arts of directing, setting, costume design, sound—*and particularly the art of the lighting designer*—conspire to metaphorically build a virtual paradox: Either Macbeth is a villain, a bloody-handed murderer or he is tragic figure, a flawed but magnificent human being.

Just as everyday logic does not apply to what may be seen and heard through the headpiece of a virtual reality device, neither does it apply to the virtual worlds created by the arts, especially theatre. Time and space, light and darkness, logic and illogic, and even good and bad have become metaphors devised to present the vision of the artist. We may come away from a successful production of *Macbeth* somehow understanding that Shakespeare's metaphorical paradox about Macbeth has dealt with *both* his evil and his magnificence—and we have come to understand something about the nature of mankind by experiencing it that we could have never understood by way of explanation.

Logic doesn't apply to the virtual world of the arts.

Adolphe Appia, a 19-20th century stage designer and theatre aesthetician, compared the virtual world of art to that of the dream. He was particularly impressed by the *freedom of the dream*, actually much the same as the freedom of virtual reality, which opens almost unending possibilities to the artist's creativity. Literal minds are left far behind. Artistic freedom allows the artist, poet, stage or lighting designer, to explore the depths of his or her imagination, to dare to imagine things the world of logic might reject. Richard Wagner, the great German operatic composer of the late 19th century gives Hans Sachs in *Die Meistersinger* this revealing line:

> *Believe me, mans' truest illusion is oft in dreams revealed!*[2]

If the designer is encouraged to imagine with the freedom of the dream, what magic may ensue?

A play in production should be, in the best of possible theatre, a virtual world into which the audience is invited by its artists, *there to experience what can not be explained—by way of "truest illusion."*

A 4-D Art with the Fluidity of Music

All arts enjoy virtuality but lighting enjoys special freedoms. It can have the fluidity of music and, even more, exists in the four-dimensional world of space and time. The designer's challenge is to envision lighting within these vast horizons.

Where Does the Designer Start?

All art, including stage lighting, must begin with a *sense of creative direction*. This may come in a flash of insight (in a "dream?") or after hours or days of research or muddling about. Nevertheless, if the effort is to proceed in the direction of art, there must be a goal. It can have many names, e.g., concept, idea, artistic goal, commanding form, vision, through line, and more. Whatever the lighting designer chooses to call it, if indeed he or she calls it anything, it will be the measure of his or her work. Of course, if the theatre's goal is to produce a simple comedy, a spectacle, or merely a money-making show, the Lighting designer's goal isn't likely to have much artistic potential. Still, a goal must exist. Without some guiding objective even the most crass of show business efforts will founder from lack of organization, its lighting included.

But our course is loftier than this and we will proceed with the assurance that it is always easier to scale down the goal-seeking effort to fit simpler theatrical pieces than it is to scale up a poorly developed goal to strive for art.

Artists explore things that logical minds reject.

Art begins with creative direction.

---

[2] Wagner, Richard. *Die Meistersinger* as quoted in Appia, *La Musique et la Mise en Scene*. Tr, W. Bellman. Original: "Glaubt mir, des Menshens wahrster Wahn wird ihm Traume aufgethan." Emphasis in translation by wb.

Concept

Art begins with a dream and, when it succeeds, it inspires yet other dreams. This metaphorical assertion simply reminds us of those moments in the theatre (or art gallery or concert hall, or…) when we felt that we were somehow given the freedom to experience a new and wonderful insight, one to be long remembered but never really described. A lighting designer's concept must assure its creator that it will become part of this audience experience as the play evolves. To do this, the designer first must first enjoy the freedom Appia described—and must reject nothing, however outrageous it may seem to a logical mind. Then, having ventured to the farthest reaches of the imagination, in the very next moment the designer turns critic. Can this dream of mine lead to lighting that will make the play more expressive, more emphatic? Or does it merely promise to illuminate the stage floor? Does it raise the art to a higher level or simply avoid being in the way?

These cycles of dreaming and evaluating may repeat over and over in the designer's mind but ultimately, if the design is ever to succeed, there must come an image of the lighting that passes the "dream test" and encourages the designer to move ahead.

From dreamer to critic

Moving from Art to Technique

As the artist's design concept grows clearer, the need to externalize takes over. Artists, after all, are communicators. They are impelled to share their insights. To even begin to put the lighting concept down as plans and specifications and to share it with the director and other designers means change. All artists' visions change as they move from concept to studio, but the lighting designer faces even greater hurdles than most. He or she must deal with such things as electrical engineering, building and safety laws, control technology, optics and the psychology and physiology of human vision, not to mention the demands of other artists and the director as they react to the sketchy bits of information they are able to derive from preliminary discussions. Therefore the changes may be massive. The final product may, at least to the designer, seem far removed from the original dream. This leads some lighting artists to argue that original concept means little; what counts is what evolves as the lighting is put together first on paper, then on the stage—a notion that either underestimates the power of the artist's original dreams or, sadly, describes his or her willingness to let expediency overcome artistic ideals. One must take refuge in the assurance that change is the essence of creative activity, but change *within the realm of the original dream*. If the art work is not changing, it is stagnating and headed for the trash bin.

The artwork must grow and change or die.

We now move ahead to the designer's next and more concrete phase, converting the general concept (the product of the dream) into the lighting plot. Although the plot itself is almost completely technical to an outsider (and even to the technical director, the crew chief and the crew itself), it is to the designer a set of plans that will enable him or her to bring the concept to fulfillment by cueing the lighting once the plot has been converted into actual equipment organized and ready for use.

Chapter 2

FROM CONCEPT TO CUES

Application of Aesthetic Concepts to Lighting Design

This chapter serves three purposes:

1. It introduces the reader to some of the most commonly used techniques for lighting the stage, particularly for dramatic productions.
2. It places aesthetic terms introduced in Chapter 1 into practical context using them to explain how lighting equipment arrangements and cues can have artistic effect.
3. It moves our description of the process of lighting a show forward through the technical interlude of mounting the equipment to the point where the designer is ready to create the cues

We begin with a study of some of the "commonplaces of lighting," schemes of lighting design that almost inevitably come to the designer's mind as he or she mentally lights the show.

"Stock" lighting schemes

The reader should be aware that this list is in no way exhaustive; each designer will contrive new ways of lighting whatever production is at hand. This chapter merely includes some of those most commonly used, indeed these are so common that one might call them the "stock in trade" of the lighting designer.

The artistic import of any of these schemes can vary from negligible to major. For instance, a technique such as sidelighting can be used in a particular show exclusively for its utilitarian value—to make the show more visible and interesting. In another production the identical lighting setup might be cued in a way that fuses it with the acting, the directing and the script making a major contribution to the artistic impact of the production.

Design should never repeat what has been done in the past.

Although the following techniques are the "commonplaces" of lighting design, no designer should adopt them simply because they are frequently used. Design, when artistically effective, is guided by insight, not slavish repetition of what has worked before. The designer's vision, blended with that of the playwright and the director, will form the designer's artistic goal for the lighting. Only if these techniques promise to bring that goal into being, should they should be adopted.

Light and the Actor

The essence of theatre is the moving, speaking actor who inhabits a virtual world into which the audience enters. If we are referring to live performance (legitimate theatre), the actors perform their magic in the immediate presence of the audience and actor-audience interaction is part of the art. In motion picture and television this interaction is lost (save for an occasional and rather artificial "studio-audience" situation). Nevertheless, from the point-of-view of the lighting designer, the manner in which the audience views the actor is vital whether the situation is "live" or not.

A beginners' list of functions of lighting almost always begins with "visibility." If the actors cannot be seen, radio drama is the result. But *being visible and being effectively lighted are two vastly different things*. Artistically effective lighting helps to determine how the audience views the actor's character—a matter vital to the art of the theatre—mere visibility will suffice for janitorial services on stage.

"Designed" visibility

Directional Light and Three Dimensionality

The majority of objects observed in life are three dimensional i.e., they have thickness as well as height and width. The degree to which this third dimension is perceived depends on lighting except for cases where the observer is close enough to sense three dimensionality using the focusing apparatus of the eyes (accommodation). Practically, this means that the observer must be quite close to the object (say, under twenty feet) if the object is the size of a human being or smaller. Perspective will aid in sensing three dimensionality of large objects at greater distances, espe-

Perception of the third dimension usually depends on the lighting.

Sensing three dimensions

Technology of Directional Light

Directional lighting is usually produced on stage by using relatively narrow-beam sources such as spotlights or beam projectors so positioned that they produce shadows clearly visible to the audience. The most important of these shadows will normally be those on the actors' faces. Only rarely will a broad source such as a floodlight, suffice. Directional lighting is arranged so that shadows produced by the principle luminaires are carefully protected from being washed out by the light from other luminaires. See "Key and Fill Lighting" below. Both intensity and color may be used to make the directionality of the lighting evident. Much of the art of lighting depends on the skill of the designer in arranging directional sources so that the shadow patterns produced are both effective and appropriate to the artistic intent of the scene.

cially if they are made up of planes and angles.

Given these exceptions, the main determinate of our perception of the three dimensionality of objects is directional light (Figure 2.1). The shadows cast by this light define the thickness of the object aiding visual perspective and the focusing of the eyes in defining the shape of the object.

Directional light determines three-dimensionality

On stage in almost all but the smallest theatres perception of three dimensionality depends mostly on light and shadows—the result of directional light.

Figure 2.1. Directional Light. Dickens' *Nicholas Nickleby* (Part II). Note the strong orientation to stage left produced by the sidelighting from that location plus the generally quarter-left facing of the actors. Produced at Carnegie Mellon Kresge Theatre. Directors, Gregory Lehane and Jed Allen Harris; set designer, Tony Mileto; costume designer, Cletus Anderson; lighting designers, Part I– Lauren Crasco, Part II– Cindy Limauro. Photo by Harold Corsini. Courtesy Cindy Limauro.

Technology of Nondirectional Lighting

Nondirectional light is usually produced by wide-source equipment such as border lights or large floodlights arranged so that any shadows produced are canceled by other luminaires. An exception to the use of wide-source equipment is the common professional theatre practice of creating a "wash" of light on the entire front of the stage by a battery of spotlights mounted low on a balcony rail and focused straight toward the stage. When properly angled and focused, any shadows produced by an individual spotlight are washed away by light from those adjacent to it. The use of spotlights makes it possible to have the flood of nondirectional light without noticeable spill light onto the proscenium arch or into the house—something borderlights could not do.

Directionality Depends on the Way Light Is Used

All light has direction; at less than astronomical distances, it travels in straight lines from its source until it strikes some reflecting, refracting or absorbing object. Directionality, however, depends on how the light is observed. When it strikes an object, it casts a shadow. If the shadow is visible to the observer in such a way that it reveals the 3-D nature of the object, the light may be termed "directional." If the shadow is invisible to the observer, because it is hidden from view or because it is overridden by other light, the light is not directional for that observer. In theatrical terms this means that any light which casts a shadow that is clearly visible to the audience is directional and any that has its shadow hidden or washed out is nondirectional.

Directional light

The only exception is the visible light beam. If the air is filled with smoke or haze so that the beam of light itself can be seen, a strong sense of directionality will be present even if the light casts no visible shadows. Powerful follow spotlights often produce this effect even without the addition of haze to the air in the theatre. However there is a caveat: Although the audience will be very aware of the direction of the beam, they may not be able to use that directionality to make out a performer's facial expression. For many in the audience, the shadows produced will be invisible and the performer will appear "flat."

Nondirectional Light

Light that illuminates, but doesn't appear to have a direction also has its functions on stage: It is the choice of the designer wherever he or she wants to obscure the three-dimensional nature of an onstage object. For example, a painted drop or cyclorama requires nondirectional light to obscure the minor imperfections in the base material. Also, in theatres short of spotlights, nondirectional light may be used as fill light (see "Key and Fill" below) making it possible to use the few spotlights available for key lighting.

Nondirectional light can hide imperfections in scenery.

The Actor As Three-Dimensional Object

It is a fact of life that all human beings are three-dimensional, they have height, width and thickness. Moreover much of what we as observers determine about a person comes through our eyes and depends on the shape, position, and movement of various parts of the person's body. If we cannot make out these details either because of darkness or because shadowless lighting obscures them, we do not get the information. What is true in life is even more true on stage where the nature of the character being created by the actor depends even more heavily on our seeing that actor, particularly his or her face, in three dimensions. If we are observing a dancer or a mime, our perception of character and, indeed, plot too, depends entirely on how we see the whole body.

Plasticity—the Objective of Key/Fill Lighting

"Plasticity"   *Plasticity* (also sometimes "modeling light" or "modeling") refers to the audience' perception of the actor in three dimensions, particularly the actor's face. In all but the most intimate of theatres plasticity depends on the directional lighting provided for the actor. This is usually provided by *key* and *fill* light.

Key light   *Key light* (Figure 2.2) is the directional light that creates the most conspicuous pattern of highlights and shadows on the actors' face (and body if the costume affords this possibility). This pattern of highlights and shadows makes it possible for the audience to sense the direction of the light.

Clearly, key light has potential symbolic value i.e., it can become part of the symbolic structure of the production. For example, in Shaw's *Saint Joan* a high-angle key light can become a symbol of Joan's faith as she renounces her previous denial of her visions and thereby condemns herself to the stake. It is hard to imagine Hamlet's *to be or not to be* speech without strong modeling on the actor's face produced by a set of specially angled key lights designed and cued to follow him as he moves through the scene. Thus the designer's consideration of key lighting—a major part of his or her design process—must grow out of his or her perception of the import being built up by the actors and the director as the action progresses.

Fill light   Fill light literally fills in the shadows cast by the key light making the details within the shadows visible. The brightness ratio between the highlights formed by the key light, and the shadows illuminated only by the

Contrast   fill light, is known as the *contrast* of the lighting. It defines the plasticity of the lighting at that particular moment. Designers often refer inter-

Key/fill ratio   changeably to the "contrast of the lighting" or the "key/fill ratio." What-

Technology of Key/Fill Lighting

Historically, key/fill lighting was provided by dividing the stage into areas capable of being covered by a single spotlight which provided the key lighting and by flooding the stage with nondirectional lighting from borderlights and footlights for the fill light. This system had the advantage of getting the most effective use out of relatively rare spotlights in an era before they became the main means of lighting actors.

Modern key/fill lighting is accomplished entirely with spotlights used in pairs normally of equal power, one serving as key and the other as fill. The luminaires are angled to illuminate the same area of the stage which is termed an "acting area." These acting areas are carefully blended into each other so that an actor crossing from one to another receives essentially the same key/fill lighting over the entire movement. Refer to Chapter 10 for details on arranging acting areas.

Ideally each acting area luminaire should be separately controllable. Thus either can serve as key or fill depending on relative brightness. This doubles the range of possible contrast settings and makes possible a wide variety of subtle color changes in the acting area lighting.

In special circumstances an additional luminaire or even two may be added to selected areas to further increase the range of lighting angles and/or color changes available to the designer.

ever the term, this combination of lighting on the actors' face and/or body comprises one of the most powerful of the designer's variables.

The Designer's Eye for Plasticity

Throughout the design process the designer must attend to plasticity. He or she must maintain sufficient shadow detail on faces and or figures to enable the audience to see their facial expressions. Where entire bodies are the expressive elements, the audience must see the details of those bodies well enough to respond kinesthetically to their actions.

Keeping the lighting plastic involves careful attention to key/fill and also to background/actor contrasts. Figure 2.2 shows one of the almost infinite variety of key/fill possibilities possible on an actor's face. Obviously in any given lighting situation, there is a limited but rather large number of possible variations available for experimentation. Thus the design of key/fill lighting depends not on trial and error but on the "vision" of the designer, his or her capability to imagine the lighted face or figure in a way that best contributes to the dramatic value of the scene. Clearly, this is an extension of the vision-critique process. The designer first envisions the lighting and then turns critic to evaluate the results. Finally the designer uses his or her technical skills to create the envisioned effect on stage. Fortunately the process of tweaking the contrast settings is usually fairly simple and contrast-controlling cues are subject to repeated change far into the rehearsal process.

Using a Single Luminaire

Any acting area can be easily reduced to a single-luminaire area by adjusting the controls if separate control is available for each luminaire. The result will be an exaggeration of the effects listed above but with the caveat that the actor must play into the light or lose much of the expressiveness of one side of his or her face. Given a scene that calls for this extreme plasticity, a single luminaire can have the dramatic power of a special while remaining part of the acting area scheme for use with other luminaries as needed.

Plasticity is vital except in the smallest theatres.

Figure 2.2. Key Light. The strong, shadow-producing light coming from the actor's right and well above his eye level is the key light. It establishes the direction of the scene, aided by the slight stage right facing of the actor. Scene from Shakespeare's *Macbeth:* "Your castle is surprised, your wife and babes savagely slaughter'd." Actor, Gilman Rankin. Lighting by author. Photo by M. Herbst.

Key/Fill and Dramatic Impact

Envisioning key/fill contrasts is part of the design process.

An examination of key/fill lighting used in dramatic scenes reveals a wide range of potentialities for artistic import. *All of these depend on the actor and ultimately the script for fulfillment* but the contribution of lighting, given this fulfillment, can be powerful. Below are some general "rules of thumb." Note that in each case the greater the contrast between the acting area and its surroundings, the greater the dramatic impact.

- As contrast between key and fill increases so does the potential for dramatic impact.
- A scene being built toward a climax by means of acting and directing techniques can be heightened even more by also increasing key/fill contrast. Pacing of the key/fill changes to fit the development of the scene is the very essence of such builds.

Crossing the key

- Adjusting dimmer settings to change the key light to a fill and vice-versa is a powerful way to aid in the giving and taking of the scene by the actors. This dimmer change is sometimes known as "crossing the key."

The vertical and horizontal angles of key/fill lighting also can have import:

- The greater the vertical angle of the acting area lighting, up to where it becomes top lighting, the greater the potential for dramatic impact.
- To a lesser but still significant degree, increasing the horizontal angle past the normal 38° (as measured from the centerline of the stage) also suggests greater dramatic tension.

Color in Acting Area Lighting

Acting area color

The technology of color in acting areas, including the very important effect on color when incandescent sources are dimmed, is detailed in Chapter 10. The artistic impact of color can vary from almost zero to powerful, However the effect is fleeting because of the physiological phenomenon which causes the eye to rapidly adapt to a color environment and cease to respond to it. The designer must take this into account. Frequent changes in the color environment are one solution to this problem.

The use of complementary or related tints in acting areas will afford the designer a wide range of possible color shifts. Shifting from predominately warm or cool colors to the opposite can have strong dramatic effect if coordinated with the action of the play.

Color and Plasticity

Complementary tints afford flexibility.

The plasticity of acting area lighting may be enhanced by the subtle use of color. (See Chapter 10 for the technology of this process.) If the left and right components of each acting area are fitted with complementary tints, the effect will be to create a warm side, a cool side and a portion of the face which exhibits the combination of the two colors. This increases plasticity by adding color contrast to the shadow contrast present on the actors' faces. The same effect will prevail on the actors' bodies if costumes will allow it. The use of related tints in acting area luminaires will have the same but lessened effect.

These adjustments in color offer the designer a chance to enhance plasticity without increasing shadow contrast.

Designers must take care that they do not inadvertently destroy the modeling effect of acting area color by dimming. Even a reduction of only 3 or 4 points on the usual dimmer scale will shift many cool acting area tints to warm by removing most of the blue light from an incandescent source. (This is known as "color shift" and will be discussed in detail later.) If dims of this magnitude or more are necessary—and they often are—the designer should add other sources (usually sidelighting) to maintain modeling. This color shift will not occur if non-incandescent sources are in use.

Red shift can eliminate color differences

Sidelighting as a Designer's Variable

Sidelighting is another major type of actor lighting. Unlike acting area lighting, it covers much larger areas of the stage than an acting area, usually an entire "slice" of acting space reaching from stage left to stage right and perhaps six to ten feet deep. Designs for dance lighting and sometimes for musicals often specify that the sidelight beams pass straight across the acting area. However the designer will often find that "front-sidelights" are more useful. These are luminaires mounted so that their beams cross the acting space from above the eye level of the actors and somewhat downstage of the acting space they illuminate. (Figure 2.3) Both varieties of sidelighting serve many purposes:

Front-sidelighting may be more effective than 90 degree sidelighting.

Adjunct to Acting Area Lighting

Sidelights adjusted to augment a row of acting areas reaching across the stage can add yet another range of variables for the designer. These lights can be added to the actors' faces and bodies or even used to replace one side of each acting area with yet stronger key lighting, possibly of a different color. See Figure 2.4.

Sidelighting can also aid in the design of cues. If there is rapid action moving over wide areas of the stage and the designer wishes to carefully control key/fill ratios on these moving actors, cueing area-to-area changes may be

Figure 2.3. Sidelighting. The strong shadow pattern creates a powerful orientation to stage right. In this case the sidelight is also located somewhat above eye level improving the modelling of the actor's face. Scene from Shakespeare's *Macbeth*: "Bring thou this fiend of Scotland and within my sword's length set him..." Actor, Gilman Rankin; lighting by author. Photo by M. Herbst.

Sidelighting can cover actors moving too fast for follow focus cues.

Figure 2.4. Acting Area Plus Sidelighting. The key/fill ratio has increased but almost all of the actor's face remains visible. Every shadow delineates his expression. Scene from Shakespeare's *Macbeth*: "O, I could play the woman with mine eyes and braggart with my tongue…" Actor, Gilman Rankin; lighting by author. Photo by M. Herbst.

impractical. Any changes that will be effective will be too fast for subtlety and very hard to execute. If sidelighting can be arranged so that it spills invisibly into the wings, it will remain essentially invisible to the audience until an actor moves into it. This creates the equivalent of a set of acting areas which turn themselves on and off as the actors pass through them but without attracting any attention to themselves. This may leave the regular acting areas available to the designer for use as additional accents.

Such use of sidelighting needs the cooperation of the director. Unless the actors are carefully blocked, there will be times when one actor's shadow will block light for another actor. The solution is to move one of the actors either down- or upstage of the other.

Sidelighting Emphasizes the Whole Figure

Although acting area lighting normally strikes the entire actor, it is designed primarily to light faces. Sidelighting is the equivalent of a much "larger paint brush." It tends to place emphasis on the entire figure of the actor or actress. This is the reason it is so effective for lighting dance where the figure is usually more important than the face.

This "broad brush" characteristic of sidelighting can be valuable to the designer as a supplement to acting area lighting. In the case of musicals and operas where dance is an integral part of the show, the combination of acting area and sidelighting makes it possible to shift from lighting faces to lighting figures, or to have any combination the designer wishes.

Technology of Sidelight

Sidelighting is normally provided by ellipsoidal reflector spotlights capable of precise shuttering to keep spill light out of the house. These luminaires are normally circuited separately stage right and left and also separated by color.

Colors chosen will usually be stronger than the acting area colors but part of the same color scheme. See Chapters 10 and 11 for details.

A Caution

As more light sources are added to the stage, the designer may be in danger of washing out most of the shadows needed for plasticity. Simply bringing in the sidelights on top of existing acting area lighting may turn out to do exactly this. The solution is to balance the brightness of the two types of lighting to maintain good modeling.

Building a Scene

This is a directorial concept wherein a number of attention-heightening techniques are used to bring audience interest to a climax. This is usually done in conjunction with a climax written into the script although a scene may be built entirely by staging techniques—a practice common in revue and musical shows. Directors of revues and musicals use such techniques as larger and more rapid actor movement, louder voices and the addition of more moving figures on the stage. Lighting can be used to further heighten the build by cueing in more rapid and more drastic changes, adding brightness, color, and movement if automated luminaire equipment is available. As such a sequence of cues builds to its end, the designer may be tempted to specify an "all to full" cue shortly before "curtain" is called. However he or she should proceed with caution; this tactic may also destroy the plasticity of the lighting by blanking out all shadow detail leaving the audience with a last impression of a mass of blank-faced performers. A well designed "build" cue requires the careful adjustment of contrast on faces and bodies—sometimes even the removal of some luminaires from the cue. The goal is to leave the audience with an image of the most sparkling stage picture possible but with faces and figures clearly defined. Once designed, such cues are as easy to effect on a modern console as a single preset.

Note that dramatic climaxes are often built by an almost opposite technique. Shakespearean soliloquies are good examples. For example: The focal character takes the stage using the techniques of acting and directing to render the other figures onstage insignificant. The actor uses his or her voice and gestures to command attention and focus. An effective way for lighting to assist this build is, paradoxically, to *eliminate* sources leaving the key figure almost isolated on the stage but with excellent plasticity. If the character moves as the scene builds, the lighting should seem to move with him or her as though it is a sort of "aura" attached to the figure. Although this kind of build may involve many cues, none of them should call attention to the lighting—they should seem to "emanate" from the character. Either increasing or decreasing the intensity of the lighting on the main figure may be effective depending on the nature of the scene.

Specials

A "Special" is a luminaire planned by the designer for a single purpose in a production such as the special lighting to build to a climax as discussed above. Although it is quite possible that additional uses will be discovered for this luminaire, its location, focus and other adjustments will be determined exclusively by the original purpose.

Working toward a climax

Adding more lights is not always a good idea.

Avoid destroying plasticity

Building by taking away light

Specials have but one design purpose.

Specials are the designer's most precise lighting. As such they most intensely reflect his or her approach to the scene. They tend to come first in the designer's thoughts with the remainder of the lighting filled in around them. Extending our earlier example, the designer creating the lighting for Shaw's *Saint Joan* might design the renunciation scene around a high angle special focused precisely for the character's position, particularly her face. Once this special is established as the central element of the lighting, the designer, with the collaboration of the director may add other specials to fill in the scene. However the high-angle special will remain the central light perceived by the audience. Ideally, it should blend so integrally with the characterization and movements of Joan that it seems to belong to her.

Specials are often key elements in the development of lighting design.

Specials may fulfill artistic purposes such as the one discussed above or they may be purely utilitarian, for instance, to light an alcove used only once in the show and out of reach of the area lighting.

Backlighting

"Halo" created by backlighting

Backlighting is lighting that comes from above and somewhat behind the actor. Its purpose is to delineate the actor from the background by producing a bright "halo" of highlights around the head and shoulders. Occasionally it can become a major design element when the designer wishes to place the actor or dancer in near-silhouette but retain accent on the character.

The effectiveness of backlight depends on the hair and costume color of the actor or actress and upon the background. Blonds have a great advantage because their light colored hair takes backlight well. Light colored costumes are also effective. A relatively dark background increases the effect of backlight.

In live theatre the need for backlight is a sometime thing. It is obviously necessary if there is a difficulty separating the actors from a light-colored background. However in many instances the light from the acting area lighting will provide sufficient separation particularly if sidelighting is being used.

The lens media are another matter. The television or movie camera has a powerful tendency to merge the foreground, including the actors, into the background. Remember that the final product is a two-dimensional picture on a screen. This makes backlighting almost a necessity. In fact, it may require more wattage to backlight the scene than to front-light it.

Planning for backlighting

If the designer is completely informed about color of settings and costumes, the hair color and makeup of the actors and the general style of the production he or she may be able to forecast the need, if any, for backlighting. If there is a probability that it will be needed, equipment must be specified on the lighting plot and control provided. Even if it is later eliminated, this procedure will probably cost less in time and production funds than installing back lighting after the show is mounted.

Design Conferences

As the designer's concept takes form, discussions with the director and other designers become increasingly important. Talking about the proposed lighting design may be frustrating and misunderstandings abound. Some designers may use sketches or computer simulations to aid them in making their still-evolving lighting design clear to others. The designer should consider this option carefully; the specificity of a drawing, even a very crude one, may lead the director or other designers to expect that the final design will match the sketch, trapping the lighting designer in a half-conceived thought. If the designer decides to use sketches or simulations despite the risk, there are several possible methods:

1. Fragmentary sketches of a light plot: These are really crude technical drawings that show the angling of one or more luminaires proposed to light actors. Such drawings will often be highly useful to the designer later when developing the final lighting plot but are apt to be almost unintelligible to others.

2. Hand-drawn sketches (Figure 2.5A). These can be as crude or as refined as the designer's drawing talents allow. Actually, since a crude drawing may be less apt to be taken as a final concept, designers may choose to make their drawing crude. Such drawings may prove to be helpful in director-designer conferences because they require less knowledge of the technology of lighting.

3. Computer simulations. Modern computer graphics programs for lighting offer a variety of simulation applications including full-stage lighting on a simulation of the setting (Figure 2.5C) Such drawings, usually in color, can achieve a high level of accuracy showing how the lighting will highlight objects and how light is to be distributed over the entire stage. Close-up details of parts of the stage are also possible but bringing the image down to illustrate the lighting on one or two actors may exceed the capability of the system to render useful facial or figure detail. Figure 2.5B illustrates the capability of one computer program to display lighting on actors. It is based on the same composition as shown in Figure 2.5A.

The designer's sketches may originate the lighting plot.

From Conferences to Light Plot

As the conferences with the director and other designers yield positive results, the technology of lighting becomes increasingly important. Before the designer can move ahead to bring the concept to the stage by creating lighting cues, the stage must be prepared. Equipment must be chosen, prepared, mounted, circuited and focused. The control console must be readied and the operator(s) trained. This process begins with the preparation of the formal light plot.

If the designer has used technical sketches as discussed above, he or she may already have the key parts of the light plot sketched out. With or without benefit of sketches, the designer converts his or her well-formed concepts into a technical drawing that instructs the crews what luminaires to place in which locations and how to equip them and interconnect them to the control system. The goal of this massive effort is to

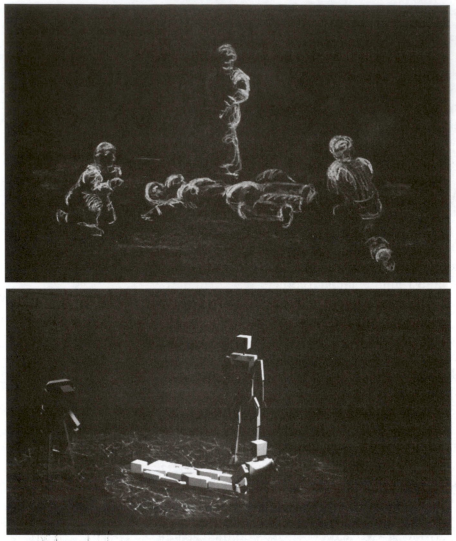

Figure 2.5A. Sketch of Proposed Lighting. This white-on-black drawing is intended to convey a rough idea of the look the designer has in mind for a particular moment in the production. Compare with Figure 2.5B. Sketch by Ellen E. Jones.

Figure 2.5B. A Computer-Drawn Version. This version of the sketch in Figure 2.5A was created by inputting lighting plot-like information from the original drawing into WYSIWYG, a computer lighting graphics program. Additional information specifying floor and background textures was added. Stock figures from WYSIWYG were used as replacements for the figures in the drawing. Note the limited amount of modeling detail, especially faces, in the figures. Computational power greater than what is available in most personal computers limits the modeling capability of many software programs like WYSIWYG. Note in Figure 2.5C how the software does a much better job modeling settings and lighting effects. Computer sketch drawn and supplied by CAST Lighting.

make it possible for the designer to bring the concept to the stage. For the duration of this interlude, the subject has shifted from art to technology.

Designers still using mechanical drafting techniques will create lighting plots on vellum, all based on a master floor plan (or multiple master plans for shows with multiple settings). Such master plans should contain all of the outlines of the setting and major properties but not be cluttered with dimensions or carpenters' instructions. The drawing will be cluttered sufficiently with lighting information. Many, perhaps most designers, will turn to one of the several very useful computer programs for creating light plots. These speed up the work, for example, by making the process of working in layers much easier to handle, by providing ready-made symbols for equipment, and by keeping track of equipment lists,

Software for creating
lighting plots

Figure 2.5C. Computer Simulation. This drawing shows proposed staging for a Canadian East Coast Music Awards Show to be presented in the Centre 200 Arena in Sidney, Nova Scotia and broadcast nationally. The lighting design is by Robert Bell and Gil Densham of CAST Lighting. This simulation illustrates the ability of computer graphics to sketch large-scale drawings for use in production conferences. Courtesy CAST Lighting.

color media and a myriad of other details that the designer would otherwise have to retrieve from the finished drawings and make into separate schedules. Some of these computer-based programs are capable of interfacing directly with a console enabling the designer and/or the operator to create cue information within the program and view its effect directly on the console and thence the stage, or conversely, to create lighting on the stage and feed the data back to the computer program. Conversion from floor plan to sectional view, determination of lighting angles and other items requiring a three-dimensional approach to the plot are facilitated. Finally, printing out the plot and its accompanying schedules is easily accomplished.

Once the designer has completed the lighting plot and associated charts, lists and specifications these are turned over to the technical director, the lighting crew chief and the various assistants who follow them to assemble the electronic giant known as the "lighting setup" or the "lighting rig." This array of control equipment, wiring both temporary and permanent, luminaires, projectors and other equipment must be assembled into a complex but highly reliable "lighting instrument," analogous to a giant pipe organ or, closer still, a huge symphony orchestra with its instruments at the ready. Only when the lighting instrument has been tested and finely tuned can the designer proceed with cue writing and this only with the equally complicated preparation of the cast and other technical crews who will together create the theatrical art work in the making.

The lighting "instrument"

Supporting the Technical Work

Fine focusing by designer

The designer's first obligation to the technical staff as it goes about its work is to make sure that these plans and specifications are as clear as possible and to be available to answer questions as needed. Toward the end of the process when the equipment has all been mounted and roughly focused, the designer or a trusted assistant will do the fine focusing. However this assumes that the designer has no other responsibilities toward the production except lighting design and that the designer is only working on a single production. Most professional designers find it necessary to be working on more than one show at a time and therefore may be at another theatre working on another show while the show at hand is being mounted.

Multiple responsibilities

It is also possible that the lighting designer's title is "designer- technical director" or "designer-technical director-educator." If this is the case, he or she is the person in charge of the technical interlude. In his or her role as technical director or lighting technician the erstwhile designer will interpret the lighting plot for the crew, checking such things as critical loading of dimmers and special circuitry and, if teaching is part of the task, instructing the crews in all of the many details of their work. While this can grow into an exhausting assignment fraught with long hours and pressures to be in several places at the same time, it does offer some time and energy saving aspects. For instance, if the designer/technologist is in charge of focusing, the entire task, including fine focusing may be done in one operation instead of waiting for the designer to come to the theatre for a special fine-focusing session. In the role of teacher, the designer can observe the performance of the crew members and begin the task of deciding on the operating crew early in the work sessions.

As the last of the fine focusing sessions are finished, the designer can resume the role of artist and begin the second most creative part of lighting design—creating the lighting cues.

Technique of Lighting Plots

The intricacies of lighting plots are covered in detail in other texts. However some notes may be helpful here:

Light plots usually consist of a plan view of the stage plus a section through the centerline of the stage for each setting. They are normally drawn at either $1/2'' = 1'\text{-}0''$ or $1/4'' = 1'\text{-}0''$. The latter size is more convenient to handle but may not afford enough space for detail. The plot should indicate the kind, wattage, location, circuitry, color medium, focus and any other special details for each luminaire to be mounted. The section should indicate trims and masking, if used, for all lighting pipes.

Additional schedules should detail hookups, control arrangements, special equipment, gel cutting instructions and plugging if the theatre's equipment forces interplugging during the production. A "magic" sheet directly indicating which controls affect which design elements of the lighting (acting areas, for example), is usually derived from the plot by the designer for his or her personal use.

CUEING THE LIGHT

Lighting Cues

Although most readers of this book will have long since operated their first light cue and many will have already designed cues, it is worthwhile to remind ourselves exactly what a light cue is before we examine some of the designer's many ways of creating them:

A light cue is a designer's order for a change in the lighting. This may be simply a mechanical change such as turning on the house lights or it may have weighty artistic import such as a complicated cue for lighting Lear's "Blow, winds, and crack your cheeks…" speech. Cues get worked out by a variety of methods ranging from the designer personally running them and adjusting them to a union situation where the designer never touches the console which is run by a specialist.

Until recently "change" in a light cue meant a change in the light output of one or more luminaires. These intensity changes often indirectly caused changes in the color, angle, distribution and other attributes of the lighting. With the introduction of automated luminaires, a much wider variety of changes can be wrought directly rather than via intensity changes.

Unless it is instantaneous, a light cue has duration—it starts at a certain time, proceeds through the change and ends at a predetermined time. Rate of change is also likely to vary within the duration of the cue. Indeed, this is one of the most important elements of lighting design—so important that many modern consoles provide special equipment to make rate-of-change adjustments.

Although a cue may be described and even graphed against clock time, *its real "clock" is the rhythm of the production*. It begins at a certain point in the dramatic time of the show and moves forward in dramatic time until its finish.

Cue: an order for a lighting change

Effect of automated luminaires

Variations within the cue are vital.

Rhythm of the play determines cue's rhythm.

Creativity on Demand

No designer should come to cue-setting sessions without a carefully and completely thought out concept for the lighting. However he or she knows all-too-well that the very act of building up the lighting on stage will evoke new ideas in his or her mind. Furthermore, the director, who may have had no way of viewing the proposed lighting until it begins to appear on stage, will almost certainly request changes, some of them substantial. At this point, the designer has arrived at one of the most challenging and, at least at times, satisfying parts of lighting design: creating lighting on the spot. Working with his or her knowledge of the lighting setup and referring to a "cheat sheet" which lists the luminaires and their artistic purpose (and often information on how they are controlled), the designer calls out control settings, requests changes from setting to setting, often repeatedly, until the effect is satisfactory whereupon it is recorded. Sometimes this will involve making notes for relocation or refocusing of equipment later which, of course means that the cue will remain incomplete until later.

Anticipating this demand for instant creativity, the wise designer will create a lighting plot that includes extra equipment mounted in strategically probable locations. Fortunately, modern robot luminaires and color changers (scrollers) can make on-the-spot design easier to do—and more tempting to directors who now can see no reason for not requesting major changes on short notice.

What Goes into a Light Cue?

The principal ingredients of light cues are:
- The designer's concept;
- The installed system of luminaires, cabling, connections and the like specified by the designer in the light plot;
- The control apparatus including the dimmers, and more importantly, the console;
- The well-trained operator(s) of the console.

The end of the cue-on-demand session is by no means the end of creating the lighting. It is important that all who view the cues at this early stage understand that what they are seeing is both preliminary and incomplete. Changes, sometimes numbering into the hundreds, are yet to come. Not only the lighting is incomplete at this stage, the setting, costumes and makeup are also almost always in preliminary stages. Only when all of these are complete will the designer be able to make final adjustments in lighting.

Two Approaches to Designing Cues

Modern lighting control began with the labors of a technician working gas valves and progressed to the work of another technician working the ominous open knife switches of the earliest switchboards. The results were relatively crude, although some were judged to be artistically effective. At that time, toward the end of the 19th and the beginning of the 20th centuries, the aesthetics of lighting was far ahead of technology.

CHAPTER 3

Such idealists as Adolphe Appia and Edward Gordon Craig envisioned subtleties in lighting far beyond the capabilities of the equipment then available. Nevertheless, the first of the two major approaches to lighting design evolved. Predictably, they grew out of the technology of the time, not the thoughts of the most advanced artists.

Preset Lighting Design

The manually operated "switchboards" of the 1910-1930 era were organized with rows of individual switches controlling the colored border and footlights circuits. The usual procedure was to set up the lighting for an upcoming scene while an act was taking place in front of the main curtain illuminated by the follow spotlight. With the main switch off, the individual color circuit switches were thrown to create whatever color pattern was needed next—i.e., they were *preset*. When the main switch was thrown, the preset color arrangement came up on the stage. Later when resistance dimmers were added to the switchboards these were used to gradually bring in the lights but the same presetting principle prevailed.

This primitive beginning quite naturally evolved into thinking of lighting as a series of stop-time snapshots. Changes were made as needed, but the focus of the designer's attention was on fixed conditions. Even when somewhat more flexible control equipment became available, designers and operators studiously avoided having more than one preset device in control of the lighting at a time except during the necessary change periods. One reason was the near impossibility of writing a cue to represent the control settings while two or more control devices were simultaneously affecting the same circuit. This is no longer a problem with modern computer-assisted consoles which can record and/or display the condition of the lighting on stage at any moment without regard for the complexity of the settings making it up.

As control equipment evolved, presetting was accepted as the "normal" way of organizing lighting. In a sort of circle of self-fulfillment, designers were motivated to think of lighting in presets by equipment designed to work that way because that was what it was understood designers wanted. As lighting designs became more complicated, more and more presets were added to accommodate more frequent changes. Consoles were designed with row upon row of controllers each row representing a preset and containing a controller for each circuit available on the console. This led to the creation of monster controlboards (Figures 3.1 and 3.2) with hundreds of individual circuit controllers arranged in ranks. This imposing field of controllers was the realm of a lighting crew specialist who did nothing but set up controllers ahead of cues so they would be ready for the cue when it arrived—a task almost certain to result in mistakes. Each row, i.e., *preset*, was under the control of a master fader or submaster. Thus the console, gigantic and confusing as it was, remained strictly in the preset mode. Finally, the introduction of computer assistance eliminated the arrays of controllers and reduced the risk of errors, but the preset concept still prevailed.

Switchboards

The first presets

Equipment designed for presets fostered thinking in terms of presets.

Figure 3.1. "Monster" Console Operating Unit. This console, originally for a television studio, illustrates the extremes to which console designers went to provide the operator with enough active presets to accommodate a series of rapidly sequenced cues. This figure shows the operator's console from which cues were executed. Note the row of 12 master handles at the lower right. These were the main means of actually taking cues. Above these are three rows of controllers making up three presets on the main console along with selector buttons that determined which preset will be active. Also included are switches to transfer the control to the preset console (Figure 3.2).

Figure 3.2. Preset Unit. This unit, operated by a second and perhaps a third person consists of ten rows of controllers, one per channel, comprising ten presets. It was the job of the operator of this console to keep these presets up-to-date with settings for upcoming cues, obviously a tedious and error-prone task! This console is now many years out of date. It has been replaced by computer-assisted equipment. Courtesy Berkey Colortran.

Many shows fit the preset scheme perfectly

Sometimes this arrangement was exactly in harmony with the needs of the show and the thought processes of the designer. Variety shows and musicals, for example, tend to be organized into discrete scenes, each requiring a specific arrangement of lighting. Many comedies and dramas require a fixed lighting situation for entire scenes or acts or need at most one or two changes per act. Such productions fit perfectly into the preset concept of lighting.

Lighting that follows characterization does not lend itself to presetting.

However as change and rhythm of change become more important to the designer, for example in a dramatic production where the lighting is conceived to be closely related to characterization—a tragedy for instance—the preset concept begins to chafe. Designers of such productions tend to think of lighting, not in snapshots but in movements over time.

Counterpoint Lighting

The world of musical composition has developed this line of artistic thought into a major creative technique. For example, a single melody may be created to evoke a relatively simple artistic experience or multiple melodies may be constructed to occupy the same time interval, interacting to create a complex and potentially artistically rewarding experience. This technique of superimposing melody upon melody is known as *counterpoint*. It is exemplified by the works of Johann S. Bach, particularly his fugues.

This artistic concept may be applied to lighting wherein two or more "melodies" of lighting may be operated onstage during the same time interval. While musical melodies are made up of notes produced by musical instruments played by musicians, melodies in light are made of *patterns* of light produced by one or more luminaires operated as a unit. Each pattern is an *element of design* that functions symbolically, first in the thoughts of the designer and, if successfully carried to artistic completion, contributes to the aesthetic experience of the audience.

Note that although a specific collection of lighting equipment can serve as the technical source of a pattern, *the pattern itself is an artistic concept.* For example, a bank of sidelights gelled with warn flesh tones and controlled together may be the source for a pattern called "warm sides left" or perhaps "the rising sun." However the sidelighting luminaires are *not* the pattern; their artistic function is. Indeed, these same luminaires may very well also be a part of another pattern with a completely different artistic purpose.

The very essence of counterpoint lighting is change. The designer thinks in terms of patterns of lighting which are changing in relationship to each other and interrelated with the rhythm of the production. The rhythmic structure of these changing patterns must be evolved by the lighting designer from the script and the rhythm of the production as it is interpreted by the director. When these rhythmic elements complement each other artistic success is imminent.

Note that there is a strong tendency on the part of the designer to give patterns names instead of abstract numbers related to the technology of the console or the location of the luminaires on the lighting plot. This reflects the artistic, as opposed to technical nature, of patterns which

> A pattern is an element of design, not a collection of equipment.

> Rhythm is an essential part of counterpoint lighting

> Patterns usually have names.

Terminology

Strictly speaking, a "pattern" is a design element which exists in the designer's mind. It is manifested in part of the lighting setup as specific equipment that will cause that pattern to appear on stage and be controlled. Therefore it is convenient to refer to the equipment setup as a "pattern," although this may not even be completely true if some parts of the setup also serve other functions. Henceforth in this text "pattern" will be used interchangeably to refer to either the design concept or the equipment but qualified whenever the difference is significant.

arise from the creative thoughts of the designer who then arranges equipment to make them appear on stage and devises cues to manipulate them. If the designer chooses to write down the sequence of patterns in a show, it is likely to seem more meaningful to do this in a playscript. The notation is apt to be derived from musical notation instead of the conventional warns and takes of preset cueing. This does not rule out standard warns and takes as part of the cues, it simply accents the fact that warns and takes are, by themselves, inadequate to the task of notating a constant interweaving of "melodies in light." The fact of the matter is that the notation of counterpoint lighting has yet to be perfected. Thus each designer must create his or her own system, ultimately depending on operator memory to fill in the details that the cues do not convey.

Recording cues at the console is equally challenging because of the lack of acceptable notation. The best operator will be one with a phenomenal memory for rhythmic structures, usually a musician, who can run a show using written cues as mnemonic devices, not as detailed instructions for operation of the console.

Large Modern Consoles: These consoles, considered "top of the line" by their manufacturers, offer every control feature considered important by their designers plus capacity to independently control a large number of channels. A still larger number of circuits may be controlled by ganging them onto the individual control channels.

Although these consoles are usually considered to be permanently installed in a lighting control room, it is also quite possible to treat them as portable. They are indeed lightweight compared to their autotransformer dimmer predecessors. See also Figure 4.3 for another large console.

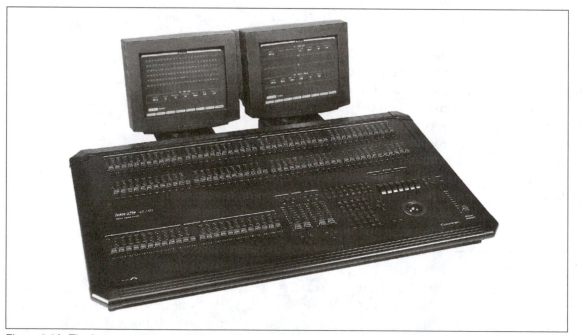

Figure 3.3A. The Innovator Console. This console manufactured by Colortran is available with 24, 48 or 72 basic control channels, each with two controllers. These may be configured to make up a 2-scene preset or may be assigned as submasters. This setup allows up to 192 submasters, no matter how many control channels are built into the desk. This array of submaster functions should be particularly interesting to those running counterpoint lighting. Additionally, the console provides "512 moving light channels," each capable of controlling a single function (e.g., color change) on a robot luminaire.

Among the many other features are: "Submaster fade times (separate up, down and dwell times) with profiles," "Two pairs of assignable playback faders with Take Control Buttons," and "maximum 600 cues per show." The console is software controlled being user reprogrammable via floppy disk. Photo courtesy Colortran.

Lighting Control for Counterpoint Lighting

The counterpoint approach to lighting implies a different arrangement of the control apparatus. Preset lighting requires means for the sequential control of a series of static lighting conditions. Counterpoint lighting requires the ability to control a number of changes taking place simultaneously over a period of time. In addition, as counterpoint lighting progresses, new patterns may be introduced and old ones dropped. One or two crossfaders cannot handle this type of lighting. Therefore the console must provide a number of "submasters," (now better labeled "pattern masters") each of which will control a single pattern. On modern consoles groups of submasters (the term is still standard) are often grouped via software into "pages" which can be brought into action by a digital command. This makes elaborate changes in patterns easily and quickly available to the operator.

Pattern masters.

Modern computer-assisted consoles offer the operator(s) a wide variety of ways of controlling lighting. There will almost always be several ways of causing the same change in the lighting to happen. The skilled operator will be able to choose the one most appropriate for the cue sequence at hand taking into consideration the preceding and following cues and their demands on the console.

The best way to operate a cue is the way that makes the next cue possible.

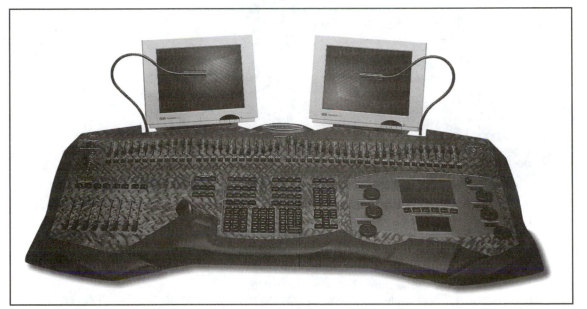

Figure 3.3B. Obsession II. This console represents one of the most advanced efforts to date to consider the ergonomics of operating lighting consoles. In addition to the main console, it features a portable designer's desk which replicates all of the programming and playback features of the main desk. Some of its many features are: Up to 3072 dimmers, 1000 cues, controls for scrollers or moving lights, and two pages of 24 submasters with labels, timing and rate attributes. Photo courtesy Electronic Theatre Controls (ETC).

Instead of operating cues in sequence by means of a "go" button or by repeatedly moving crossfaders to bring in one cue after another, the operator(s) will be operating a number of control devices simultaneously causing a number of patterns to move through time at once. Some patterns with simple time lines may be operated by autofaders. This can be a major "assist" for the operator(s) who are thus freed to handle other, more complicated patterns, manually checking and updating the auto-fade-controlled patterns occasionally if necessary.

Note that it is quite likely that more than one operator will be needed to operate complex counterpoint lighting. Each will handle several patterns, the "team" maintaining the kind of artistic cooperation found in, say, a good string quartet. These operators need a special artistic skill: They must begin with a clear understanding of the sequence and rhythm of the pattern of changes planned by the designer and then be able to exploit the potentialities of the console to "play" the lighting as the drama

Multiple operators are often needed.

Consoles Evolved Within the Concert World. The following consoles reflect a quite different approach to lighting from that in the legitimate theatre—one that often treats lighting as an independent art. However the borders between legitimate theatre and the concert world are blurring. These consoles reflect an attempt to satisfy both markets.

Figure 3.3C. The Virtuoso. The makers, Vari-Lite, Inc., state that this system "equally addresses the automated and conventional needs of theatre, television, corporate theatre and concert touring..."

Control capacity is extensive. For example: 2000 multiple parameter channels, 2000–10,000 cues for fixtures, 2000 cues for DMX devices, 1000 board cues, 1000 effects, 1000 presets, 100 beam selects, and 300 color selects

The console has 10 main submasters and 20 auxiliary submasters with page controls and a manual rate override. Individual channel selection for manual control is via a field of 100 push buttons (top left). A built in 3-D graphics display (top right) provides the operator with an image of whatever part of the lighting is selected. The group-select panel offers choice of any of the 400 groups. Presets may record all parameter data (moving lights attributes) including timing. Courtesy Vari-Lite, Inc.

progresses. This calls for an excellent memory for the details of the rhythmic structures and an intimate knowledge of the various potentialities of the console. Although this may seem to be an awesome assignment, many students master it and, indeed, come to enjoy it. Many of these folks are musicians.

Musicians tend to make good counterpoint operators.

Pattern Control on Preset Consoles

Theoretically, any counterpoint lighting sequence could be operated using nothing but presets. All it would take is enough discrete presets to cause the lighting on stage to appear to be constantly flowing as designed. But this is usually a practical impossibility—the number of presets would be staggering and the time it would take to work them out would be greater than the time available to the designer and operator(s) between rehearsals. More important, this approach would be at cross purposes with the thought processes of the designer who is thinking of the light-

Figure 3.3D. The Whole Hog Console. This console evolved out of the rock concert world and is refreshingly devoid of "traditional" approaches to cueing lighting. Note in the following sketch of its capabilities how many of them could be applicable to counterpoint lighting or a combination of counterpoint and preset control.

The console consists of two parts, the main console (left) and the expansion unit (right) which provides additional masters. The Main unit features two LED display panels which are touch sensitive, adding immensely to the instant selectivity. Fixture, group and preset selection is done at these displays. Typical of concert lighting needs, "favorite arrangements" can be named and assigned to "on view" buttons for instant display. Timing of operations is unlimited and the dwell time within a timed cue can be manually controlled. [Note the built-in adaptability to the live and often nearly random lighting needs of the concert world.] The console will operate in either track or "cue only" (no settings carry over) mode. Each master operates its own cue list and there are 8 plus over 100 other masters creatable via software. Page sizes are flexible with instant page changing. Within a cue each channel can have independent timing and fade path settings.

The displays can include cue list, cue contents, actual output, spreadsheet, the (lighting) rigging schematic, and the floor plan. Its capacity is 2000 DMX512 channels and dimmer channels, and it will allow an unlimited number of simultaneous crossfades. Perhaps most important to future console design: "All items can be given useful names to simplify operation. Courtesy High End/ Whole Hog.

ing as a series of flowing patterns of change, not as snapshots. It could also engulf the operator(s) in such a morass of presets, many almost simultaneous with each other, that he or she could grasp no clear picture of the lighting the designer wants. The chances for making mistakes in operating the lighting would increase greatly.

If the theatre is saddled with an early computer-assisted console designed exclusively for preset lighting, the designer and operator(s) will have to conspire against its design. Usually there will be a number of "submasters" with ranks of controllers assignable to them. These were originally planned to facilitate the building up of preset cues before installing them into memory or to operate cues directly without using the memory.

Loading each of these submasters with the ingredients of a pattern and then operating directly from the submaster bank(s) and the individual circuit controllers when necessary may make a modicum of pattern control possible. The designer will have to understand that there will be a limit to the number of patterns available at any one time and to the ability of the operator to bring in new patterns and retire old ones.

Both the designer and the operator will soon long for the availability of many computerized "pages" of submasters and for a number of automated faders which can take over the operation of patterns whose timing allows automation.

Small and Medium Sized Modern Consoles. The following is a sampling of the many consoles made for small theatres and other facilities that need to control the lighting, but not at the "do it all" level of the consoles in Figure 3.3. These consoles provide for at least two-scene presetting and memory-assisted lighting control, but with a modest number of available cues and configurations.

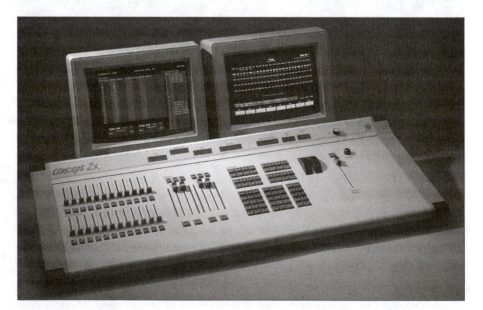

Figure 3.4A. Concept 2X Console. This medium-sized console is adequate for many theatres. In manual mode it provides 12 channels in two-scene preset configuration. In memory mode it provides control over several hundred channels. Note the dual "Wheel" controller at the right. When assigned to a wheel, a channel may be adjusted either up or down from its assigned reading. The new reading can be entered into memory if needed. Courtesy ETC.

Combining Design Concepts

There is nothing to be lost and much to be gained by combining preset and pattern control if the show requires it. Creating a lighting design in which the "master cue" for an act or scene is a preset but within which counterpoint cues handle the details is a perfectly natural way to proceed, providing the console will handle this much complexity. The only reason that this approach demands special mention is the history of consoles exclusively dedicated to preset control and the carry-over of preset terminology into modern systems. Many modern consoles offer the potential for elaborate counterpoint control but hide it by giving the controllers names pointing toward presetting. A skilled operator will soon learn how to exploit the flexibility of the system and ignore the terminology.

Given these approaches to lighting design, how do the designer and operator go about bringing the lighting into actualization?

The Mechanics of Setting Cues

While the lighting begins its artistic life in the mind of the designer, it must eventually be communicated to those operating the console and recorded in such a way that it can be faithfully reproduced every performance of the run. The process by which this is accomplished will depend

Figure 3.4B. The Status Console. This console is made with either 24 or 48 individual controllers which can either be configured into a two-scene manual mode with a split cross-fader or into a multi-scene memory mode. Either 12 or 24 submasters are provided. It can handle 118 cues in memory plus two on manual and can control up to 512 dimmers. Photo courtesy Colortran.

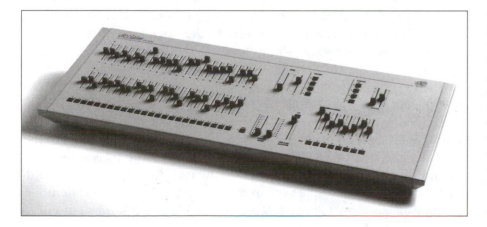

Figure 3.4C. The Acclaim Console. The modern replacement for portable two-scene preset control boards, this console is available in 12, 48, 72 or 96 dimmer capacities. It provides two-scene preset capability plus eight overlapping proportional submasters which give access to eight submaster memories. The console can interface with any DMX512 dimmer rack. Courtesy ETC.

on the style of the show, the control equipment available in the theatre, the designer's concept of the lighting, the training and ability of the operator(s) and, particularly in the professional theatre, the amount of time available for this part of the lighting process. The following discussion begins with methods adapted to the preset mode and then with the more complicated task of creating counterpoint cues. This discussion presupposes a regular script-controlled production. Improvisation will be dealt with later:

• Cues written in advance

This process works best in the professional theatre where highly trained operators are available, often these are operators who are used to working with the designer and know his or her "language" of cues. It is also best adapted to shows designed around the preset concept of lighting. Obviously, the subtleties of counterpoint lighting which defy accurate notation, cannot be handled this way.

The cues are prepared by the designer in a format agreeable to both designer and operator and adapted to the vagaries of the control system. The operator then enters into the system the necessary data for running the cues and lighting rehearsals begin. This can be a highly efficient process that saves much stage time, a matter of great concern in the professional theatre.

Modern computer-assisted consoles that use standardized computer language as the basis of their cue-recording function offer the designer a more sophisticated way of writing cues in advance: The entire sequence of cues for a show may be prepared on the designer's personal computer at home or office, stored on disk and loaded into the console computer before the first lighting rehearsal. After rehearsal, the designer may take a copy of the cues as changed during the rehearsal and make further alterations as he or she feels necessary. This new version of the cues is then loaded into the console for the next rehearsal. Clearly, the operator will need to review the changed cues before attempting to run the show unless the changes are all small intensity adjustments.

• "Dry tech" cues

To dry-tech the lighting of a show the lighting designer and crew need complete control over the stage and house but no actors need be present. The director may or may not attend. If scenery shifts are involved, the stage crew must be available. Some of the more discrete and obvious cues may be planned in advance and handed to the operator or presented on disk, but most of the show will be cued as the dry tech rehearsal proceeds.

The designer, operating from a position near the center of the house either dictates the cue settings over an intercom system or, if the system is equipped with a designer's console, enters the cue data directly. As the lighting is brought up on stage, the designer makes adjustments until the particular cue is satisfactory. Then the command "write it" is given. The operator does this either by writing it in the cue sheet and/or by recording control settings into the system memory under an assigned number. Timing data, such as "take on a ten-count" or "take on John's entrance" are written on the lighting cue sheet unless the console allows notes to be attached to each cue.

This approach is best fitted to the preset approach to lighting where it can prove to be very efficient although still time consuming because of the many adjustments the designer will need to make. He or she will want to adjust dimmer settings within each preset and, when these are established, set the timing and rhythm of the transitions between cues. Moreover, no dry tech can finish off the cueing process. This requires the presence of the setting, properties and, most important, the actors in costume and makeup. "Final" changes are then possible.

Adjustments may seem endless

"Dry teching" a show using counterpoint lighting is, at best, only partially possible. Only the beginning and ending settings of each element of the counterpoint may be set in advance. The rhythm of the lighting will have to be synchronized with that of the acting and directing—something only possible in a full-cast rehearsal with the actors playing their parts in the rhythm established by the director.

• Setting cues during rehearsals

When counterpoint lighting is the style it is ideal to set light cues during rehearsals with actors. It is also quite possible to establish preset cues or at least to fine tune settings during rehearsals. In either case, this will require the approval of the director who may fear too much interruption of the rehearsal. Directors should be assured that both time and artistic improvement are to be had by allowing lighting to be changed during rehearsals. Artistically, the operator(s) will have a much better grasp of the relationship between the lighting and the acting/directing. Technically, a successful job of setting cues while a rehearsal is in progress can eliminate many hours from the time required in technical rehearsals.

The theatre must be equipped with intercommunications equipment between the house, the lighting control area and backstage that allows unobtrusive conversations—a squawk box will not do! The operator(s) must be familiar with the lighting setup and the console, able to recognize every preset as it appears on stage and/or to recognize each pattern. Professional operators should do this automatically, students may need the "follow-focus" training sessions outlined below.

Good communications are essential.

Follow-Focus

Actually this is a lighting technique often used in situations such as theatre of improvisation, where the blocking of the actors is only partially known. However it is also an excellent training technique for novice console operators during rehearsals. Note that only one operator should work the console at a time even if it is anticipated that there will be a team of operators working the show. Directors should be assured that there will be no drastic changes in light levels as the training proceeds, only shifts of focus which may, at first, not exactly follow the blocking.

Directors must understand the procedure.

Follow-focus consists of the operator, without benefit of cues, keeping the brightest point in the lighting at the dramatic focus of the scene as it plays. To do this the operator must have a good sense of the way blocking is used by directors to focus the audience' attention on the proper character(s) at the proper time. Fortunately, if the directing is well done, the center of focus should be obvious. Given the ability to recognize the focal point, the operator needs to know the arrangement of the lighting, particularly the acting area and sidelighting, well enough to recognize what equipment to adjust and know the console well enough to make the necessary adjustments promptly.

Keeping the lighting accent at the director's focal point

The usual approach when this technique is used for training purposes, is to adjust all acting areas to, say, 8 on a standard dimmer scale (10 being full). Then the current focal point is brought to 10 and the action progresses. As the characters move about and the focus changes from character to character, the operator endeavors to bring up the new location to 10 and fade the outgoing one to 8. This will take considerable concentration. However, if the operator has talent for this job a few run-throughs will be enough for him or her to gain proficiency in handling the console and to learn the blocking. Once the operator is proficient, the designer can proceed with setting the actual cues for the show.

Design Procedures: Criteria

Clearly, there is no generally established sequence to the job of setting lighting cues. The approach outlined here is simply a commonly used one. What is most important is the designer's awareness of the vital link between lighting and the artistic success of the production: In the dramatic theatre both comedy and tragedy depend on characterization. This is first the responsibility of the actors and the director. However only the audible part of characterization will reach the audience if they cannot clearly see the facial features of the actors and, when the costumes are so designed, their body language. From the beginning of the development of the lighting, but particularly as the cues are set, the designer should keep in mind:

Plasticity

- The plasticity of the lighting plays a large part in the audience' perception of characterization. Therefore well-lighted faces should be the most important consideration for the designer. (Dance and spectacle are exceptions to this rule.)

Focus

- One of the characteristics of good directing is that the audience is motivated to focus its attention where the director wishes. Good lighting is usually depended on to make a major contribution to focus by placing the brightest illumination at the point on stage where the director has created the focus.

Back ground levels alter key/fill appearance.

As the designer sets out to achieve these goals, he or she must deal with an important characteristic of human vision: The perception of brightness is always in proportion to the overall brightness of the stage. This applies to both character-to-background ratios and key-to-fill ratios on actors' faces. If, for example, an actor is standing in an acting area on an otherwise unlit stage, even a very low key/fill contrast ratio, say 4:5 will be clearly seen and will provide plasticity to aid the audience in its perception of characterization. However as the background brightness is increased, the perception of key/fill contrasts lessens. At the "normal" level of background lighting on most scenes, the contrast on the actor's face may have to be adjusted to as much as 4:1 to achieve what 4:5 produced on the dark stage. This means that the designer will often find it necessary to create cues calling for contrast changes that, as far as the audience is concerned, simply maintain a consistent key/fill ratio.

With this contrast phenomenon in mind, many designers will begin their cue setting by establishing the background against which the acting area lighting will play. This can be done by actually setting the background lighting, e.g., the cyclorama settings if an outdoor scene is being lit, and then moving on to actor lighting. Or the designer can simply have the operator bring in whatever lighting is available to fill the background to the level the designer anticipates using. In either case, the designer will anticipate refining both the background and the actor-lighting as the design develops.

Setting background

Establishing Acting Area Lighting

After setting the background to the proper brightness the designer proceeds to cue the acting areas. A common starting place is to set up a full-stage cue first and then work from it. This is done by bringing all the acting areas to full. Any brightness adjustments that are needed to produce an evenly lit stage are made and this setting recorded as a reference cue. Even though it may never appear in the show, it will be a useful starting point as other cues are established.

Dividing Up the Show

Designers, directors and actors all have need to refer to parts of the show smaller than those labeled "act" or "scene." Directors and actors often refer to "French scenes." A French scene begins whenever a character enters the stage and ends when one leaves. There is a kind of dramatic logic to this in that entrances and exits are often the motivation for what takes place in the scene. Sometimes French scenes are also useful to the lighting designer, but not always. Lighting changes have a way of including several French scenes within one "movement," much as several melodies may occur in one musical movement. Clearly the lighting designer needs a reference system adapted to the particular show and not tied to the limitations of French scenes. There is no accepted term for these divisions although there is a temptation to adopt the musical term, "movement." If all lighting were in the counterpoint mode, this would be quite satisfactory but, since this is not the case, the more neutral term, "segment" is hereby offered. A "segment" is simply any division of the lighting that makes sense to the designer and can be clearly communicated to the operator(s) and possibly the director. It is a function of the design process not the control system. Segments may be given numbers, letter names or names in words such as "the love scene" or "chaos and cataclysm."

At this point the designer has two options, depending on the nature of the show. If it fits into the preset mode because it consists of scenes which contain few, if any, internal lighting changes, the designer moves to the first of these scenes and creates its cue by altering the basic full-stage setting, creating accent(s) where needed and removing or reducing lighting on unused parts of the stage. When completed, the dimmer settings are given a cue number and possibly a descriptive title and recorded in memory. The cue number and its title, if one is used, will also be recorded *in pencil* in the stage manager's or cue caller's book making clear exactly when the cue begins, its probable duration and rhythmic pattern, if any, and its ending. Obviously, all of this data is subject to change. The designer then moves on to the next scene and follows the same procedure.

If the show is being designed in the counterpoint style, a procedure by which the designer creates the beginnings of each segment first and then, in further rehearsals, fills in the details is likely to serve better:

1. Patterns that are part of the opening of the show are brought up one at a time and adjusted to the designer's satisfaction. These are then adjusted in relationship to each other to establish the beginnings of the segment. These settings are given a name and cue number and recorded in memory.

2. The designer then skips to the point where an additional pattern is to be added or an active one is to be dropped. Again the active patterns are brought up and adjusted until the designer approves. These settings are also recorded. This process is continued throughout the show.

3. At the next rehearsal, the designer begins the process of filling in the details of changes between the points already established. He or she may, for example, call for changes in the key/fill ratio of certain acting areas as a dramatic scene builds. These additions and adjustments are recorded in memory where they are static enough to allow and are noted in the cues as the beginnings of the "scenario of cues" the operators will have to learn.

4. During subsequent rehearsals the sequences of change are further refined and notated.

This process gradually gives the operator(s) a grasp of the lighting that the designer wants to create. It also gives the designer the opportunity to refine the lighting as his or her concept becomes more and more specific. When the process works well the operators are firmly in control of the pattern sequences, know what they are to make appear on stage, and the exact timing for it. The cues and notations (see below) will serve as mnemonics for the operators who refer to them as needed but focus most of their attention on the lighting they are creating on stage.

Recording Cues

The following discussion is focused on counterpoint lighting—the most complex of all cueing problems.

"Cue" has a specific and simple meaning when applied to preset lighting: It is a command for a change to be made in a very specific way over a well-established period of time. This does not necessarily apply to counterpoint lighting. A counterpoint cue may refer to a whole series of changes, some occurring simultaneously and others in sequence. Such a cue might read:

Cue 44: follow Hamlet during *To be or not to be* soliloquy.
Begin: 10/8; end: 7/2. Areas: 7 -> 8 -> 9 -> 5 -> 4.

Executing this cue might involve a series of perhaps five or six changes involving luminaires focused to pick up Hamlet at various points in the soliloquy. At the same time the various luminaires are being brought in or taken out, the key/fill contrast ratio is being altered from 10/8 to 7/2—somewhat dimmer but much more contrasty lighting. Note that the very complicated timing of this cue is not recorded at all. It depends on Hamlet's rhythm of movement which in turn depends on the pacing of the show set by the director. Within small but significant limits, this rhythmic pattern will vary from performance to performance and the operator(s) must adjust the cue accordingly to maintain the artistic unity between the acting and the lighting. Note that this standard assumes the very high degree of actor discipline more often found in the professional theatre. Many groups will not be able to achieve this consistency and, on occasion, the operator(s) will have to be able to adjust by using different luminaires as the actor moves in a different and unexpected path, ideally with no perceptible break in the rhythm of the cue.

Timing depends on actor movement

Counterpoint cues may be recorded on a cue sheet, in the margins of a copy of the script or even in a scrolling device in the console. Whatever the method, the ideal is to provide the operator(s) with the cue information as they need it and in a way that jogs their memory to fill in the details of the lighting they have memorized. Any attempt to write out every detail of the counterpoint flux of changes would be self-defeating— it would be so wordy that the operator(s) would not be able to read it in the time they have between cues. Moreover, the cue's changeability would frustrate such detail.

To perform the soliloquy cue in the example above, the operator would have to work out a somewhat complicated movement of a series of controllers to handle both elements of the cue: changes to follow the actor and, at the same time make the change in key/fill contrast. Also, this follow cue may be only one of several changes happening during the Hamlet soliloquy. Background lighting, for instance, may be changing in both color and brightness. The operator(s), will be challenged to work out the most effective way to run such cue sequences on the console in use.

The console will determine the operator's ease in operating the cue.

Operators often find this kind of lighting fascinating. They have a far more active part in the production than that played by the operator of preset lighting whose console operations may consist of a series of takes on a "Go" button or occasionally moving a split fader.

The successful use of counterpoint lighting depends on its proper application to the right script and production concept, the enthusiastic cooperation of the director and actors, the presence of the proper control equipment, and on the availability of enough rehearsal time to perfect the lighting.

All Is Tentative

All visible elements must be complete to enable the designer to complete the lighting.

Whether the lighting style is counterpoint or preset, the operator(s) and all those involved with the lighting (and the rest of the cast and crew, for that matter) should constantly bear in mind that all settings and timings are tentative. If the designer is working with stand-ins or even if the actors themselves are present but not in costume or makeup, things are even more tentative. Moreover, many conferences between lighting designer and director are still to occur because artistic decisions remain in a developmental state. Counterpoint lighting is particularly susceptible to fine-tuning right up to opening night.

Follow-Focus As Part of Counterpoint Lighting

Follow-focus, a technique of training console operators, may, under certain circumstances, be applied to a production itself. It can be advantageously applied when the operators are skilled and the movements of the actor(s) are numerous, come rapidly one after the other but are generally predictable. A follow-focus sequence cue specifies the beginning and ending of the sequence and the contrast to be maintained between the point of focus and the rest of the stage. For example, the cue for Hamlet's *To be or not to be…* soliloquy might be:

Follow focus for rapid sequence cues

Follow Hamlet soliloquy. Start: 2 point; end: 5 point.

Hamlet K/F start: 8/6; end: 6/2

This would translate to: "Follow Hamlet keeping his key light 2 dimmer points higher than the rest of the stage at the start of the sequence and ending with a 5 point difference. At the same time start Hamlet's area at a key/fill ratio of 8 to 6 and end the sequence with the key/fill ratio at 6 to 2." Note that this will have the effect of almost isolating Hamlet on a nearly dark stage by the end of the sequence if the background lighting is at a low level.

Use pages to quickly change setup.

On many consoles, this cue would require two operators, one to handle follow-focus and another to adjust the key/fill. Depending on the arrangement of the console, it may be necessary to run the follow-focus on submasters, and to adjust the key/fill on individual circuit controllers. Such an arrangement would likely be placed on a single page of the submaster system, to be activated when needed and replaced when the sequence is finished. A more sophisticated console may allow the operator to create key/fill masters that will control the key/fill function for all areas in use.

Details of timing depend on operator

This same lighting sequence could be broken into a series of separate counterpoint cues, each notated separately although this would create a series of cues coming with such rapidity that there would be little time to read the cues. In either case, note that the moment-to-moment timing of the changes remains unspecified in the cue(s). The operator(s) must understand the intent of the designer and then follow the actor as he moves, not always at the same pace, through the soliloquy.

Greater contrast makes lighting changes more obvious.

Follow-focus is possible if the designer is willing to trust a skilled operator to maintain proper focus and to do so without placing more emphasis on the lighting fluctuations than the designer wishes. Subtlety of the lighting will depend on the skill of the operator(s) and upon the brightness difference between the accented area and the rest of the stage. The greater the difference, the more obvious the changes will be. Follow-focus is usually a full time job for an operator. Therefore, if other cues are being operated at the same time, a series of presets simulating a sunset for example, another operator will be needed unless the other cues can be handled on autofaders.

Relating Cues to the Action of the Play

Whenever the designer opts for a style of lighting that consistently relates the cues to the action, moving the focal point of the lighting to match the focus of the scene as staged by the director and the actors, timing of cues must blend with the action so closely that the light following the actor seems a part of his or her character. This remains true whether follow-focus is in effect or whether each change in the acting area lighting is separately cued. Such integration of acting, directing and lighting depends heavily on the actors. The consistency of their blocking from performance to performance, their understanding of the intent of the lighting, and their willingness to "play into" the lighting using its effect on their faces and bodies, will determine whether the lighting succeeds or turns out to be a distraction. If the actors cannot reach this level of integration with the lighting, the designer will have to reduce the contrast between accent and background and perhaps create large lighting areas out of two or more small ones. These large areas will then be treated as if they were one acting area by combining the cues for the component luminaires. This will give the actors more space in which to move without seeming to work against the lighting.

Actor cooperation is vital.

Adjusting for unpredictable actor movement.

Given the necessary actor cooperation and skill, this type of lighting also depends heavily on the training and ability of the console operator(s). Although the pacing of a well-rehearsed show done at the professional level should only vary over a very small range, the operators must be sensitive to these variations and adjust the pacing of the lighting cues to match.

Lighting in the Theatre of Improvisation

Improvisation is a type of theatre; sometimes it is merely an exercise in the acting studio, sometimes a performance technique wherein the actors make up the dialogue and action as they go. There is no written script, although there may be a scenario, theme, or topic. Sometimes a script is generated out of improvisation, other times no written form ever appears.

One of the most important parts of improvisation as a theatrical form is that it must be the product of an *ensemble* of artists (actors, designers, director, musicians, etc.) who have worked together for an extended period of time and who are so familiar with each other's approach to an improvisation topic that they can almost predict what their fellow artists are going to do.

Ensemble is the key.

Lighting enters into improvisation only when an audience is involved. When this happens, the lighting designer must ideally be a part of the ensemble and as intimately privy to their collective thoughts as any of the

The lighting director should be a member of the ensemble.

actors. As the improvisation proceeds and the actors are thinking in terms of their interaction with each other as characters, the lighting designer is thinking of making the lighting interact with them.

There are a number of possible assists:

Pre-planned lighting

Follow focus

Use sidelighting

Use "all stage" lighting for everything

- The designer may set up a number of presets in advance that seem likely to serve many of the needs of the show. If each of these covers a major part of the acting space and includes good plastic lighting, the actors should be reasonably well lit although the focus of the lighting will not consistently follow that of the action.

- The technique of follow-focus may be utilized but with the contrast between the focal point and the rest of the stage kept purposely low so that mismatches between the focal point of the lighting and that of the action will be less noticeable and more easily corrected.

- Well-designed sidelighting can make a major contribution to this kind of lighting. It can provide good facial contrast over a wide stage area and has the advantage of not being very visible to the audience until an actor steps into it. (Particularly if the sides of the stage are designed to mask the spill from the sidelights).

- The lighting can be set up as an "all stage" coverage with the same key/fill ratio over the entire area, in effect giving the actors a work light situation but with good plasticity. This option is the only recourse for the designer who is not privy to the ensemble.

Style in Lighting

Style: how something is done

Style is the *way* something is done as opposed to *what* is done. It can be applied to almost any activity, e.g., in basketball a player may be praised by saying that he made the basket *with style*., i.e., with a flourish. Note that it is quite possible that a player could make a basket *without style*. The score would be the same but the flourish would not have occurred. Thus style in sports can be easily separated from the final result. In art, the result and the way it is accomplished cannot be separated. An attempt, for example, to separate the style of Keats' *Ode On A Grecian Urn* from its artistic import will have the effect of obliterating both. This does not mean that style cannot be usefully discussed in connection with art but it does mean that a discussion that purports to separate style from "content" is probably futile.

In art, style and import are inseparable

Style in theatrical production is further complicated by the fact that the end product is the result of efforts of many artists working in collaboration. The guiding style of a production may, for example, come from one or more of the following:

1. The script—which can indicate style by its period, its literary style, its stage directions, and the import of the lines themselves
2. The director—who may adopt the style expressed by the script reinforcing and interpreting it or who may impose his or her own style on the production in spite of the script. As the production is developed, the director may dictate style or it may be developed under his or her guidance by the artistic team.

3. The producer—The style may be established from the very beginning by a producer who uses the power of the financing to determine the kind of a show he or she wishes to produce. The director and other artists are hired with the understanding that they will create this kind of a show.
4. Tradition—Such forms as the American Musical and the revue have their style well established in the past development of the form.
5. History—A style of a past production may be copied, the process being guided by the director and or the artistic team. E.g. a 19th Century melodrama may be staged in the style of its original performance

The lighting designer may have a significant role in determining the style as a member of the artistic team or may simply try to follow the stylistic dictates of the director. Whatever its source, the style of the lighting can be a major factor in the style of the entire production.

Lighting plays an important role in style.

Style in Lighting the Dramatic Theatre

As noted above, some types of dramatic scripts provide strong indications of the style of the lighting and thereby impose limits on the lighting designer. Others offer challenge and much greater freedom for the designer's creativity. Dramatic scripts fall into two categories:

Style based on the script

1. Naturalism to selective realism—All of these scripts have in common the use of life outside the theatre as the source of the environment of their action. They vary mainly in the degree of emphasis placed on this environment.

    These styles may be arranged on a continuum extending from naturalism through realism and ending with selective realism. Every possible degree of variation within these categories may be found, which means that the lines dividing the categories are fuzzy indeed.
2. Expressionism, impressionism, symbolism, et al.—Scripts in this category create their own environment of the action with little or no regard for the possibility that such an environment might exist outside the theatre. Language, literary style and the stipulation for the environment of the action are created by the author.

    No continuum exists in this category. As regards design, these scripts have in common only the characteristic that the author has either envisioned an environment of the action which he or she feels fits the dramatic intent of the script, left the environment to the production team to devise, or even stipulated that the be "no environment" (Wilder's *Our Town,* for example).

    Style names abound in this category, many seeking to express something about the attitude of the script toward life, for example, "expressionism," "symbolism," "impressionism," etc. The limits of such styles blend into each other in a way that makes it possible for one authority to place a script in a category while another chooses a different one.

Designers should approach categorization of scripts with caution. Even the category names themselves may engender more confusion than understanding, particularly when they turn up in designer-director conferences. The best approach is to treat terms such as "expressionism" or "realism" as signs that the user has a style in mind but that the listener has, at the moment, only a vague idea of what it is. Further discussion aimed at developing specific examples may bring clarity to what might otherwise be a dangerous discussion leading to major disagreements later in the production process.

Naturalism

This form seeks to imitate life outside of the theatre with photographic accuracy. Dialogue in a naturalistic script is usually carefully written to reflect the era, nationality and social status of the characters. The environment of the action, often painstakingly detailed in the script, may be as influential as a major character. The rhythms of the action are, as closely as the author can make them, the rhythms of real life. An example of this kind of script is *The Lower Depths* by Gorky.

Find the environment and copy it.

Designing the scenery and lighting for such a script is normally approached with the eye of a museum artist creating a diorama. The impression given to the audience should be that an appropriate environment was found in real life and meticulously copied on stage. In a naturalistic setting stoves often work, sinks have running water and dirt and grime are "real."

Making light imitate nature

Distribution of light on the naturalistic stage is determined by "motivating sources," scenery or property items that would be light sources in real life such as windows, illuminated chandeliers, and lanterns. These items are practical—they work. Since lamps and lanterns cannot really produce the amount of light needed to light the stage and would be far too glaring even if operated at their full normal intensity, luminaires ("cover spots") are arranged to create the illusion that the light on the actors' faces actually comes from these sources. This motivated light forms the main share of the acting area lighting. Color media for these lu-

Finding the Light

This is a technique which should be second nature to experienced actors. Its purpose is to enable the actor to know when he or she is in the light, not in a shadowy area of the stage. Clearly it would be out of character for an actor to move about on stage looking up at the spotlights overhead. (If the spotlights are very powerful, they will also temporarily blind the actor.) Therefore the actor needs to sense the flare of light from his or her eyebrows and move into the light if the flare is not present.

It is sometimes helpful if the lighting designer or an assistant moves about with the actors on the lighted stage pointing out to inexperienced actors where "their light" is and explaining how to tell if they are in it without getting out of character.

Figure 3.5A. Naturalism/Realism in Lighting. This setting is categorized by its designer as "selective realism." Lighting designer, Richard Devin has designed the lighting based on motivating sources. Note that each of the three practical lamps is lit and provided with "cover lighting" to suggest the light from the lamps. The overhead light fixture also serves to motivate much center-stage lighting. *Born Yesterday* (Garson Kanin) as staged by the Seattle Repertory Theatre. Director, Burke Walker; scenery, James Joy; costumes, Laura Crow. Photo by Richard Devin.

minaires will be chosen to match colors found in nature in a similar situation. For example, a setting might have a window that admits "daylight" and a lighted lamp on a table. Acting area colors, usually in complementary tints (Chapter 10) will be arranged so that the cool side of each acting area appears to come from the window and the warm sides of the areas will match the lamp light. Thus designing naturalistic lighting consists of studying natural situations resembling those to be reproduced on stage and arranging equipment to achieve that effect.

Light for actors' faces must fall within the limits of naturalistic motivation and the actors must find it and use it within these bounds. Similarly, changes in lighting for the purpose of focus of attention, if attempted at all, must be extremely subtle and/or appear to be motivated by visible natural sources such as change of time of day, weather, a lamp brought onstage by a character, etc. Achieving good focus of attention and naturalism at the same time is one of the most difficult design problems the lighting designer may encounter

Realism and Selective Realism

Realism follows the same path as naturalism but does not carry exactitude as far. This relaxed approach affords the designer a wider choice of options making some subtle use of lighting provided only for plasticity and focus of attention possible. Actors need to "find their light" is lessened but

Imitating nature but not so rigorously

Figure 3.5B. *Julius Caesar* (Shakespeare) as staged at the American Conservatory Theatre. Note that the lighting has no realistic motivation; instead it is motivated by the vision of the designer and the nature of the dramatic scene (the murder of Caesar). Director, Edward Payson Call; scenery, Richard Seger; costumes, John Conklin; lighting, Richard Devin. Photo by Richard Devin.

by no means removed.

Selective realism moves even further from the rigors of naturalism. Visual elements not central to the script are omitted or merely suggested. On the other hand, elements of dramatic importance may be treated with the same precise detail found in a naturalistic production.

This leaves room for many theatrical maneuvers on the part of the lighting designer. Motivating sources will still be present, particularly when they are part of the environment selected for complete development. However the fragmentary nature of the setting makes it possible to rationalize the presence of additional but invisible motivating sources. This leaves the way open for the lighting designer to provide additional lighting for plasticity and focus of attention without breaking out of stylistic limits. Such lighting must be cued with subtlety. Colors chosen for acting area lighting under selective realism must still follow the general "rules" of naturalism but with more latitude for the designer who may rationalize a wider color palette just as he or she rationalizes invisible motivating sources.

Naturalism only where needed

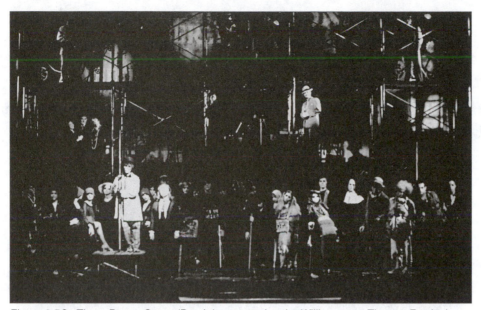

Figure 3.5C. *Three Penny Opera* (Brecht) as staged at the Williamstown Theatre Festival. Categorized as a constructivist setting by lighting designer Richard Devin. Note that the stage space is arranged purely for the function of the action of the play. Lighting follows the same pattern focus of attention following the needs of the drama—primary and secondary focal points sharply control where the audience is looking. Scenery and costumes, John Conklin; lighting, Richard Devin. Photo by Richard Devin.

Expressionistic Theatre

At this point the continuum of dramatic style mentioned above breaks. Imitation of nature is no longer the paramount concern. Instead, the script is built upon its writer's thoughts, feelings and opinions. Stage directions may even challenge the scene designer and the director to create an environment for the action unlike anything ever before staged.

The challenge of designing new worlds

These productions also challenge the lighting designer. Within the usually broad limits of the director's concept (usually, but not always, derived from the script) the lighting designer is free to place light anywhere on the stage he or she feels is artistically necessary and to use whatever colors satisfy that same artistic need. Lighting cues need no motivation from natural cause, instead they are used to focus attention as needed and to provide the actors with the kind of plasticity needed to further the development of character. Note that this is not a license to blatantly assail the audience with distracting lighting. Lighting design still remains subservient to the drama and must function artistically within its context.

This category of styles is often described as "theatrical," meaning that the audience is frankly invited to participate in a theatrical situation, con-

Theatricality

Figure 3.5D. Expressionism. This design by Joseph Svoboda is for a production of Strindberg's *Dream Play*, directed by Jarka Burian, produced at State University of New York at Albany. Photo courtesy Jarka Burian.

trived for that audience and openly labeled as such. For example, the lighting equipment may hang in clear view of the audience who, if they bother to look, can see luminaires brightening or darkening as the cues proceed. Similarly, actors may directly address the audience in their character or, in some cases in the character of an actor playing the role (See Wilder's *The Skin of Our Teeth*, for example).

While these forms, compared with naturalism, seem to free the designer from many restrictions, they are also in many ways more rigorous. The designer of naturalism need only research and copy; the designer of expressionism and its related forms must create new theatrical worlds with their own logic and then rigorously maintain that logic.

The Lighting Designer's Personal Style

Given the above restrictions and repetitions of the fact that lighting is a dependent art when used for the dramatic theatre, the student may wonder where personal style enters the picture, if indeed it does. Clearly the lighting designer has little of the opportunity for flamboyant personal expression allowed his or her compatriots in the concert lighting world. However these free souls pay for their freedom by being forced to work with theatrical material of limited depth and artistic import. Personal style in dramatic lighting must be more subtle but it gains from the depth of the dramatic material for which it is designed and to which it can make a significant contribution.

Individual style in lighting is often expressed through variations in the following:

- Color of the acting area lighting
- Color and contrast of background lighting
- Overall brightness
- Contrast between acting areas and background
- Degree to which light cues are intentionally apparent to the audience
- Size and blend of acting areas
- Use of dark areas
- The use of sidelighting
- The use of moving lights (automated luminaires)

Personal Touches within the Limits of Naturalism

Even naturalism leaves some room for personal expression and the other forms offer more. For instance, the designer of naturalistic lighting will find that there are a number of possible variations in the way faces are lit, all within the realm of naturalism: The lighting might be brittle and brilliant, the actors' features displayed in sharply chiseled highlights and with filled-in shadows. Or the actors faces, while still delineated by good plasticity, might be displayed with soft-edged but bright highlights contrasted with shadows dimly filled with warm light. The angling of the acting area lighting will also reveal the designer's approach. Although angling is often circumscribed by the architecture of the building, a wide range of angles is almost always available within which the designer can offer his or her personal touch. For example in different productions of the same play, one designer may favor relatively low angles for acting area lighting, making for more open, less shadowed faces, another may opt for higher angles increasing plasticity and thus emphasizing the dramatic qualities of the production. Additionally, one designer may favor sidelighting at quite high brightness levels while another may depend almost entirely on acting area lighting.

Other theatrical forms, such as selective realism or expressionism leave far more latitude for individual expression on the part of the lighting designer, although he or she will still usually achieve that expression by varying the elements listed above.

Personal touches within naturalism

Greater freedom in expressionistic forms

Chapter 4

THE CONTROL CONSOLE

Developing the cues for operating the lighting is one of the most important steps in lighting design. Clearly, the very nature of the cues, the designers' approach to them and the manner in which they are recorded and operated depend on the design of the console. The more flexible the console design is and the greater the capacity of the computer which assists it in its operations, the more freedom the designer will have to develop sophisticated and artistically effective lighting. Moreover, a modern console will also save a great deal of time and money by speeding up the cue recording process.

The Evolution of Presetting

Lighting control began with the gas valve before electricity was introduced into the theatre. Gas lights were controlled by a backstage array of valves which controlled the flow of gas to the rows of gas burners that made up the dangerous borderlights and striplights of the 19th century theatre. The valves had one advantage, they could be turned up or down to adjust the amount of light the burners put out—the earliest "dimmer." However, if the gas was turned completely off, it had to be relit producing a very obvious flare of light.

The switchboard

Soon after ways were developed to produce enough electrical current, electric lamps were installed in theatres to eliminate the fire hazard of gas lights. Electric lamps were simply substituted for the gas burners in the long rows ("borderlights") hanging over the stage and in the footlights. The electrical circuits were controlled by "on-off" switches installed on a "switchboard." This was a slab of slate or marble upon which were mounted open knife switches—electrocution waiting to happen.

The beginning of presetting

The possibility of gradual adjustment of the light output vanished with the introduction of the "on-off" switches, but "presetting" came into being. The switches were grouped according to the color and location of the lamps they operated. (e.g., "Red footlights" "Blue first border," etc.) Each group was controlled by a color master switch and the whole switchboard was controlled by a "main switch." Thus there was a "red master," a "blue master," and a "white master." The electrician could preset the colors on stage while the curtain was down and an act was taking place on the apron illuminated by the limelight follow spotlight. When the next full-stage act opened, the electrician threw the proper master switch or even the main to bring up the color arrangement he (female electricians were unknown at this time) had preset. Thinking of lighting as series of internally static presets was on its way.

Although resistance dimmers were installed in a theatre in London almost as soon as electricity was introduced, most theatres were equipped with the switchboard first and dimmers considerably later.

Resistance dimmers

These were not part of the switchboard but existed as a separate rack to be operated by another electrician.

Later the resistance dimmers and switches were incorporated into a single but very large unit. A safety factor was added: The entire front of the device was enclosed in metal preventing any possible contact with live parts (see Figure 4.1). The back and sides were covered with metal mesh to allow the heat from the dimmers to dissipate. This arrangement was touted as "dead front." The unit was now called a "controlboard."

Dimmers made it possible to adjust the light output of the border-lights and footlights providing gradual color changes and also to begin and end scenes with a fade-in or fade-out. The dimmers were all installed on a common shaft to which they could be locked, making it possible to move an entire row at the same time. Unfortunately all of them had to be

Mechanical
interlocking

The Now-Obsolete Resistance Dimmer

Resistance dimmers work by adding resistance in series with the lamps thereby cutting down current flow. When about 3 to 4 times the resistance of the lamps has been added, the current will be reduced to the point where the lamps produce no more visible light. A considerable amount of the current that was being used by the lamps is converted into heat making the dimmers run very hot, particularly at half-dim settings.

Since the amount or resistance needed to black out the lamps varies with the resistance of the lamps, a given dimmer can dim out only a relatively narrow range of lamp loads. Too much load will cause the dimmer to take the lamps out prematurely and too little will make it impossible to dim them out to black. Thus the dimmers must be matched to the loads or, loads must be adjusted to fit the dimmers by adding extra lamps known as ghost loads. In addition to having the proper amount of resistance, the dimmer must be designed to carry the current up to, and usually well above its rated load.

Load sensitivity, heat and size made the now totally obsolete resistance dimmer an undesirable stage lighting control device. Its only advantage was that it was nearly indestructible—a questionable advantage when it came time to persuade theatre owners to replace them.

at the same reading to be interlocked. The entire set of several rows of dimmers could also be interlocked on many of these early dimmer racks, although this made an exceedingly heavy mass of interlocked machinery. It could only be operated by means of an extra long lever or, for long slow fades, by operating a special worm gear drive device controlled by a wheel. Much later, resistance dimmers were replaced by autotransformer dimmers eliminating the many electrical and mechanical problems of the resistance dimmers (see Figure 4.2). However, at least in large installations, the mechanical arrangement and backstage location of the dimmers and switches remained basically the same.

Autotransformer dimmers

Direct Control

Throughout all of this period of lighting history the control was direct, i.e., there was a mechanical connection between the handle of the dimmer and the current-carrying parts of the dimmer. This meant that the dimmers and switches and all other direct control apparatus had to be large enough and heavy enough to handle the current, well enough insulated to protect the user, and designed to dissipate the very considerable heat when resistance dimmers were in use. This resulted in very bulky controlboards which were always placed backstage to shorten the

Backstage controlboards

Figure 4.1. This photo shows the face of a typical resistance dimmer. The Nichrome resistance wire is imbedded in a ceramic layer installed on the inside of the dish-like steel enclosure. The wire is arranged in a zigzag pattern making it possible for the brass contacts, which extended up through the ceramic, to have several inches of wire between each adjacent pair As the contact arm was rotated, resistance wire was added or subtracted from the circuit.

The scraping of the moving contacts over the fixed ones often made these dimmers noisy to operate. They also produced heat in significant quantities, particularly at partial settings. Note that the face of the dimmer presented live contacts accessible to anyone foolish or careless enough to touch them. For this reason the dimmer racks were enclosed in metal mesh or steel covering to achieve a "dead front." Although now a forbidden practice, resistance dimmers were often circuited into the grounded neutral of the lamp loads making it possible for a single large dimmer to dim a number of load circuits even if they were fed from different phases.

expensive runs of wiring needed and to place the operators where they could take cues from the stage manager. This used up valuable backstage space and located the operators where they could see little of the results of their work—so little that cueing was sometimes done by telephone from a back-of-house location and relayed to the people running the board.

Remote Control

In engineering terms, remote control means that the device handled by the operator does not actually control the current supplying whatever device is being controlled. Instead, the control mechanism sends an electrical signal, usually a tiny current compared to what is being controlled, to the remote device which reacts to the signal and effects the control. Some of the advantages of this arrangement are:

- Lighting control devices for remote control applications can be designed and sized to fit the needs of the operator, not to satisfy the engineering needs of heat dissipation, insulation and the like. This has turned out to be the most significant advantage of remote control for stage lighting purposes.
- Multiple control locations and complicated interlocking controls become possible at reasonable cost and with good reliability.

Figure 4.2. This photo shows the working parts of two autotransformer dimmers, 6 kW and 100 Watts. The 6 kW unit was commonly installed as a replacement for resistance dimmers and was made to fit into the same space. The 100 watt unit served as a master controller for ranks of resistance-based individual circuit controllers in early preset consoles.

Note the coils of copper wire in both units They are wrapped around an inner core of laminated soft iron plates that serves to concentrate the magnetic field making the back EMF more effective. Voltage adjustments are made by rotating the sliding graphite contact (most visible on the 100 W unit) over an exposed part of the copper coil. Without load, either of these dimmers will draw only a minuscule amount of current.

As made for setting voltage in an electronics laboratory, ATDs were equipped with a knob which required about 340° turn to go from full-on to full-off. This motion is awkward and not very useful for making long, smooth theatrical dims. Therefore the dimmers were equipped with rack-and-pinion devices by which a handle could move the dimmer over its entire range as the handle moved perhaps 45° to 60°. For the large dimmers, this arrangement could be further mechanically interconnected by inserting it into the same shaft-and-dog system then used for resistance dimmers. Although now obsolete, autotransformer dimmers are still in use.

The Autotransformer Dimmer (ATD)

The autotransformer dimmer (Figure 4.2), a non-load-sensitive voltage-setting device, replaced the resistance dimmer in the 1940s and early 1950s. Early ATDs were simply laboratory instruments imported to the theatre. They were operated by rotating a dial over about 340 degrees—a movement nearly impossible to perform with one motion of the hand. Although there was no way to mechanically master them, electrical mastering was possible.

ATDs were designed to output voltage linearly from 0 to 120 volts which left them with a less than ideal operating characteristic for theatrical use. Incandescent lamps respond to increasing voltage non-linearly. Therefore movement of the dial at the low voltage end produced little change but movement near the full voltage end caused rapid change. Later, some ATDs made specially for theatrical use were constructed to avoid this problem. These later ATDs were also designed to be mechanically mastered and to fit into the same controlboard framework that was already in use for resistance dimmers. This resulted in the installation of many controlboards with the same bulky size as controlboards containing resistance dimmers despite the fact that heat dissipation was no longer a problem. Some of these remain in use.

Some autotransformer-equipped "portable" package units (they were actually very heavy) were manufactured containing six 1000 watt dimmers plus a 6000 watt master. A switching arrangement allowed the six 1000 watt units to be operated from the output of the large dimmer or independently, as needed. When in the master-dimmer mode the unit provided completely proportional dimming—the six individual dimmers could each be placed at any setting and dimmed by the master maintaining the proportional settings until the attached lamps were either full-up or full off—a function impossible with mechanical mastering. Also directions were circulated by manufacturers of autotransformer dimmers for building homemade units for small theatres. Either of these options made it possible to locate the controls at the back of the theatre if wiring were available. However, back-of-house control was considered radical and dangerous by some authorities because of the possible breaks in communication with the stage manager.

During their heyday, ATDs were considered very desirable because of their lack of load sensitivity, the fact that they produced almost no heat and could be adapted to electrical mastering. Unfortunately ATDs were also very heavy, somewhat noisy and not as durable as their predecessors. They were soon replaced by electronic dimmers.

- Noisy and/or heat producing equipment can be located where noise and/or heat will not bother. For example, stage main switches are large and best operated by an electromagnetic device (called a "relay") which will open or close them accurately but noisily. These relays are best located in the basement far from the stage. Dimming equipment can also be noisy. Locating it away from the stage can be advantageous.
- Until recently, lighting control equipment was bulky and precious backstage space could be saved by locating it elsewhere.
- Expensive runs of heavy wire to feed the stage supply can be shortened substantially by locating the dimmer bank and associated switching mechanisms near the building power service entry.

Remote control dimming

Although remote on-off control had been common in electrical engineering applications for many years, it was only after World War II that electronic equipment became available from which remote control dimmers could be economically and reliably made. The next decade saw a rapid evolution through electronic tube ("thyristor" or "thyratron") dimmers to silicon controlled rectifier dimmers (SCRs) to today's modern refinements of SCRs (see Chapter 12). The result was smaller, lighter, less noisy and much more reliable remote control dimmers which are presently almost "invisible" to the console operator.

The "remote" end of a remote control system consists of whatever arrangement of signaling devices is appropriate to the system being controlled. Because it carries only a small amount of current, mostly at low voltages, it can be compact, light in weight and therefore portable, and designed to fit the needs of the operator. For example, a tiny push-button can signal a huge, noisy stage- main relay to turn on or off thousands of amperes of current.

"Consoles" or "desks"

The introduction of the remote control dimmer changed even the terminology of lighting control. The operator(s) no longer struggle backstage at a "switchboard" or "controlboard," instead they work at a "console" (often called a "desk") located at the back of the house where they can see exactly what changes they are making in the lighting. Remote control also effectively separated the problem of selecting a console from that of selecting dimmers. Standardized digital signaling systems (protocols) such as DMX512 have made it possible for most consoles to signal most dimmers.

Console design

The development of the remote control dimmer also brought into existence the art and craft of console design—the creation of consoles adapted to the needs of the operator(s) instead of meeting the engineering requirements of a power handling device. For a considerable period of time this art moved ahead without the benefit of the computer, which was still in its infancy. During this pre-computer era both the designer and the operator(s) were frustrated by the console's limited ability to handle cue information. At first there was no way to store cue information except by writing it down, just as had been done for direct control systems. Operators looked at the cue sheet when warned of an oncoming cue, organized their hands on the controls, and moved them on "take."

Per-computer console designs

Very soon consoles were devised whereby an extremely limited amount of cue information could be stored in rows of controllers, each row representing one complete set of dimmer readings for the entire console. These controllers had to be set individually by hand while the row was inactive. A single row represented the data for one cue which could be brought to the stage by activating the entire row and deactivating the row that previously controlled the stage. At first two rows ("two-scene preset") were provided. It was soon apparent that there were many cue situations where there wasn't time between cues to reset the inactive row before the next cue was called. The immediate solution was to add more rows creating multiple scene presetting, eventually up to ten scenes! The result was monstrous consoles with bewildering arrays of controllers and a special crew member who did nothing but readjust the preset knobs to stay ahead of the operator. Errors abounded and were nearly impossible to correct because it was so difficult to find which controller was off its setting. This was presetting at its worst (see Figure 3.2).

Early attempts to simplify this data entry task resulted in such things as stacks of punch cards (easily dropped and scrambled) each containing the information for a single cue, and even a system in which a number of portable racks of controllers, each representing one cue, rode on an endless chain arrangement that moved them into position and inserted them into the system so the cue could be run.

Computer-Assisted Consoles

The earliest attempts at handling cue information by computer were limited because computer memory was limited and expensive. Not enough cues could be stored to get through an entire show unless it was very simple. Therefore the memory had to be reloaded between acts. Thankfully this era is long gone.

Huge memories make modern consoles possible.

The modern computer has proven to be a near-ideal solution to the problem of handling cue data. It can accurately store huge amounts of data and bring it back for change or operation almost instantly. Modern computer memory has become economical and available in huge quantities, eliminating any need for reloading. In fact, some systems allow cues for several shows to be stored in memory at the same time. Additionally, removable storage devices with huge capacity make it possible to store any amount of cue data outside the computer and/or to take it from console to console with ease.

Total automation of lighting is not applicable to legitimate theatre.

It is important to note what "computer-assisted" means: The computer does the same job that was so poorly done by pre-computer devices handling cue data. It keeps the cues in order and makes the data available to the operator as needed—*it does not run the show*, although it could. Total automation is not desirable in live theatre where actor-audience interaction is of the essence and where subtle but very important changes may be made by the operators during each performance to synchronize the lighting with the show. Nevertheless, equipment to operate completely computer-run shows is standard in suppliers catalogues. Such shows are found in amusement parks where the entire shows are automated and the actors, if there are any, must follow a prescribed pattern of movements on an exact time line. While spontaneity has little to do with this arrangement, consistency and economics do.

The Ideal Console

The ideal console should resemble a musical instrument as far as its relationship with the operator is concerned. A fine violin is so designed that it allows a master violinist to completely command it, making it seem to vanish from the listener's and musicians's attention leaving the artist and the music as a seamless experience. Similarly, the ideal control console should be so well adapted to the operation of the lighting that the operator can concentrate on the lighting he or she is "playing" while the console remains in the background. Clearly, modern consoles still do not reach this ideal state, although they come much closer than any from the past.

Console compared to a musical instrument

Some General Concepts of Lighting Control

As lighting control has developed from the crude beginnings with resistance dimmers controlling border lighting, the following control concepts have evolved. They are common to most modern consoles:

Proportional dimming

Historically, this concept was a much longed-for improvement over the mechanical mastering provided by the practice of mounting resistance dimmers on a common shaft to which they could be attached by means of a metal rod (a "dog") that fitted into a notch running the length of the shaft. This rod was spring loaded but could be locked in its up position keeping it clear of the shaft or could be released allowing the dog to engage the shaft when the notch lined up with the dimmer rod. Thus all interlocked dimmers had to be at the same reading. With this arrangement it was common practice to perform a fade-up by locking in the dimmer which was at the lowest reading and setting the remaining dimmers to latch as the shaft rotated and picked them up. The result was that as the fade-up progressed all of the dimmers were brought to the same setting, destroying the ratios previously set between the individual dimmers.

Mechanical dimming—all dimmers at same setting

The introduction of the ATD brought the first real prospect of true proportional dimming where the ratio between the individual circuits could be maintained until the circuits reached either full up or full out depending on the direction of the fade. This was first done by providing a large ATD capable of handling the total load of the smaller dimmers to be mastered by it. A switching arrangement was usually provided that allowed the master dimmer to control individual dimmers up to its capacity or, if mastering was not needed, to use the large dimmer to control a large load such as house lighting. Note that this circuitry could be applied using resistance dimmers but the result would be that any change in one of the individual dimmers would also cause the rest to change (unless the master dimmer was at full on) because of the load sensitivity of the master resistance dimmer. Nevertheless such systems were occasionally constructed and used although they were frustrating for operators.

Large ATD as master

Proportional dimming is now the assumed standard for all consoles. However, it is no longer accomplished by huge dimmers capable of carrying the load of many individual circuits. Remote control electronics has solved that problem by doing the mastering at the control level where,

Remote control
eliminates the need
for large master
dimmers.

in fact, the same circuitry may be found, but in tiny controllers which master each other by setting voltages, not carrying loads. Digital circuitry can also accomplish mastering using even less current and providing still greater flexibility.

Pile-on

The term pile-on describes the situation where an individual circuit controller is controlled by two or more masters at the same time—a common occurrence when the same channel is part of two or more presets operating simultaneously. The usual practice is to engineer this situation so that whichever master controller is at the highest setting takes control of the individual circuit. There is no adding together of the control signals. This is often described as "highest reading takes precedence."

Highest reading takes
precedence

However there is also on many consoles another possibility: "last takes precedence." Whichever master is last moved establishes the setting for the piled-on circuits. Last action may be selectable over the entire console or may apply only to certain designated channels Obviously this makes for a different kind of cueing. For example, a cue might begin with one master at 8, the other at 4, and the piled-on circuit at 10. The master reading 8 is the last one moved and the piled-on circuit is at 8. Consider the effect of moving the other master *up* from 4 to 6: The piled-on circuit will be to dimmed *down* to 6 because this is the last movement. This type of control provides the chance for an *up* motion of a fader to cause *down* movements of some circuits while effecting up movements in others The reverse is, of course, also possible.

Moving a master up
can cause a
downward effect in
the piled-on circuit.

This type of control can effect changes that otherwise cannot be done with a single control handle without executing a cross fade between presets that removes one set of readings while adding another. Obviously, both operators and designers must be very sure which mode they are using when establishing cues.

Intensity vs. rate control

"Normal" controllers, submasters and masters set the brightness of the luminaires they control. The rate of change depends on the speed and rhythm of the movement of the controller. However it is also possible, and sometimes desirable, to have controllers which adjust the *rate* of change instead of the intensity.

Rate control offers the operator a degree of subtlety different from simple intensity control. The end effect of the cue remains the same as it would if controlled only by an intensity controller. However, varying the rate will change the duration of the cue, thus affecting its rhythm. Rate control may be applied to a wheel control and thereby control the rate of all channels assigned to that wheel. This kind of control is particularly effective for making adjustments to account for variations in the pace and rhythm of a production from performance to performance.

Rate changes alter
the rhythm of the cue.

Preset vs. tracking

In a typical example of the evolution of console terminology, an addition has been made to the definition of the word preset. This has come about with the development and promotion of "tracking" as a desirable feature in modern consoles. Tracking simply means that once a channel is set at a reading, it will continue through subsequent cues at that reading until changed by another cue. For example, if the warm sidelights are set at 80% in cue 3, they will continue to appear at that setting in all future cues until changed by another cue setting them, for instance, to zero. Actually, this concept is no different than what now obsolete manual boards provided; a dimmer, once set, remained at that setting until moved. However modern tracking is a computer-assisted function that offers not only basic tracking, but also the possibility of isolating a single channel or package of channels from the cues memory and examining its settings throughout the show. Changes can be made globally on tracked cues or by segments. Some consoles may allow tracking to be selected or deselected, depending on the designer or operator's needs.

With computer-assisted tracking came the need for a term describing its opposite. "Preset" is the favored term. This is logical because on old-fashioned manual set preset banks no settings carried over from one row of controllers unless they were reset.

Tracking can be a convenience to the operator or a nuisance, depending on how the cues are interrelated in the show. If it remains in effect, the operator who is setting cues must take extra precautions to black out channels not wanted when moving from cue to cue. Indeed, some operators routinely include a "blocker" cue as the first cue in each scene which sets all channels back to zero. Then the new cue may be built up knowing that no tracked channels lurk in the background.

Modern Consoles as "Platforms"

In the jargon of the computer specialist, "platform" refers to the device itself (e.g., Macintosh, IBM, etc.) combined with the basic operating system ("OS") that determines how the machine will operate. However a platform can do nothing until it has been loaded with a program of software such as "Microsoft Word," or "Pagemaker" which determines what it can do. This arrangement makes the computer an exceedingly flexible machine capable of a wide variety of functions, depending on which programs are loaded into it.

Unlike computers, most lighting consoles, with the exception of some of the most modern, are hard wired. This means that the program is built into its electronics and cannot be easily changed. Thus the early console, "Lightboard," operated only within one set of instructions. Changing its program would have required extensive electronic reworking. On the other hand, some modern consoles are structured more like their computer relatives. Rather than having their various functions built in, their functions depend on the software installed in them and that software can be easily changed.

Hard wired vs. software

Depending on the brand, consoles may be considered as being pure "platforms," almost totally subject to reconfiguration by the software or they may be partially "hard wired" which means that some control configurations are permanent parts of the console and others subject to alteration by changing the software.

Consoles As Related to Dimmers

Electronic and mechanical dimmers respond to the same commands

In terms of engineering, the entire console is a "remote control device." It only handles very small amounts of electrical current using it mainly to send electrical signals to electronic or mechanical dimmers and operate pilot lights. Electronic dimmers (Chapter 12) are usually located in some space close to but not on stage where the heat and noise (both mechanical and electronic) can be controlled and the dimmers protected from mishandling and overheating. Mechanical dimmers (really motor-driven shutter-like devices) are found built into automated luminaires. The console devices which control either type of dimmer can be identical and interchangeable.

Fortunately dimmers are normally "transparent," i.e., they impose no special concerns on the operator or designer except to see that they are properly circuited when the lighting equipment is installed and, if loads are changed during the show, that they are not overloaded.

The Effect of Automated Equipment on Console Design

Color changers (one type is known as "scrollers") were introduced into the theatre many years ago but have only recently become common. Automated luminaires, sometimes known as "wiggle lights" or "robot luminaires," are a still more recent addition. They were first used in the concert lighting world which contributed much to their development and are now moving into the legitimate theatre. (See Chapter 8 for details on these luminaires.) These devices have multiplied the number of variables handled by a console many times over. In the past, all changes commanded by the console varied the light output of luminaires and only indirectly changed the color and distribution of the light on stage, automated luminaires can directly vary a number of attributes (sometimes called parameters, variables, functions, etc.) of the light produced. Although the number, nature, and names of these attributes vary from manufacturer to manufacturer, the following list is typical:

Originally one kind of control: intensity

- Mechanical dimming
- Movement of beam (pan and tilt)
- Color varied by dichroic or standard filters on a color wheel or by subtractive color mixing with dichroic filters
- Beam shaping
- Selectable beam angle
- Beam rotation
- Adjust for hard/soft beam edge
- Strobe effects
- Gobo (or slide) selection
- Movement of gobo (or slide)
- Variable focus of gobo (sharp or soft)

Designers of lighting for opera and musical theatre, in particular, will find the artistic potential of these luminaires overwhelming. However devising adequate control for these complex applications proves to be a challenge. Early solutions to this control problem, devised by the pop concert industry, consisted of multiple presets which could be rapidly sequenced to create a light spectacle to go with the music. Note the description of the "touch plate" below. Elaborate electronically generated "chases" were also often added to bring still more movement and glitter into the concerts.

Overwhelming new potentialities for lighting control

Rapidly changing presets for pop music

However this kind of control offers little to the designer of legitimate theatre lighting. The great artistic potential that these luminaires promise can be achieved only if the console can provide *individual control over each variable for each luminaire*. Although the beginnings of this kind of console development are now evident, the ultimate console for handling this awesome array of control variables remains a dream of the future. See Figure 3.3 for some current partial solutions to this problem.

Individual control over functions is necessary.

Devices Commonly Found on Consoles

In the "generation" of consoles just prior to the present each of the devices listed below appeared as a separate physical device. In consoles of the "platform" variety these devices may exist as software functions assignable to one or more controller-like mechanisms. Thus the function "submaster," for example, may, for different productions using different software, appear on different parts of the console. It is even possible that these functions may shift position during a single show.

Not all of the items on this list will be available on every console or with every software package. Unfortunately the names given to these devices vary from manufacturer to manufacturer. It is up to the potential user to determine exactly what they do. Figure 4.3 illustrates a top-of-the-line console.

Controller: This is the most basic unit of control. It affects only one electrical channel, making it possible to dim that circuit up or down or, if the circuit under control handles an attribute of a moving light, controls that one variable for the luminaires on that channel. Note that however many luminaires are attached, they will all operate as one. Controllers found on most consoles are slider devices usually calibrated 1–10. These may be physically identical to and interchangeable with other sliders used for the functions below.

In consoles where functions are determined by software, rows of sliders are often provided which take on the function of "controller" whenever the software commands, but can also serve other functions if so designated. Such rows of multiple-function controllers may be referred to as "submasters" in manufacturers' literature.

Submaster: A device or assignable function that controls a group of individual circuits each of which also has individual control. In turn, a group of submasters may be assigned to a master.

Note that controllers, submasters and masters may all have the same mechanical appearance and that, in many cases, the same device can serve any of these functions depending on software commands. On consoles where the functions are hard wired, each of these will be represented by a mechanical device specially designed to serve its function, although the internal parts may actually be about the same.

Page(s): Refers to programmable consoles only. A typical statement in the specifications for a console might read: "Twenty pages of submasters are supplied."

A "page" of submasters is a configuration of submasters and circuits assigned to them that exists as a unit of memory in the computer. It can be brought into play making a highly specialized package of control available to the operator. While the page is in control, the operator has the advantage of the particular pattern

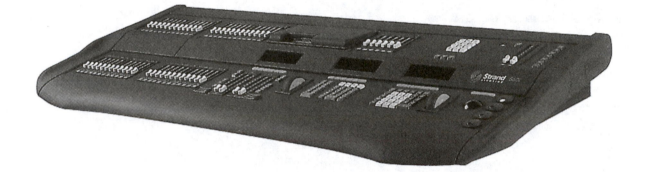

Figure 4.3. Control Console Components. This highly sophisticated console, the Strand 550i, illustrates the appearance and organization of controls on modern consoles. Note that no individual channel controllers are present, although, they would look about like the submasters. Instead, individual channels may be digitally called up, given an intensity setting and assigned to any of a wide variety of controls. Submasters however abound, supplemented in this console by bump buttons that allow instant on-off action of the channels controlled by the submaster, and by LEDs that indicate active or inactive status. Note the six supermasters with their liquid crystal displays that allow labeling to indicate what channels are being controlled. A grand master controller and a blackout or stop button are also present.

The Playback section consists of two split cross faders capable of a variety of actions including automation, depending on software. Adjacent to them is a wheel which can vary the rate of progress of any cue(s) assigned to it. This playback section can be split into two control packages, one for moving lights and one for fixed lighting equipment.

The Moving Lights section features a trackball to which one or more moving lights may be assigned and their pan and tilt controlled, or any other attribute appropriate to control by trackball. Note also the four fingerhole knobs. These are also for motion control.

This console is software configured and can, by itself, control as many as 6000 intensity channels and 2000 scroller or moving lights channels. In addition, a number of these consoles can be interconnected to afford control over very large facilities and/or large numbers of moving lights plus regular lighting. Photo courtesy Strand Lighting.

of control he or she predetermined. When that configuration is no longer needed, another page can be activated making a new organization of the submasters available for use. Thus pages are a major way of reorganizing the console as the operator(s) run the lighting cues. It is advantageous to have a number of pages available on a console. Note that shifting from page to page is a common way of altering the function of many of the devices on the console, for example, changing the function of an erstwhile controller into that of a submaster.

Master: This is a device (or function) which effects control over a number of individual controllers and thereby controls a number of channels.

Grand Master: A master-like device that controls all or almost all of the circuitry on the console. This can be a very powerful control—if it is so circuited, the entire stage may be blacked out by operating it.

Pages configure control for specific lighting situations.

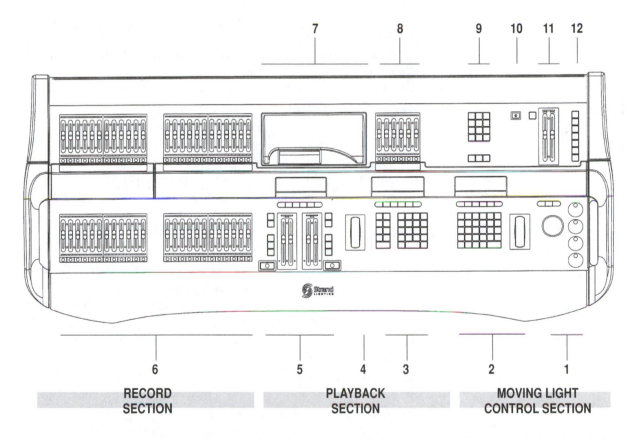

RECORD
SECTION

PLAYBACK
SECTION

MOVING LIGHT
CONTROL SECTION

1. Tracker ball, rotary controls (fingerhole knobs) and option keys for moving light control

2. Command keypad, multifunction wheel, context sensitive soft keys and graphics LCD

3. Function keypad, effects keypad, effects soft keys and graphics LCD

4. Rate wheel

5. Playbacks, 'GO' buttons, context sensitive soft keys and graphics LCD

6. Submasters, bump buttons, 'active' and 'loaded' LED indicators

7. Floppy disk drive

8. Supermasters or extra submasters

9. Display and command routing key pad

10. Power On/Off

11. Grandmasters and 'stop' button

12. User programmable keys

Fader (Crossfader): This is a slider-operated device that shifts control from one package of control to another. Unlike the controller and master controller, crossfaders have no "off" position (unless one end is purposely left unloaded). Moving the slider from one end of its travel to the other gradually shifts the control from one group of settings to another. In its intermediate positions, both sets of controllers and master(s) have control, the degree depending on the location of the slider.

A wide variety of controllers, submasters and even masters may be assigned to either end of a crossfader. This makes the crossfader one of the most-used devices found on the playback part of the console.

Split Fader: This device could be thought of as two masters installed so that the "off" position of one is mechanically adjacent to the "on" position of the other. One may assign all of the "up" movements in a cue to one half of the split fader and the "down" movements to the other. This makes it possible to control the outgoing part of the cue at a different pace and over a different time period than the oncoming part of the cue, something highly desirable in most lighting situations.

Autofader: This may be either a single fader or a split fader. The distinction is that this device will automatically time a fade once it is signaled to start the movement. The most sophisticated autofaders allow the rate of change to be programmed to follow a predetermined time pattern. A variety of these "fade curves" is usually available and custom curves may be possible. Faders can be used to control intensity, the usual arrangement, or they may control rate of fade.

Wheel: This device is literally a knurled wheel part of whose perimeter extends through the surface of the console. Any one or more of the various control devices or functions on the console may be assigned to the wheel. While assigned, their setting may be altered either up- or downward from wherever it was when the device was assigned. Once changed, the new setting may be recorded into the current cue, made into a new cue, or abandoned in favor of the original setting. This flexibility makes the wheel a desirable device for quickly changing settings "live." Note that the wheel has no stopping point. Its movement simply raises or lowers the setting from its present amount.

Touch Plate: This device is rare on consoles designed for the legitimate theatre but common on those designed for the concert field. It consists of a rectangular metal plate that only needs to be touched to cause it to function. Its purpose is to make it possible for the operator to "play" a series of presets rapidly and in random sequence. Changes are usually as near to instantaneous as the luminaires will allow. Also touching a plate could serve as a "go" signal for an automated cue sequence.

Trackballs and *Fingerhole Knobs*: These are special controllers normally used to control the movement of automated luminaires. The trackball may be simply the same device often found in place of a mouse on computers. The fingerhole knob is a conveniently large knob with a finger hole in its face to allow the operator to rotate it smoothly over a complete circle. Either of these devices make it possible for the operator to angle one or more luminaires over a wide range, the limitation being the capability of the luminaire itself.

Organization of Consoles

The pervasive influence of the preset concept is reflected in the organization and labeling of many consoles. One section is often entitled "recording" and another "playback." (Figure 4.3) The recording portion is arranged to facilitate the creation and storing of preset cues. It will usually contain a bank of controllers, sometimes one per channel, sometimes a lesser number to which any load circuit or circuits may be assigned by computer. Many consoles contain what amounts to a manual two-scene preset controlboard which is intended to enable the operator to create and record cues and also to run simple shows directly from the console without previously creating presets. The two-scene setup provides two controllers for each circuit under control making it possible not only to create preset cues but also to design and record the transitions between cues. On many consoles, this two-scene preset arrangement will handle only a fraction of the total number of channels in the system unless several are loaded onto each controller. When not being used to build up cues, these same controllers can be digitally reassigned, frequently as submasters.

Record and playback sections of a console

The "record" portion of the console will also contain or be adjacent to the apparatus needed to assign cue numbers and sometimes names, and then to record them into memory. Transitions between cues may also be recorded on the more elaborate consoles. Note that almost every console available provides facilities for the insertion of additional cues between those previously recorded.

Inserting additional cues into the sequence

"Playback" Section of Consoles

The playback part of the console (Figure 4.3) will contain facilities for calling up cues, assigning them to a control device and then taking the cue at the proper moment in the production. Cross faders are the commonest device for this operation. Cues are sequentially assigned to the inactive end of the cross fader and brought up when the fader handle is moved to that end. If the console is set in its "sequential mode," as soon as the fader has reached the limit of its traverse, the next cue in memory will be called up and assigned to the inactive end. This makes it possible to move from cue to cue as fast as the fader handle can be moved back and forth. Obviously, this arrangement is ideal for operating preset cues. The ultimate in this sort of automation is for the transitions to be recorded into the cues taking even the timing of the transitions out of the hands of the operator who has only to press a "go" button (or move the autofader lever slightly) to initiate the cue.

Sequence mode

Using Modern Consoles for Counterpoint Lighting

Although the labeling and outward arrangement of most modern consoles reflects their history as preset devices, all but the most primitive offer a wide variety of ways to operate counterpoint lighting or, even better, to combine preset and counterpoint lighting. The designer and operator(s) must simply ignore the labels such as "record" and "playback" and use the functions provided.

Ignore "record" and "playback."

One of the most useful functions of a modern console is the previously mentioned "page" arrangement for re-configuring the channels operated by "submasters." Despite the name, an adequate number of these devices provides an ideal way to set up pattern control, provided that the submasters actually exist or can be made to exist on the console and are not merely software. The usual procedure is to assign a number of individual channel controllers to a submaster to make up a pattern. If these controllers are actually present on the console, they may also be used to tweak settings within the pattern. Most modern systems allow the same load circuit to be assigned to more than one control path at once making it possible for an individual circuit to serve more than one pattern at a time.

Pages of submasters offer ideal flexibility.

Patterns for an individual segment of the show can be built up on a single page and, when the time comes to add or drop one or more patterns, this can be accomplished by setting up the new arrangement on another page and switching between the two. "Live" page changing should be possible on any console intended for use with counterpoint cueing. Although the usual number of patterns being changed at any given moment during a production will usually not exceed three or four, as many as ten patterns may need to be available on pages to allow for rapid shifting instantly from one working group of patterns to another.

While counterpoint is being operated via the pages of submasters, one or more presets can be operating to care for the static or near-static portions of the lighting. These will, of course, carry through without being affected by the pattern changes.

Presets can run along with patterns.

Note that this scheme almost reverses the apparent intent of the console designer's labels. The "playback" section becomes the control for whatever presets are in effect and may require relatively little of the operators' attention. Meanwhile the counterpoint lighting will be effected on the "record" section, often with intense activity. Those considering the purchase of a new console may wish to keep this in mind giving those consoles which provide adequate space for this activity an advantage over those which crowd the "record" section into the smallest possible space.

Other Parts of Consoles

A wide variety of features is offered by most manufacturers, particularly for their more elaborate (and expensive) consoles. Here are some of them:

Tracking: In addition to offering the designer and console operator a way of making a channel setting or settings continue automatically from cue to cue until changed, tracking affords the technician a way of searching through the cues to discover why something mysteriously goes wrong with a channel at some as-yet-unknown point in the show.

Global Change or *Cancel*: This function, associated with tracking enables the operator to change the reading of the identified circuit over the entire show or to cancel that circuit out completely. "Cancel" is particularly useful during the run when a luminaire gets knocked out of focus and light is striking where it is not intended. The offender can be canceled out until repairs can be effected.

Flash or *Bump*: This is an electronic means of identifying a luminaire or luminaires on a single circuit so that changes can be made. Flash causes the circuit to flash on and off enabling the crew to identify the luminaires associated with it. Bump temporarily brings the luminaire(s) to full thus making it stand out from the many others presently on. Both of these features are helpful during focusing sessions and when making changes between rehearsals.

Using tracking to solve problems

Utility Controls

Although not a direct part of lighting design and operation, such items as house lighting, work lights, orchestra pit lighting and, of course the lighting for the console itself, must be controlled. Many consoles can be ordered with controls for these items installed ready to be hooked up. In other cases, the controls for these utilities will be mounted adjacent to the console but not as part of it.

Emergency Controls

The theatre building emergency lighting system will automatically come on in case of power failure without any action on the part of the lighting personnel. Indeed, the emergency system is intentionally kept entirely separate from the theatrical lighting system and even utilizes a separate set of lamps mounted in the house and throughout the building. Its automatic controls are installed well away from the stage lighting system. However, many municipalities also require a "panic" system controllable from a number of legally specified locations including the lighting control area, backstage right and left and the house manager's office. Panic buttons are engineered to transfer the house lighting from its normal dimmer-operated source to a constant and separate power supply, thereby providing house lighting in the event of a complete failure of the stage system, but not of the entire building supply. The panic button in the lighting control area should be installed near the console, although legally it cannot, in most instances, be a part of the console. Operators should be well informed about its purpose and also about the emergency system.

Chapter 5

THE NATURE OF LIGHT

Light as Radiant Energy

Light is the very essence of our art, yet there is much that is unknown about its physical nature and the way the human body responds to it. A study of the physics of light leads almost directly to the great cosmological questions of our time and to some very complicated concepts. Visible light is but a tiny part of a vast array of "radiant energy" which is known as the electromagnetic spectrum. All of this radiation travels at approximately 186,200 miles per second (300,000 kilometers/sec.) through space and through man-made vacuums, and at lesser speeds through other media. The speed of light in a vacuum is one of the fundamental constants of our universe and therefore figures importantly in the theory known as quantum mechanics. Although not a complete "theory of everything," quantum mechanics accounts for the behavior of particles near the atom's size and is quite well substantiated by its close conformity with observable data.

The speed of light

Quantum mechanics

Wave Length: Spectra

Wave length is a measurement of the distance between any point in a wave to the next point where the motion or activity begins to repeat itself. In water waves, for example, if the first point is the very peak (top) of the water wave, the wave length will be measured from that point to the point where the wave again peaks (Figure 11.3). A spectrum is a display of wave phenomena arranged by wave length.

Wave length

Spectrum

The electromagnetic spectrum is roughly diagramed on Plate II along with a color image of that part of it which is visible to the normal human eye. Note that the wave lengths included in the complete spectrum range from miles in length (some radio waves) to exceedingly short wave lengths (X-rays and gamma rays).

While much is known about the electromagnetic spectrum, when physicists attempt to explain the nature of what is radiated they run into a conundrum: light sometimes behaves as though it were wave motion and at other times as though it were a stream of particles. The very fact that instruments can be devised to display it as a spectrum seems to indicate that electromagnetic energy consists of wave motion. Treating light as wave motion enables scientists to explain many things about it, including how lenses and dichroic filters work. However there are other phenomena related to light (and other parts of the electromagnetic spectrum) that cannot be explained by considering it to be wave motion but can be explained by considering it to be a stream of packets of energy (particles) known as photons. For instance, the photon theory is required to explain how light causes a solar cell to generate electrical current.

Light as wave motion

Particle theory

Physicists and cosmologists are able to reconcile these two apparently contradictory sets of data by referring to quantum mechanics which (much simplified) allows them to consider light to have both wave properties and the characteristics of particles at the same time. Although the complexities of this theory place it out of reach of this text, the lighting technician and designer will not be able to avoid reference to it completely. At several key points in any discussion of the technology of lighting, quantum mechanics lies just below the surface. For instance, the explanation of the fact that the color of the light produced by an incandescent body varies with its temperature depends on quantum theory.

Quantum theory

Human Color Vision

Although not based on quantum mechanics, the status of our knowledge of the physiology of vision is much the same as that of the physics of light. Much research is occurring in this area, largely based on new techniques for scanning the living brain to determine what parts are active under various stimuli. The concept of the three basic color sensors in the eye still applies but with new understanding and complication brought about by the discovery that the way the brain processes color sensations from the eyes is much more complex than once thought. This will be developed in Chapter 9.

Physiology of vision

Visible Light As a Physical Phenomenon

Visible light, as already noted, is but a tiny part of the total electromagnetic spectrum. It includes energy whose "wave length" (referring to the wave motion part of the theory of the nature of light) ranges from about 4/10,000 of a millimeter to about 7/10,000 of a millimeter (400 to 700 nanometers). However the human body can detect the presence of considerably more of the electromagnetic spectrum. At the "long wave" (700 nm) end of the visible spectrum there is a considerable range of radiation known as "infrared." These waves are the "radiant heat" often referred to in discussions of insulation and very much at the center of our upcoming discussions about the efficiency of lamps and the effects of heat on equipment. Infrared light is felt by the body as heat and is often used to "relieve" sore muscles because it penetrates deeply into flesh. As one moves on up the spectrum toward still longer wave lengths, the

Visible spectrum

Infrared light

infrared "light" gradually becomes ultrashort radio waves (microwaves) and the body no longer detects them although it can be affected by them.

It is very important to note that as wave lengths become shorter, the amount of energy the photons carry increases, and dangers from the effects of this radiation increases. At the "short wave" 400 nm end of the visible spectrum is found the ultraviolet radiation (UV). The entire UV spectrum extends roughly from 100 nm to 400 nm where visible light begins. This spectrum is divided roughly into the following categories, based mainly on the effect of these rays on the human body:

UVA: 400–315 nm (Near UV)
UVB: 315–280 nm (Middle UV)
UVC: 280–100 nm (Far UV)

All of these wave lengths are found in sunlight along with visible light. UVA, the "black light" used for theatrical effects, can cause parts of the body such as teeth or the vitreous humor of the eyes to fluoresce. It is usually considered harmless although there is some controversy on this subject. UVB, which, fortunately for us, is mostly filtered out of sunlight by the ozone layer before it reaches the surface of the earth, can cause serious damage to human skin, which can lead to cancer. UVC, which is even more dangerous, is almost completely absorbed by air within a few hundred meters, thus none of it reaches the surface of the earth from the sun.

Unfortunately all three types are also produced by many HID sources used in the theatre. Caution is necessary when dealing with light sources which produce "middle" or "far" UV which can be dangerous if not properly filtered out. Beyond the UV portion of the spectrum lies the region of high-energy radiation including X-rays and gamma rays—even more dangerous than UV radiation. Obviously man has found ways to indirectly detect the entire electromagnetic spectrum or we would have no knowledge of the existence of these "rays."

Kinds of Spectra

The spectrum in Plate II resembles a portion of a rainbow; the colors blend smoothly from one to another with no breaks between them. This is characteristic of a continuous spectrum and indicates that it contains all wave lengths. The most common source of continuous spectra is incandescence.

However, if the light source is an ionized gas, such as that in a neon sign, the spectrum will be quite different; it will consist of a series of a series of sharply delineated bands of color representing small groups or even single wave lengths of light separated by total blackness. This is known as a line spectrum and is characteristic of spectra produced by gases which are ionized, for instance, by passing an electrical current through them. Line spectra are very important to scientists because every element produces a characteristic pattern of lines that can serve to identify it. This has resulted in the development of spectroscopy—the science of identifying the presence of elements, often in very small quantities or at astronomical distances. Line spectra are also important to the theatre because they are produced by a number of the non-incandescent sources of light now in use.

Scientists refer to light by wave length. Since fractional numbers, e.g., 4/10,000 mm, are awkward a more convenient unit of measurement, the *nanometer* (nm), has been adopted. A nanometer is 10^9 meters. Earlier units of measurement, sometimes still in use, are the *Angstrom unit*, (10^{-10} meters) and the millimicron, synonymous to nanometer. For example, the scientific description of the two wave lengths of yellow light which produce the bright yellow often seen in street lighting is: 598.9 nm and 589.0 nm. In earlier references these might have read 5989 and 5890 angstroms

Although a wave length figure can exactly locate a beam of light on the spectrum, it gives no indication of the amount of light present, either as energy or as a physiological effect on the eye. Measurements of both are complicated.

Energy Measurements: The energy in a light beam, known as *radiant flux*, is expressed in watts (sometimes "lightwatts"). It varies inversely with the wave length of the light being measured, the shorter the wave length, the more energy it carries. This is what makes X-rays and gamma rays so powerful and dangerous. However, measurements citing radiant flux are of little value to the artist or lighting technician. They incompletely describe color sensations and only indirectly quantify the sensation of brightness, the amount of sensation produced in the eye by light.

Measuring Brightness: Brightness refers to the sensations produced in the eye by varying amounts of light. However the strength of these sensations also depends on the wave length of the light, the eye being most sensitive at a point near the center of the visible spectrum (yellow-green at about 555 nm) and tapering off to zero at about 400 nm (blue-purple) and 700 nm (deep red). Thus brightness readings must be either related to a kind of white light which contains equal energy at all visible wave lengths ("equal energy white") or to specific wave lengths. Brightness is cited in several ways, *luminous flux* being the most basic. Luminous flux measurements are often referred to as *photopic flux* which is balanced to the 555 nm sensitivity peak of the normal eye. Although there is another scientific variety of luminous flux (scotopic flux, which is balanced to the dark-adapted eye) theatre technologists and lighting equipment engineers commonly refer to "luminous flux" without qualifying it as "photopic" and, furthermore, commonly refer to brightness in terms of lumens.

Brightness measurements of white light are made by comparing the light to be measured against the light output of a standard source. This source was once literally a "standard candle," a precisely made candle of special wax. Now the standard is a much more accurately reproducible source; an incandescent piece of platinum metal of a specified size and temperature. Instead of its output being called a "standard candle," it is called the candela. *Webster's Third New International Dictionary of the English Language Unabridged* (1981) defines it as:

"An international unit of luminous intensity equal to the luminous intensity of five square millimeters of platinum at its solidification point of 1773.5° C also called an international candle."

Nanometer

Angstrom Unit

Radiant flux= actual energy

Brightness measurements

Candle

Candela

THE NATURE OF LIGHT

Other brightness units are defined by referring to the candela. A bit of geometry is involved:

Steradian: This is defined as a solid angle, whose vertex is at the center of a sphere, and which cuts off an area equal to the square of the sphere's radius. Thus, if the sphere has a radius of one foot, one-steradian will delineate one square foot of the surface of the sphere. Similarly, a steradian in a one-meter sphere will delineate one square meter of surface. Figure 5.1.

Lumen: (See Figure 5.2) If a one-candela source is placed at the vertex of a one-steradian cone it will illuminate one square foot of spherical surface at a distance of one foot with luminous flux equal to one *lumen* (also known as one foot candle, if English measurements are being used). At one meter distant from the same source one lumen of luminous flux will extend over one square meter of surface. At greater distances, the same amount of luminous flux will be spread over increasingly greater surface area in inverse proportion to the square of the distance from the source. This is known as the *law of squares*. Its effect is to rapidly dissipate light as it moves away from its source.

Thus a lumen can be described in any of these ways:

1. that amount of flux emitted over one steradian from a source of one candela;
2. that amount of luminous flux found over one spherical square foot of surface at a distance of one foot from a source of one candela;

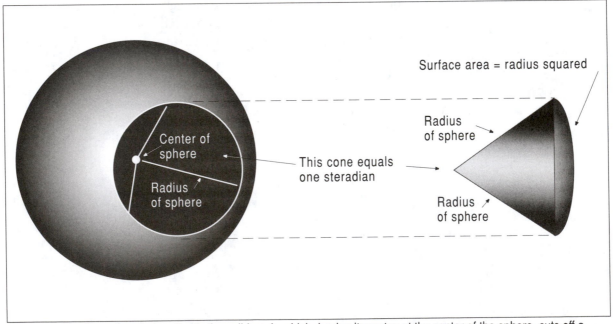

Figure 5.1. The Steradian. A steradian is the solid angle which, having its vertex at the center of the sphere, cuts off a surface area equal to the square of the radius of the sphere.

3. that amount of luminous flux found over one square meter of spherical surface at a distance of one meter from the source of one candela.

Foot Candle: This term is most accurately a synonym for lumen per square foot, however it may also refer, albeit somewhat loosely, to the brightness at any point on a surface illuminated by one lumen of luminous flux.

Foot candle

These units represent small amounts of light. Note that about 30 lm/ft² would be an appropriate brightness for reading text such as this book.

The term "lumen" is much used by manufacturers to describe the efficiency of lamps and lighting apparatus. Lamps are often rated in "initial lumens" which describes the total lumens emitted in all directions by the lamp. It is up to the user to collect this light and direct it in the best possible way. "Lumens per watt" also refers to the total output of the lamp but does some mathematics for the user. Obviously, if initial lumens and wattage are known, initial lumens per watt can be calculated.

Initial lumens

Lumens per watt

A "lumen hour" is the amount of light produced by a lamp emitting one lumen of light for one hour—a very small amount of light. "Cost per million lumen hours" can be a useful figure. The manufacturer has figured in the cost of the lamp, the electricity and (maybe) the cost of relamping and spread this over whatever time it takes for the lamp to produce a million lumen hours. This figure can give the user an idea of the efficiency of the lamp. (Note that a million lumen hours is approximately the total amount of light produced by a 100 watt general service lamp over its entire life.)

Lumen hour

Million lumen hours

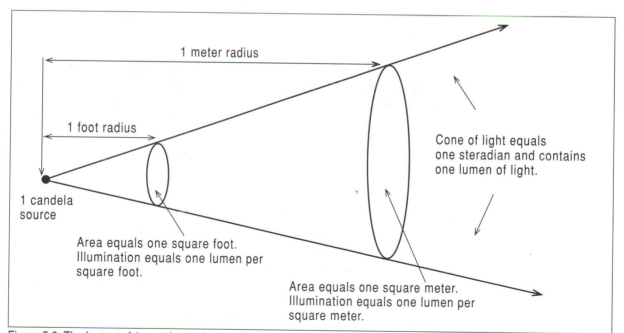

Figure 5.2. The Lumen. A lumen is a unit of irradiation. Beam lumens, defined as the radiation from a one candela (foot candle) source in a solid angle defined as a steradian (Figure 5.1). Note that the lumen refers to a specific quantity of radiation which may be distributed over any area. Thus it is always necessary to define both the area and the number of lumens striking it (e.g., 10 lumens per square foot).

Beam lumens (also "beam candlepower") is a more controversial term. It is much used by manufacturers to describe the efficiency of their luminaires, particularly spotlights, by stipulating the total number of lumens within the beam. The problem is encountered defining the edge of the beam. Only the most precise and expensive scientific optical equipment can be said to approach producing a knife-edge beam which passes from full intensity to total darkness over the "width" of a geometric line. Beam edges of stage lighting equipment always taper off toward darkness over considerable distance and not always evenly. One useful way to

avoid part of this difficulty is to define the "edge" of the beam as the locus of those points where the beam intensity reads 10 percent of the main part of the beam, sometimes called "the brightest part of the beam." This leads to the phrase, "beam lumens to 10% beam candlepower" which is more accurate than trying to define the edge of the beam. Done properly, this "edge" is established by averaging brightness readings over the central part of the beam and using 10% of this number to define the beam edge. Clearly, this averaging technique is subject to variation as is the part of the beam used as the reference.

Since many modern spotlights are equipped with "zoom" devices to change the beam spread over a considerable range, it is also necessary that comparisons between competing luminaires be made at like beam spreads, better still, at a number of like beam spreads.

Spectrograms

A recording spectrophotometer is a precision machine that measures the amount of energy (lightwatts) in light at each wave length present in the sample and reports it in a graphical form known as a *spectrogram*. Precision spectrograms are considered the most scientifically accurate way of defining colored light.

Manufacturers of theatrical color media offer booklets containing samples of their color filters accompanied by simplified spectrograms (Plate III) sometimes labeled "spectral distribution curves." The descrip-

tion may specify that the light passing through the filter was compared with equal energy white light or may merely indicate "percent transmission." These are discussed in Chapter 9.

Producing Light by Incandescence

Not long ago it was safe to say that the incandescent lamp was the source of 99% of the light seen on stage, at least in the USA. This is no longer true. Gaseous discharge sources have taken over an increasing share of stage lighting. Nevertheless, the incandescent lamp remains a major light source which must be understood before one can proceed to other, more exotic and complicated sources.

Incandescence is a way of producing light by converting heat energy into radiant energy. Although this conversion process occurs at any temperature above absolute zero (approximately -273° C) the term "incandescence" is commonly used to describe the process when the radiation produced is near or in the visible range. Very simply explained, the process consists of using the energy of heat to raise electrons attached to atoms to higher energy states. When they return to their normal condition, they emit photons (light) at a wide variety of wavelengths. The relationship between the energy input and the wavelengths of the emitted light is grounded in quantum physics, well beyond the scope of this text.

As the amount of heat applied increases, the wave length of this radiation moves toward the visible part of the spectrum until the heated object begins to emit visible light, beginning at the red end of the spectrum. At this point, the hot object is commonly said to begin to "incandesce." Still higher temperatures cause the matter to radiate the entire visible spectrum and yet higher temperatures can cause it to emit ultraviolet light, X-rays and even gamma rays, phenomena often detected in stars. Of course the matter will have long since melted and, changed to a gaseous state, and ultimately to plasma as the temperature is increased.

Increasing heat causes radiation at shorter wave lengths.

Incandescent Sources

Man's first "artificial" light source was probably incandescent: a pitch knot set afire. All early light sources, torches, oil lamps, candles, various lanterns and the like, produce their light by incandescence. These sources combine the heat producer and the radiant material. For instance, white-hot soot is both the source of light in a flame and part of the burning fuel that produces the heat. The soot particles are heated to incandescence and almost immediately burned up.

Note that no energy is lost in this process and no matter is destroyed. Both matter and energy are simply redistributed to different forms. However incandescence from a flame is not very efficient when the goal is to produce usable visible light. Most of the energy produced in a candle flame, for example, remains as heat and is dissipated with the fumes from the flame. We shall soon see that incandescent lamps are also not very efficient at converting electrical energy into useful light.

• The Coleman lantern

An examination of the Coleman lantern may help the reader to understand the distinction between a heat source and the material which incandesces: This lantern is commonly used by campers and others who need a good source of light while away from electrical lines. The heat source in the lantern is the flame of a gasoline blowtorch which, by itself, produces only a dim bluish glow of little use to a person needing light. The incandescent material consists of a part of the lantern known as the "mantle." This is a delicate whitish structure of mineral ash which was installed around the snout of the blowtorch as a special fabric bag. The first time the flame is lit, the fabric part of the bag burns away leaving the mineral structure in place. When the blowtorch flame heats this mantle, it emits a strong and very useful amount of white light. Note that the mantle is not consumed by the flame— it could theoretically last forever. Thus we have the two parts of the incandescent process clearly defined: a source of heat, i.e., energy to be converted, and matter that can be heated to a temperature high enough to effect the conversion of heat into visible light.

• Electric arc lights

Electric arc light

The electric arc is another early incandescent source, one much used in earlier theatres and also as an early street lighting device. It was invented early in the 19th century by Sir Humphrey Davy but was not used in the theatre until later. It was the first electrical light source in the theatre.

The carbon arc light consists of two rods of carbon, a conductor of electrical current, inserted into an electrical circuit in such a way that the current can flow from one rod to the other. If these rods are touched together and carefully moved a little distance apart, an electrical spark (arc) will form between them and continue to burn as long as the distance between the rods is maintained constant and the current flows. The energy source is the electrical flow which is converted into heat in the arc. Contained within the arc are two types of incandescent material: the heated ends of the carbon rods and bits of carbon (soot) torn from the rods and carried into the arc. This soot incandesces brilliantly before burning at the outer edges of the arc. The result is an intense incandescent source and, naturally, a great deal of heat. Also produced but not visible, is a quantity of carbon monoxide gas produced by the burning of the carbon. This gas

Carbon monoxide dangers

is odorless, colorless, and poisonous. It can seriously injure or kill without any warning. Even if death does not result, the damage done to the brain from carbon monoxide poisoning may be irreversible. Therefore all spotlight booths and/or projection booths equipped for the use of carbon arcs are required by law to have special exhaust systems. However, a particular caution is necessary concerning the use of portable equipment. Although they should now be considered obsolete, it is quite possible that there are still carbon arc follow spotlights available for borrowing or rental. Temporary installation of such equipment in an enclosed space can be deadly—the gas must be exhausted to the outside and fresh air provided for the operator.

"Cored" carbons

While early carbon arcs used rods composed only of carbon, later ones used "cored" rods which had a special center of minerals chosen for their efficiency in converting heat into visible light. This increased efficiency significantly.

Because the arc gradually burns away the carbons, an arc light must have constant adjustment and the carbons need replacement at frequent intervals. This meant that carbon arc lights needed an operator. Actually this was no great hardship because the carbon arc was used almost exclusively as a source for follow spotlights—the powerful luminaires mounted at the back of the theatre and directed to light the "lead" or "star" on stage as he or she moved about. The operator followed the artist, kept the arc in adjustment and replaced the burned carbons as needed.

Although some are still in use, carbon arcs must now be considered obsolete as sources for both follow spotlighting and motion picture projection. Modern follow spotlights and projectors utilize short-arc gaseous discharge lamps, sources of far greater efficiency and safety than the carbon arc. These will be discussed later.

Properties of Incandescent Light

The incandescent lamp is still a major source of light on stage and also serves as a basis of comparison for discussion of more efficient sources. Before discussing the incandescent lamp in detail it will be helpful to understand the characteristics of incandescent light and know how it is described.

If white incandescent light is analyzed by a spectroscope the result will be a continuous spectrum; wave lengths blending from one to another creating a smooth band of color such as that shown in Plate II. This indicates that the light contains all visible wavelengths rather than being made up of bands of wavelengths which would produce a line spectrum. As we have seen, spectral analysis can provide a very accurate description of the wave length content of any light source. It is regularly used in the theatre to describe the properties of color filters, although in a very simplified form.

However the description of white and near-white incandescent light is more commonly done by a comparison process: A standard source is heated until its light exactly matches the sample being described. The temperature of the standard, stated in kelvin (K), is used to describe the *color temperature* of the sample. The standard is a *standard black body*, a source that is theoretically capable of emitting all wave lengths equally. Practical standard black bodies come very close to the theoretical standard. The temperature scale used to describe the light is the kelvin scale named after Lord Kelvin, an early scientist. This scale measures heat beginning at absolute zero, that point where an object no longer contains any heat energy. This is about -273 degrees C. Any matter, when heated above zero K, will emit radiation. At low temperatures this lies in the far infrared range. As the temperature of the object rises, the energy it emits includes shorter and shorter wave lengths until visible light is emitted at about 600–1000 K.

Standard black body

Kelvin scale

Absolute zero

The color temperature system is illustrated by the blackbody locus near the center of Plate I. There is no theoretical upper limit. Although it is difficult to produce extremely high source temperatures in the laboratory, astronomers routinely cite color temperatures into millions of kelvins.

Although very high kelvin numbers are used to describe blue-white and blue light, a source need not operate at these temperatures to produce this light. It can be produced by filtering light of a lower color temperature as long as the source light actually contains the wave lengths needed to make up the high kelvin temperature light. The filter will remove (and waste) much of the energy in the light, but the result will be light at a much higher kelvin reading.

Changing color temperature by filtering

Color Terminology

One of the ironies of color terminology is that the terms used to describe the psychological effects of colored light are in direct contradiction to the kelvin temperatures associated with those colors. Thus a blue-white light (high kelvin reading) will be termed "cool white," and a rose or pink (low kelvin reading) will be called a "warm pink."

"Warm" and "cool" versus color temperature

It is important to note that the kelvin scale has no bearing on the amount of light being produced. One might have a stage full of light at 2000 K or only the emission of a single candle. Similarly, an entire cyclorama might be lit with a very cool blue-white, say 4500 K, or only a tiny highlight on the set. This rather logical set of facts is confused by a characteristic of incandescent lamps. As these lamps are dimmed to produce less light, they also inevitably change color, shifting toward the warm (red) end of the spectrum. Conversely, increasing the power fed to the lamp increases light output and also makes the resultant light cooler. This relationship is almost instinctive with lighting designers who have spent a large share of their careers using only incandescent lamps. However the nature of things is changing. Now the stage may be lit with a mix of incandescent and gaseous discharge sources. The non-incandescent sources, to the dismay of the habituated lighting designer, do not, in most cases, change color temperature as they are dimmed.

Incandescent color
shift with dimming

Non-shifting color
temperatures in non-
incandescent sources

All incandescent sources used on stage are deficient in blue light as compared to the red end of the spectrum. Dimming, as noted above, aggravates this deficiency. This means that the production of large quantities of blue light on stage, e.g., for a cyclorama, is a costly affair requiring many high-wattage lamps to get the effect wanted. This is one of the reasons that many European theatres have converted to fluorescent lamps for cyc lighting—they produce a much higher percentage of blue light, are cheaper to operate, and last longer.

The production of really pure blue light on stage has only recently become possible. Not only were incandescent lamps poor sources of blue light, the media (absorption filters) used to separate this light from the rest of the spectrum were notoriously impure and inefficient. The result has been weak and impure blue light. The recent introduction of gaseous discharge sources and dichroic filters (see Chapters 6 and 9) has now made it possible to have really pure blue light on stage and in useful quantities.

The Incandescent Lamp

The first incandescent light source used in the theatre was the carbon arc lamp discussed above. It entered the theatre about the middle of the 19th century. The first practical filament incandescent lamp was invented by Thomas Edison in 1879 and was soon used in the theatre. Edison's first lamp consisted of a carbon filament enclosed in an evacuated glass bulb. It produced about 1.4 lumens of light per watt of electricity at a relatively low color temperature. After much experimentation, Edison chose to use a carbon filament because of its favorable electrical conduction and high melting point.

Original carbon
filament

The theory of Edison's lamp and all incandescent lamps since produced, is quite simple: An electrically conductive wire of relatively high resistance is enclosed in an evacuated glass bulb. When an electrical current is passed through the wire in the proper amount, the wire will be heated up to the point where it glows white-hot, i.e., it incandesces. The vacuum prevents the wire (filament) from burning up by combining with oxygen in the air and, theoretically, the filament should last indefinitely.

Actually, the filament will deteriorate quite rapidly if it is operated at a very high temperature because of a phenomenon known as *sublimation*. This is a process whereby solids can be converted into gases without first melting. For example, ice cubes will slowly shrink and eventually vanish in a refrigerator even though the temperature of the freezer remains constantly well below freezing. All materials sublimate if the conditions are right. The rate of sublimation varies with the material, increases with temperature and in inverse ratio to the pressure of any gases surrounding the material. This set of circumstances was what held Edison's early lamps to their low efficiency. The pressure on the filament was very near zero (a perfect vacuum) and the temperature was high. Edison quickly discovered that the higher the temperature of the filament, up to the point where the filament might melt, the greater the efficiency but also the faster the sublimation. To maintain a practically useful life, Edison had to run his lamps at low filament temperatures making them inefficient and giving them low color temperatures.

Sublimation

The race was soon on to find more efficient materials for making filaments. Osmium, tantalum and even platinum were tested and found to work but they were prohibitively expensive. Ultimately, in 1907 tungsten filaments were introduced. Tungsten is relatively abundant and has a very high melting point (6120° F). It has the favorable property of emitting much of its radiation in the visible spectrum. Thus it rapidly became the standard material for making filaments. Unfortunately tungsten is naturally a very brittle metal, hard to form into wire. As we shall see below, this caused problems with early lamps.

Tungsten filaments

In 1913 another partial solution to the sublimation problem was introduced. If, instead of a vacuum, an inert gas was introduced into the bulb, the pressure on the filament could be increased slowing sublimation significantly. Nitrogen was first used for this purpose. More recently a mixture of inert gases is used because it has more favorable heat conduction properties. Introducing inert gas into the bulb has the negative effect of moving heat away from the filament more rapidly than it moves through a vacuum. This reduces the efficiency of the lamp. Despite this loss, the use of inert gas makes it possible to operate the filament at a much higher temperature producing more light per watt and at a more useful color temperature. Early gas-filled lamps had about ten times the efficiency of Edison's first lamp—about 14 lumens per watt. Additional improvements in filament design and increases in gas pressure have now brought the efficiency up to well over 20 lumens per watt.

Gas-filled lamps

Concentrated Filament Lamps

Early electrical lamps, while used in the theatre in the place of gas burners in footlights and borderlights with a great improvement in the safe operation of theatres, were of little use as sources for spotlights. The problem with the early lamps was the size and shape of the filament. It was an elongated clothesline-like wire that occupied a considerable space at the center of the bulb. If this lamp were placed behind a lens in an attempt to make a spotlight, the result was an out-of-focus image of the filament instead of a useful pool of light. So from before the time of the

Early filaments
useless for spotlight

invention of the incandescent lamps until about 1920, the only sources for spotlights were carbon arcs and the limelight, a nonelectric source consisting of a piece of limestone heated to incandescence by a gas torch.

This situation changed about 1920 with the invention of the concentrated filament lamp. This invention hinged on the development of relatively ductile tungsten wire which replaced the very brittle wire makers of early lamps were forced to use. When ductile wire was invented and a means devised to coil that wire into tight spirals the *concentrated filament* was invented. It had two advantages: it was a small, compact light source that could be used with a lens to make a spotlight and it was more efficient than previous filaments because the close proximity of the parts of the filament conserved the heat thus causing more of it to be converted into usable light.

Concentrated filament lamps

This tightly packed filament immediately led to the invention of the incandescent spotlight—the first one being a powerful 100 watt model. Other versions of this same filament made possible incandescent slide and motion picture projectors and ultimately such lamps as the modern reflector lamps (types "R" and "PAR") now the backbone of concert lighting.

Lamp technology progressed rapidly. Soon the coiled filament was coiled once again producing a yet tighter source of still greater efficiency known as the "coiled coil filament." Lamp wattage also soon increased to 2000 watts. As various sizes of lamps became available terminology for spotlights became more complex. The original 100 watt spotlight and the soon-developed 250 watt spotlight became known as "baby spotlights" and the larger 1000-2000 models were simply "spotlights."

Coiled coil filament

All of these early lamps were gas-filled and had globular glass envelopes. They were known as "G" type lamps and were the standard lamp for all early spotlights equipped with plano-convex lenses and, within a few years of their invention, with spherical concave metal reflectors for increased efficiency. As lamp wattage increased it became necessary to specify that they be operated "base down to horizontal" to avoid melting the cement that held the base to the glass. Filament supports were designed with this position of operation in mind and if the instructions were not followed, not only might the base come loose, the filament might sag and short itself out.

Restricted operating position

Lamp Life

Edison struggled to produce a lamp that would produce a usable amount of light and have a useful life. The problem still remains with modern lamp engineers, but it is vastly improved. The tungsten filament and the use of a gas fill in the bulb were the two first steps in improving the efficiency/life dilemma. With these two improvements, early general service lamps were made to average 600-1000 hours of life but produced less than 20 lumens per watt. However concentrated filament spotlight lamps were, from the beginning, designed to favor efficiency over life. Thus a "long-life" spotlight lamp had a life of about 200 hours and produced over 20 lumens per watt. Higher efficiency lamps for projection service were made with a rated life of 50 hours. This situation prevailed until the 1950s when the tungsten-halogen lamp became available (see below).

Lamp life vs. efficiency

Lamps for More Efficient Luminaires

During the 1930s it became obvious that the plano-convex lens spotlight was not very efficient and could not be much improved by means then available. Therefore two new types of luminaires were invented, both of which demanded special lamps: the ellipsoidal reflector spotlight and the fresnel spotlight (See Chapter 8 for details on their operation.). The fresnel spotlight in particular requires a very close lamp-to-lens distance. This fostered the development of the tubular (Type "T") lamp which almost replaced the early globular (Type "G") lamp except in very large wattages used in the movie industry. The type "T" lamps not only have tubular bulbs instead of globes, they also have a different filament structure. Filaments for "G" lamps were constructed in a circular form which suited the needs of early plano-convex spotlights and did not need very precise positioning in the luminaire. "T" lamp filaments are flat and may be either monoplanes, one row of filament coils, or biplane type, two closely spaced rows of filament parts. These lamps must be accurately positioned in the luminaire so that the flat side of the filament faces the lens or reflector.

Type T lamps

Monoplane and biplane filaments

The design of the early ellipsoidal reflector spotlight for high efficiency not only required a tubular lamp, but also required that the lamp operate base up. This meant that the lamp had to be built with a securely-fastened base made to take high temperatures and that the filament had to be designed to operate base up without sagging and breaking. Moreover, the operating temperature of these new lamp types was so high that they had to be fashioned out of special high-melting-point hard glass. Even this glass often bulged if the luminaire was out of adjustment.

Base-up operation

With the introduction of tungsten-halogen lamps, the "T" lamp itself is growing obsolete. T-H lamps can operate in any position and are also physically much smaller than the "T" lamps. "T" lamps are still being sold and used in older luminaires although many of these can be retrofitted to take T-H lamps.

Parts of Lamps

With the exception of lamp bases, the parts of a lamp have remained much the same for even the most modern incandescent lamps. Note the configuration of the filament. This will vary considerably with various types and brands but all will represent attempts to engineer the tightest possible filament consistent with reasonably long life and for precise placement of the filament where it should be in the luminaire for which it is designed.

Although a complete lamp catalogue from a major manufacturer will list literally hundreds of base-socket combinations, only a few appear on stage. Two types predominate for use in spotlights: *prefocus* and *bipost*. These are available in two sizes for conventional lamps and the bipost type in a special "bipin" version for smaller T-H lamps. Larger wattages, high heat situations and the need to precisely locate the filament with regards the lens and/or the reflector rule out the common screw base found on general service lamps. Base and socket size engineered for specific lamps depend on the electrical and mechanical stresses placed on them.

• Prefocus base

The prefocus base was specifically designed for situations where the filament must face a lens or reflector precisely, such as a fresnel spotlight. At wattages under 1000 it is usually supplied in the medium prefocus size; larger wattages come with mogul prefocus bases. Both types work the same way. The lamp must be inserted into the base by aligning the fins on the sides of the base with slots in the socket—it goes in only one way. When aligned, the lamp must be pushed toward the bottom of the socket and turned a short distance to lock the fins under the flange of the base. When the lamp is in its proper location a slight click will be felt indicating that it is in place. Forcing the lamp to turn further may break the base or detach the bulb from the base of the lamp. Technicians should also note that it is possible to align the lamp with the base in such a way that only one of the fins actually is inserted into the base. The lamp may even click normally when it is turned, but it will be out of alignment with the lens and reflector and will not be making a proper electrical contact. Careful inspection after insertion of the lamp should prevent this occurrence.

It is common for the technician to encounter a prefocus socket in which the stops that prevent the lamp from turning too far have been broken. If there is not time to immediately replace the socket, the technician may be able to carefully position the lamp so that the flat surface of the filament faces the lens and thereby continue to use the luminaire until a repair can be effected.

• Bipost base

Although the mogul prefocus base can handle considerable current, it has its limits. When these limits are exceeded or when an even sturdier base is required, the bipost base is used. If properly used, this base-socket combination can handle the largest lamp wattages presently supplied. It also serves to align the lamp properly. There are two types, clamp and spring. In the clamp type the lamp is inserted into the base and a screw tightened to improve the electrical contact and hold the lamp firmly in place. To use the spring type the lamp is inserted into a spring-loaded base which holds it in place. Clearly, the clamp type is more secure if properly tightened. Beginning technicians should be cautioned to make sure that bipost lamps are securely clamped in their sockets, particularly in luminaires that operate base-up. It is not uncommon to find a lamp lying loose in the bottom of the reflector of an ellipsoidal reflector spotlight—the result of poor tightening.

Lamp Life

As already noted, lamp life is commonly stated in hours. The stated figure is an average determined by testing the life of many lamps under carefully controlled conditions (voltage, ambient temperature etc.) and averaging the resulting data. Note that the manufacturer does not guarantee that every lamp in a shipment will last the stated life, only that a large number of lamps properly operated will average out to this figure. Normally a manufacturer of very expensive theatrical lamps will make good on lamps that fail within a few hours of start-up and might also make good on a large batch if it can be proven that they did not meet the average life stipulated. However stage conditions which cause the lamps to be dimmed to a variety of readings make it next to impossible to show how the lamps might have performed under standard conditions.

Lamp Life and Efficiency

There are two types of efficiency data relative to lamps used in the theatre: *initial lumens* and *lumen maintenance*. Initial lumens: the total lumen output of the lamp when it is new often stated as a total figure such as: "Initial lumens = 80,000." This figure would describe the output of a rather large lamp. The same data may be reported as lumens per watt, E.g., "Lumens per watt = 20." If this figure refers to the hypothetical lamp mentioned above it would refer to a 4000 watt lamp (4000 x 20 = 80,000). All lamps, as they age, decrease in lumen output, conventional lamps quite drastically. Therefore the "initial lumens" figure is not particularly helpful to the user trying to find the best buy.

Initial lumens

Lumen maintenance is a more helpful figure. It is best stated as a graph showing the drop-off in output as the lamp ages. However it is more likely to be found as a figure entitled "average lumens." This figure gives the user an idea of the amount of light to be expected from the lamp over its rated life but does not indicate the rapidity of the drop-off.

Lumen maintenance

Lamp Failures

Despite the relatively short rated life of stage lamps, most of them have relatively long lives in actual service. This is because they are operated at reduced voltages much of the time. A rough rule-of-thumb states that every decrease in operating voltage of 1 volt will result in an increase in lamp life of 10%. Note that this rule also works the other way: An increase in operating voltage will rapidly shorten lamp life. However many lamps come to an untimely end for reasons other than normal aging.

The natural end of a lamp's life comes when it burns out. There is often confusion about what this means. In the case of normal failure, no actual burning, that is combining with oxygen, has taken place. The tungsten of the filament has simply been removed by sublimation and deposited on the inside of the glass envelope. It remains pure tungsten (not "soot" as sometimes has been alleged) but it is in the wrong place. When a lamp, conventional or T-H, literally "burns out"—that is, the tungsten combines with oxygen—the inside of the bulb will be coated with a yellowish deposit of tungsten oxide. Examination of such a lamp will usually reveal that the seal has broken where the current carrying wires enter the envelope, letting in air, or that the base has been distorted by excessive pressure when inserting the lamp and that the glass has cracked. The tungsten oxide will be most evident when the lamp with air in it was brought up slowly on a dimmer.

Deposit on envelope

Air inside the envelope

Other kinds of rough handling can also end the life of a lamp abruptly. Vibration or physical shock, particularly while operating can cause the closely spaced parts of the filament to touch creating a short circuit which destroys the lamp. Crew members should be cautioned against bumping luminaires at any time and particularly while the lamp is on. There is often a temptation to push or prod a luminaire into proper aim after it has become hot, even poking it with a stage brace. This practice can ruin lamps rapidly. Unfortunately for the security of the show, these failures do not necessarily happen immediately when the lamp is bumped. They may come hours or minutes later when the show is running.

Problems with Lamp Life and Efficiency

Lamp designers' dilemma

Lamp makers, beginning with Edison himself, have found that lamps can be built with high efficiency or with long life, but not both at the same time. The reason for this is that the tungsten filament sublimates. Sublimation varies directly with temperature and inversely with the gas pressure surrounding the filament. Efficient conversion of electrical current into visible light requires that the filament operate at the highest temperature possible without melting. Gas pressure can be only so high before the lamps become explosive. Thus the dilemma persists. A major breakthrough came in the early fifties with the introduction of the tungsten-halogen (T-H) lamp.

The T-H Lamp

A T-H lamp is an incandescent lamp

The filament of a T-H lamp is basically the same as that of a normal incandescent lamp, although the exact configuration may be changed to meet the needs of new, more efficient reflector/lens combinations designed for its use. It is important to note that the T-H lamp is basically an incandescent lamp—it makes light by converting the energy of electrically produced heat into visible and infrared light. The difference between it and earlier lamps is that the conditions that control the sublimation of the tungsten filament have been altered to improve performance. The inert gas atmosphere surrounding the filament contains a halogen. A halogen is a member of the chemical family of elements that contains, among others iodine, bromine chlorine and fluorine, all extremely active elements which tend to combine chemically with a wide variety of other elements. Iodine and bromine are commonly used in incandescent lamps. The first used was iodine which led to the first name for these lamps:

"Quartz-iodine" lamps

quartz-iodine. The name came from the fact that iodine was introduced into the atmosphere surrounding the filament and that the bulb had to be made of quartz to enable it to operate at a high enough temperature to make the halogen cycle work—ordinary glass would soften at such temperatures. This name is now a misnomer on both counts: The iodine has been mostly replaced by bromine and the bulbs are now made of hard glass instead of quartz. The present name is "tungsten-halogen" which

Modern name: tungsten-halogen

recognizes that the filament is still present (and thus it is an incandescent lamp) and that the gas contains a halogen, probably bromine. The "halogen cycle" describes the basic operation of all T-H lamps and, since it depends on the operating conditions of the lamp, it is important that the theatre designer or technician understand its basics.

The Halogen Cycle

The cycle works as follows:

1. When the lamp operates at full voltage the tungsten sublimates just as it would in a conventional lamp. This happens at the very high temperature of the filament, which approaches the melting point of tungsten, about 1774° C or 3223° F.

2. The sublimated tungsten deposits on the relatively cool, about +600° C, hard glass envelope.

3. As the gaseous halogen (Either bromine or iodine become gases at much lower temperatures than those found inside an operating lamp.) encounters the solid tungsten on the inside of the bulb, it combines with it to form a gas, tungsten halide. This reaction can happen only above about 600° C, thus the need for the hard glass envelope.

4. This gas circulates around inside the lamp and eventually passes near the hot filament. At filament temperature, the gas is broken down into tungsten and halogen. The tungsten is redeposited on the filament and the halogen freed to circulate again.

This process has the effect of transporting the tungsten back to the filament and thus removing it from the path of light passing out of the lamp. It also places the tungsten back on the filament, although not at the exact point from which it originally sublimated. Nevertheless a major improvement has occurred: The lamp has superb lumen maintenance because the sublimated tungsten no longer blocks light leaving the lamp. The filament, while not perfectly "repaired" still gains an immense increase in life. Theoretically this process could continue indefinitely as long as current is supplied to energize it. Actually T-H lamps eventually fail because:

1. The filaments break because weak spots develop where insufficient tungsten is replaced or because the tungsten "whiskers" that form on the filament as the tungsten is redeposited form a short circuit which destroys the filament.

2. The seals of the lamp fail letting in air which destroys the filament. Seal failure is a much greater problem in T-H lamps than in conventional lamps because the temperature of the envelope must be about 600° C to maintain the halogen cycle. At this high temperature, the interaction between the metal lead-in wires and the hard glass tends to cause erosion of the wire which eventually allows air to enter the bulb destroying the lamp. Note that the typical yellow deposit of tungsten oxide on the interior of the lamp is a symptom of this type of failure. Additionally the longer life of T-H lamps allows more time for seal failure caused by oxygen entering from the outside of the seal.

Filament problems await a "final solution" by the engineers; seal problems have been alleviated but not eliminated by the design of base/socket combinations that control the heat at the seals and reduce the oxidation of the lead-ins. Users should be cautioned that if a bad seal problem develops, they should carefully examine the socket and lamp base to see if any overheating and-or pitting is evident. If so, both the lamp and the socket must be replaced or the now-defective socket will promptly ruin the new lamp.

T-H lamp failure

Replace both lamp and socket to prevent further seal failures.

Note that any type of operation that tends to increase the operating temperature of the lamp beyond design values is apt to bring on both filament and seal problems. If, for example, a T-H lamp is being operated at overvoltage in a scenic projector, ventilation must be designed to remove the extra heat effectively if acceptable lamp life is to be expected.

Dimming T-H Lamps

Logic would indicate that if a T-H lamp is operated for an extended time at a low dimmer reading, the T-H cycle will shut down. Tungsten will deposit on the inside of the lamp and the halogen, being at too low a temperature, will not remove it. This does happen. The solution is to occasionally operate the lamp at full to allow the halogen cycle to restore the lamp to its proper condition. The effect of this type of operation on lamp life appears to be negligible.

Note that operating a T-H lamp on a chase or other system that never allows the lamp to get hot will have the same effect as operating it on a dimmer at low readings. The cure is also the same.

T-H lamps blacken on long dim cycles

Life of T-H Lamps

The introduction of a halogen into the atmosphere of an incandescent lamp improves life ratings from four to ten times. Lumen maintenance is also much improved. This makes possible a whole new set of options for lamp engineering:

1. *Long-life lamps*
    Long-life T-H lamps. These can now have life ratings of about 2000 hours and color temperature of about 3000 K. Light output is low compared to the shorter life versions below but thanks to high lumen maintenance (no deposit on the bulb) total life lumens remains high.
2. *Medium life lamps*
    Medium-life lamps. Life is in the 200 hour range. These have a color temperature of about 3200 K and are considerably more efficient than the long-life lamps.
3. *Short life lamps*
    Short-life lamps. Life is about 50 hours. Color temperature is 3450 K. These lamps are most used in the photographic world where their color temperature matches the needs of the "indoor" type of color film.

    They can, of course be used in the theatre but their short life will mean many burnouts during the run of the show—something the theatre can do without. They are also expensive to operate because of the high cost of lamp replacement. These lamps may be exactly what is required when maximum efficiency is needed, say, in scenic projection equipment. Such users should maintain a log of lamp hours in use and be prepared to replace them on a regular schedule to avoid burnouts at critical times.

The above categories represent the general division of available lamps. Those actually available may vary as efforts at energy conservation bring additional wattages on the market.

Types of T-H Lamps

T-H lamps (Figure 5.3) are presently available in a wide variety of wattages, base/socket types and ratings. T-H lamps are also available in double-ended configurations for use in small floodlights and similar applications. Actually the double-end configuration predates the single-ended lamps because it is easier to solve socket heating problems when only half of the heat is imposed on each socket.

• Ordering lamps: design configurations

Driven by the pressure for higher efficiency in the name of energy conservation, both lamp and lighting equipment manufacturers are constantly improving their products and finding ways of improving the equipment already in use. Therefore the only way to be sure of ordering proper lamps is to consult the current catalogue of the equipment manufacturer (or better still, one of its representatives). If the luminaires are more than a few years old, the buyer should double-check with their manufacturer and/or with the lamp supplier to see if there is a later, more effective lamp for the luminaires.

Users coming into a new job should be particularly cautioned against simply ordering what was ordered last time. The previously used lamps may not be the best choice for a given luminaire and situation although they may still work.

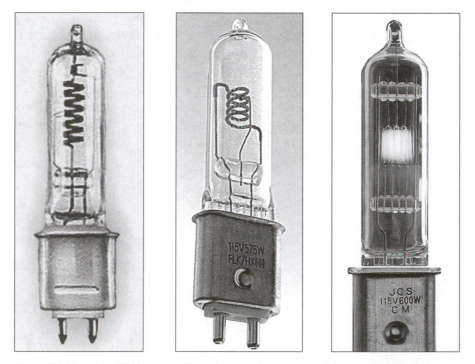

Figure 5.3. Theatrical T-H Lamps. These lamps, shown at near full size, are typical of the many T-H lamps used on stage in ellipsoidal reflector spotlights. Note the specially formed coiled-coil filaments on the left and middle lamps which are designed for efficiency with ellipsoidal reflectors. The lamp on the right has a biplane filament; note its compactness. Photos courtesy GE (left) and USHIO (right and center).

• Operating Positions for T-H Lamps

Conventional lamps, mostly in the "T" configuration, are restricted as to operating position: either "base down to horizontal" or "base up." T-H lamps generally have no such restrictions. Indeed, some of the most efficient designs of spotlights now utilize an "axial" mount wherein the lamp lies on the axis of the housing and is thus angled to whatever angle is given to the luminaire. Older ellipsoidal reflector luminaires had the socket housing and socket installed at an angle to the axis of the spotlight to cause the lamp to operate at near base up when used in its typical downward angled position.

Although most retrofit T-H lamps carry no mounting position cautions, it will be wise for users of old-style ellipsoidal reflector spotlights to still observe the "base up to horizontal" limitation when installing old-style spotlights that have been upgraded with T-H lamps. The reason for this caution is the design of the ventilation in these spotlights. They may not cool properly if mounted other than with the socket housing pointing upward.

Observe ventilation arrangements on old spotlights

• Mixing T-H and Conventional Lamps

Many theatres forced to operate with an assortment of luminaires of varying ages and with limited budgets for upgrading lamps, may find it necessary to hang shows using a combination of luminaires equipped with conventional lamps and T-H lamps. Clearly the color temperatures produced by these lamps will not match. The lighting designer can easily adjust for this by choosing gels that compensate for the mismatch. This can be done by setting up a luminaire with each type of source and checking gels visually to get a match or by consulting a computer program (Chapter 9) that allows the user to choose gels that will equalize the color temperature differences. If lamps must be changed from one type to another during the run, a similar process should be followed; crews should be instructed not to simply change the lamp and use the same gel.

The designer may gain some advantage out of a mismatched assortment of lamps by installing the high color temperature lamps where cool light is needed, thus taking advantage of their better efficiency in this range.

Chapter 6

NON-INCANDESCENT LIGHT SOURCES ON STAGE

There are a number of ways of calculating the theoretical number of lumens that could be obtained by the perfect conversion of a watt of electricity into light. One such calculation puts the amount at 673 lumens per watt. Other calculations go as high as 692 lm/watt. (Note that the energy in a lumen is dependent on the wave length of the light being examined.) Whatever the figure, it dwarfs the best of incandescent lamps which produce less than thirty lumens of visible light per watt. Outside of the theatre, modern energy saving approaches to lighting have resulted in tremendous savings in energy costs and effect on the environment. The stage, however, lags far behind, mostly because it remains committed to the concentrated filament incandescent lamp which is easy and safe to use and can be dimmed by relatively simple electronic equipment with only minor color shift problems. Also the theatre has a huge investment in equipment designed around the incandescent lamp.

Incandescent lamps are very poor at converting electrical energy into visible light.

The incandescent lamp's inefficiency, which results in most of the energy it consumes being converted into heat, costs the theatre double; once for the power to operate the lamps and again for the extra air conditioning needed to remove the excess heat from the building. The heat also is destructive to color media and equipment. Additionally, it is a constant annoyance to actors, singers and anyone on stage.

The incandescent lamp is a very poor source of cool colors, particularly pure blue. This increases lamp and power costs because much more power is needed to produce usable quantities of blue light. Moreover, while the concentrated filament is a reasonably small source, it is still far from a theoretical point, particularly in large wattage lamps which must have larger filaments. This makes collection of its light difficult and inefficient.

Incandescent lamps are inefficient in the production of blue light

For the above reasons, there is great pressure on the theatre to move to a more efficient light source. In Europe, where cost of electrical current is several times what it is in the USA, major theatres have long since given up incandescent lighting of cycloramas (one of the biggest power loads in the theatre) in favor of fluorescent lamps which are much more efficient than incandescents, particularly in the cool-light range.

Ironically, the European standard voltage (220-240 vac) makes their incandescent lamps even more inefficient than ours. It is more difficult to make a compact concentrated filament when the filament wire is half the diameter or twice as long as that in a 120 v lamp. This problem is so acute that many theatres use step-down transformers to enable them to operate luminaires at 120 v. These transformers also use some power and add huge amounts of weight to the rigging system (they are installed at the luminaires to avoid voltage drop.).

Clearly there is a real need for a better point source of light for the theatre. This need is being met by gaseous discharge lamps.

Gaseous Discharge Lamps

Ionizing gases causes them to emit light.

It has long been known that any gas which is ionized by electrical current, will emit radiant energy, usually much of it in the visible range. This phenomenon is found in nature in the northern lights and can be easily reproduced on a small scale by enclosing any gas or combination of gases in a glass tube equipped with electrodes and applying sufficient voltage to cause current to flow through the gas. The result will be a glow of wave length(s) typical for the gas(es) used. A spectroanalysis of this light will reveal that it is made up of narrow lines representing individual or closely spaced groups of wavelengths with darkness between—a line spectrum.

The practical requirements for making light by gaseous discharge are quite different from those for operating an incandescent lamp. First, the gas must be completely enclosed in the tube, not polluted by air or any other unintended gases. Electrodes must be installed at the ends of the tube and carefully sealed to prevent either the escape of the interior gas or the intrusion of air. If the gas is at relatively low pressure and the tube is long, considerable voltage will be needed to start the flow of electrical current. However, once the flow begins, the resistance of the ionized gas drops to near zero and some outside means must be used to control the amount of current that flows. These requirements mean that, compared to the incandescent lamp, operating a gaseous discharge lamp requires special equipment. Usually a *starter* is needed to provide the pulse of high voltage needed to ionize the gas and a *ballast* is needed to control the flow of current, once started. These items add to the cost of luminaires using a gaseous sources and also consume current, reducing overall efficiency.

Starter and ballast

Despite these complications, gaseous sources have proved efficient and economical. They are widely used for general illumination and, more recently, as stage lighting sources. Two general types of gaseous discharge lamps are presently in use: *long-arc lamps* which include fluorescent lamps and a variety of general illumination sources such as street lighting lamps, and *short-arc lamps*, which qualify as point sources.

Long-arc and short-arc lamps

Fluorescent Lamps on Stage

Although they are basically long-arc gaseous discharge lamps, fluorescent lamps are a special category because of their complicated energy conversion process. They are found in almost every architectural lighting situation requiring a high level of illumination at reduced cost of operation but find only limited use on stage, mainly as cyclorama lighting. This is because they cannot be made into a point source.

The operation of the fluorescent lamp involves two energy conversions: first from electrical current to ultraviolet light and then from ultraviolet light to visible light. Both of these steps are much more efficient than the conversions performed by an incandescent lamp (current-heat-light) and despite the need for an energy consuming ballast, the overall result is a source which is as much as 3-4 times as efficient as an incandescent lamp. They work as follows:

Two-step energy conversion

1. The inside of the fluorescent tube consists of a long-arc gaseous lamp using mercury vapor as the gas. Pressure and temperature range are adjusted so that maximum energy from the current passed through the tube is converted into the ultraviolet lines of the mercury line spectrum. This conversion is based on quantum theory: Atoms of the gas are driven to a higher than normal level of energy by the electrical current. When the atoms return to their normal energy level, each one releases a photon. These photons make up the UV light generated inside of the tube. Only a minimum of energy is converted into visible (purple) light. The UV light lies in the middle and far areas of the UV spectrum and could be potentially dangerous, therefore none of it is allowed to escape the tube. This is accomplished by using glass for the tubes that is opaque to the dangerous wave lengths.

The mercury-arc

2. The UV light produced as above is absorbed by phosphors bonded to the inside of the tube. Phosphors are chemicals that can absorb UV energy and emit visible light. This conversion is known as fluorescence, hence the name of the lamps. The visible light emitted is mostly in the form of continuous-band spectra. Each band includes only a part of the total visible spectrum, therefore to produce a normal looking light several different phosphors are mixed to additively produce the sensation of white light (see Chapter 9 for details about color mixing). This visible light is transmitted through the glass of the tube and is the light output of the lamp. Note that little heat is produced in this process.

Phosphors are activated by the UV light—fluorescence.

Advantages of the fluorescent source are:
- high efficiency;
- low heat output;
- good color rendition (if proper blend of phosphors is used);
- efficient in blue range;
- long lamp life.

Disadvantages are:
- usable as flood source only;
- deficient in red-yellow range;
- may flicker on start-up unless special equipment is installed;

- failure of lamp or auxiliary equipment may result in flickering instead of a simple outage.

Although European theatres, particularly large opera houses have consistently installed single-color fluorescent lighting to produce daylight effects on cycloramas saving very significant amounts of electrical costs, this practice has not caught on in the U.S. However a more flexible possibility now exists: the use of fluorescent three-color primary cyclorama lighting. Just as three-color incandescent cyc lighting requires three sets of circuits and controls (sometimes four if the blue circuit is doubled), three-color primary fluorescent cyc lighting will require three circuits and three dimmer ways. Such systems have found some acceptance in television studios where lighting loads tend to be very heavy and where air conditioning loads (much increased by waste heat from incandescent lamps) can mount up to a huge expense. The lamps used for this purpose are fluorescent tubes equipped with special phosphors (and sometimes also filters) that produce only red, green or blue visible light instead of a mixture. Electrically they are the same as normal tubes.

It seems obvious that, as the pressure for greater efficiency and better energy conservation grows, the use of fluorescent cyclorama lighting will increase.

Ultraviolet Sources for the Stage

Fluorescent tubes can be designed to produce large amounts of ultraviolet light by altering the phosphors. This light can be used to cause a wide variety of materials to fluoresce, although in many cases with limited efficiency. Some of these fluorescent materials are made up into stage paints, makeup, crayons, and treated fabrics. Spectacular transformation effects can be created by painting or drawing on scenic elements which can have two radically different appearances depending on whether they are viewed by ordinary light or ultraviolet light. The light that activates these effects is "UVA" or "near UV" light, commonly called "black light."

Several commercial suppliers offer to make up drops up to full stage sizes that can be transformed by shifting from white light to black light. Those wishing to prepare their own effects will find several sources of paint and related products.

There are three light sources commonly used to activate black light pigments:
- black light fluorescent tubes
- mercury vapor lamps
- HID source follow spotlights

All of these sources produce visible light in varying amounts which must be filtered away if the effect of the fluorescent pigments is to be seen. The fluorescent UV process is unique in that its use involves a three-step energy conversion process:

Three-step energy conversion

1. Energy from electrical current is converted into far and middle UV light inside a standard fluorescent tube. Note that the tube glass is specially formulated to contain the potentially dangerous UVB and UVC.

2. This UV is then converted into near-UV by the special phosphors bonded to the inside of the tube.

3. This near-UV (black light) passes through the tube and is used to illuminate the specially painted scenery, makeup, fabrics etc. where other phosphors make a third conversion into visible light, usually in narrow bands of color producing striking effects.

Black light fluorescent tubes are electrically the same as regular tubes of the same size, bulb configuration, and wattage. They can be dimmed by any dimmer rated for fluorescent lamp dimming and can be operated in any luminaire designed for fluorescent lamps. However, luminaires equipped with polished metal reflectors are more efficient than those with white enameled reflectors.

Black light fluorescent tubes produce a considerable amount of visible light, mostly in the violet range which must be filtered out to make the fluorescent effects visible. Some tubes may be purchased already equipped with filters, tubular filters can be separately purchased and installed, or filters may be installed at the front of the luminaire. Note that some theatrical color media in the amber range will serve as emergency filters for this purpose.

If an entire stage must be illuminated with UV light, fluorescent tubes are by far the most efficient and economical method. However if a defined pool of UV light is needed, fluorescent UV will not work. Mercury vapor lamps in a PAR-spot configuration offer a possible solution. They produce a fairly well-defined pool of UV that tapers off into darkness over a considerable distance. They also produce some spill. Therefore, if a tight spotlight effect is needed, they are best operated in a PAR can or a funnel-type housing that cuts off the spill and the outer part of the beam. Like all gaseous discharge lamps, these must be operated with a ballast to control current flow. Because these lamps also produce a large amount of cold-blue visible light, they must be operated with a special filter that blocks the visible light and transmits the UV. This filter will run hot; it must absorb all of the energy in the visible range. Units that include the ballast and a housing for the lamp are available, made for the landscape illumination market where the cold blue-green light is used because it flatters foliage at night. UV filters are available for these fixtures and funnels can be devised.

Mercury UV lamps delay starting for a period of time after the current is applied and then come on gradually and unevenly; fluorescent lamps sometimes flicker on starting. Thus the best way to use either type on stage is to turn them on and let them warm up before the curtain goes up. Any moderate-to-high level of stage lighting will obliterate the fluorescence they cause, masking their presence until the visible light is dimmed. Then the UV scene will appear, almost as if by magic. The fluorescent scene can be ended simply by bringing back the visible light. Note that mercury UV lamps should not be turned off until they are no longer needed. Once heated up, they must cool down before they can be reliably started again. This may take as long as twenty minutes.

If a pool of UV must follow the action of the play and/or must be sharply defined, the best solution is a follow spotlight that has a UV producing source and a filter to cut off the visible light. Modern follow spot-

Filtering unwanted light

Flooding the stage with black light

Producing a defined pool of black light

Lamps will not start when hot

Black light follow spotlight

lights, with the exception of small incandescent-source types, are powered by high intensity discharge (HID) lamps (discussed in detail below). In addition to visible light, these lamps produce radiation throughout the UV range including near-UV. Normally the lens glass for these luminaires is chosen to block UVB and UVC and may also block some of the UVA. Nevertheless enough will usually remain to create very effective black light spotlighting. A special filter will be needed that blocks visible light but passes UVA.

Other Long-Arc Sources

Although the fluorescent lamp has found considerable use on stage, other long-arc sources have not. Such sources include neon signs, sodium vapor lamps, mercury vapor lamps, and a number of more exotic types used for scientific experimentation. The efficiency of these lamps has, however, led to their use in a variety of lighting situations such as street lighting and the illumination of large spaces such as warehouses. Those most commonly in use are sodium vapor lamps (pure yellow light), high pressure sodium vapor lamps (pinkish-yellow), mercury vapor (cold, often greenish, white), and long-arc xenon (cool white). These sources almost never appear on stage unless there is a need to introduce this particular light as a plot requirement.

Short-Arc High Intensity Discharge Lamps—HID Lamps

High intensity discharge lamps are short-arc lamps. Their arc is confined to a very small space in a compact-arc tube instead of being extended such as the arc in a neon tube or a fluorescent lamp. The basic structure of these lamps consists of a relatively small tube of quartz, fitted with two electrodes with a small gap between them. The tube, filled with whatever gas or gases are desired, operates at high pressure and temperature, therefore it is further enclosed in an outer glass envelope.

Pulse starting

Starting is usually accomplished by sending a short but very high voltage pulse through the lamp which ionizes the starter gas, usually argon. Once the arc has started to flow through the argon, the other elements are heated and become the main light source in the arc. Once started and heated up, most HID lamps must cool after being shut off before they will restart.

High pressure mercury lamp

The earliest HID lamp that came into common use was the high pressure mercury vapor lamp. While very efficient, its color made it useless for stage use. The first lamp adaptable to the stage was the xenon lamp which produces a cool white light. It soon found use as a source for both scenic and motion picture projection. Early lamps were dangerous, particularly in larger wattages. They emitted dangerous amounts of far- and middle-UV light which in addition to being dangerous itself, caused part of the oxygen in the air surrounding the lamp to be converted into ozone, a poisonous gas. The lamps themselves operated at very high pressure, as much as 40 atmospheres which made them explosive. Xenon lamps are still in use and still dangerous, although they have been "tamed" somewhat. Ozone-free varieties are

Hazards of xenon lamps

available and research has reduced the possibility that the glass envelope will suddenly fail ("devitrify" in the euphemistic language of the engineers), throwing fragments of glass around at the speed of a pistol bullet. Their use on stage is becoming increasingly rare because there are safer substitutes (metal halide lamps), although the highest powered scenic projectors and follow spotlights may still utilize them

The category, HID lamps, still includes both the xenon and high pressure mercury vapor lamps but now also encompasses a large and fast growing family of metal halide lamps. Electrically these lamps are similar to mercury vapor lamps, indeed their basic fill is mercury with argon added as a starter. However the essential part of the fill is a carefully measured "dose" of metal halides, usually iodides of metals chosen for their efficiency and color of radiation in the visible spectrum. The result is a very complicated line spectrum displaying all of the various spectral lines of the elements in the arc. Metal halide lamps

Metal halide lamps produce light that is essentially white to the eye although it is made up of a complex mixture of spectra from the various metals introduced into the arc plus the basic spectra of mercury and argon. This light is described by means of a *correlated color temperature rating*—a way of describing the apparent color temperature of non-incandescent sources whose spectra are made up of lines and/or, in some cases, bands of color. It is specified by citing the kelvin temperature of a true incandescent source which produces the same visual effect as that of the mixture of line spectra. Some of the characteristic of metal halide lamps are: Correlated color temperature rating

- high efficiency
- produce essentially white light described in terms of correlated color temperature
- relatively long life
- can serve as a point source for use with lenses and precision reflectors
- high gas pressure inside bulb—may be dangerous
- most are not electrically dimmable
- many produce dangerous UV radiation
- most have limited operating positions
- need auxiliary equipment
- most cannot be immediately restarted after being shut down.

Halide lamps are made in a wide variety of types and sizes and find use in many applications outside of the theatre because of their efficiency, long life, and good color rendering properties. Most of these general service HID lamps will not work well with lenses or precision reflectors, however a few are made especially for use in precision optical equipment, including sophisticated modern theatrical luminaires. They are practically the only lamp used in modern automated luminaires with high light output ratings and are finding their way into top-of-the-line non-automated luminaires.

Metal halide lamps normally are made with a double envelope. The outer glass envelope serves to stabilize the temperature of the inner-arc tube and to at least partially contain dangerous radiation. Although the lamp will operate with the outer envelope broken, this is exceedingly Dangers of metal halide lamps dangerous. When an outer envelope is broken, the lamp should be immediately shut off. Indeed, many types of lamps are equipped to self-extinguish within fifteen minutes of failure of the outer envelope.

The inner envelope is the *arc tube*. It is normally made of quartz and operates at high pressure (up to 50 p.s.i.) and temperatures as high as 1800° F (1000° C). If this tube is broken while the lamp is at operating temperature, hot particles of quartz may be thrown around at high velocity. The lamps must therefore be operated only in an enclosure capable of controlling such an explosion without allowing any fragments of quartz to escape.

In addition to the hazards from high pressure, the lamp, even with the outer envelope intact, radiates dangerous quantities of middle- and far- UV which can cause serious skin burns, eye damage and even cancer. Therefore the housing should contain the unfiltered light from the lamp allowing only safe light to be emitted. Either the lens must be made of special UV-blocking glass or a special UV filter must be installed. Clearly, halide lamps should be operated only in an approved, enclosed fixture designed for this purpose.

Halide lamps should be handled only with cotton gloved hands to avoid any fingerprints, grease or oils getting on their outer surface. If they do become soiled, they must be carefully cleaned with alcohol. Used lamps should be disposed of following the manufacturer's instructions, not simply thrown into the trash.

Explosion danger (margin note)

Handling precautions (margin note)

Operating Conditions

All HID lamps, including metal halide types require special ballast equipment to control the flow of current through them. Unlike an incandescent lamp, whose resistance increases as the filament heats up, gaseous discharge lamps have a "negative resistance characteristic." This means that as the arc is developed through the gaseous medium in the arc tube, the resistance drops precipitously, approaching zero. Thus, as the lamp "fires" it becomes a short circuit in the system. To prevent it from destroying itself and parts of the electrical supply system, an external current limiting device known as a ballast must be inserted in series with the arc. Such ballasts must be designed to fit the current carrying characteristics of the variety of lamp being used. Therefore lamps are listed in catalogues with the proper ballast specified. Use of an improper ballast can result in early lamps failure or even in the explosive destruction of the lamp. *HID lamps are not interchangeable, in the same way incandescent lamps* are.

Most HID lamps, including the metal halide varieties, have limited operating positions. These are determined by the internal structure of the lamp and cannot be ignored without severely shortening the life of the lamp. This is one of the reasons that many automated luminaires are built to be mounted in a horizontal position and the beam directed toward the stage by a moveable mirror. A few metal halide lamps are listed as "universal burn" and can be mounted in any position and/or moved to any position as the luminaire is angled.

Compared to even the best tungsten halogen incandescent lamps, metal halide lamps are phenomenally efficient. For example, a number of

Lamps must be operated with the proper ballast (margin note)

Operating position limitations (margin note)

commonly used 250 watt metal halide lamps are rated at an initial output of 20,000 lumens and mean lumens at 15,500. Commonly used 250 watt T-H lamps are rated at 4800-5000 lumens. There is also a huge difference in rated life. Halide lamps are rated at 8-10,000 hours compared to T-H lamps whose life ratings are in the vicinity of 250 hours. However it must be noted that the long life of the halide lamps decreases significantly if the lamps are repeatedly shut off and restarted instead of being run continuously.

Best life expectancy when run continuously

Applications of Halide Lamps

Engineering and safety restrictions make it unsafe to simply install a metal halide lamp in a luminaire originally designed for a T-H lamp. New types of luminaires are, however being made to satisfy the requirements for using HID lamps. For instance, almost all automated luminaires except those of the lowest power, utilize HID lamps. Also, fresnel and ellipsoidal luminaires are presently being manufactured which are designed to operate with metal halide lamps. These powerful luminaires are currently in use in the film industry where their high price can be justified. It is almost inevitable that these fixtures will enter the theatre service as they become more economical. And, as already noted, modern follow spotlights, again excepting those of lowest power, utilize HID sources.

Chapter 7

CONTROLLING LIGHT

Over less than astronomical distances, light travels in straight lines moving outward from its source at a speed of approximately 186,200 miles per second (approximately 3×10^8 meters per second) if it is traveling in a vacuum. Its speed is negligibly slower in air. It continues traveling in straight lines until it is absorbed by something in its path or deviated from that path. Light emanating from a source disperses in proportion to the square of the distance from the source and decreases in brightness in inverse proportion to that distance (Figure 7.1). This is known as the law of squares. Its effect is to rapidly diminish the usefulness of radiating light as distance from the source increases.

Law of squares

The basic objective of all luminaires is to gather up (collect) as much of the light being radiated from the lamp as possible and redirect it to

Collection

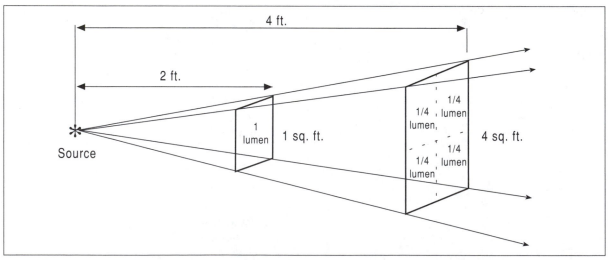

Figure 7.1. Law of Inverse Squares. Light radiates from a source such that its brightness decreases by the inverse of the square of the distance from the source. Note that if there is a brightness of one lumen at a distance of two feet from the source, the brightness will be one-quarter lumen at a distance of four feet

where it is needed. Reflectors and lenses are the means used in the theatre to effect this control. When the light from the source cannot be usefully directed, it must be blocked off to avoid lighting areas that should not be lit. This is wasteful and usually results in the conversion of the wasted light into heat where heat is not wanted.

Heat from "waste" light

In theory, the illumination engineer begins with a perfect point source that radiates light spherically. In fact, no source is really a point and the light does not radiate equally in every direction. Nevertheless most theatrical sources, incandescent or high intensity discharge lamps, can be treated as if they were point sources but better results can be had by adjusting the reflectors that collect the light to account for the size and shape of the filament or arc. However the radiation from the source is configured, the illumination engineer must solve the basic problem of collecting and redirecting it in a way that makes use of as much as possible. This is done by engineering a combination of reflectors and lenses to fit the situation. This engineering is made more difficult by the need for theatrical luminaires to operate over a wide range of distances with a broad assortment of beam sizes and characteristics. Additionally, theatrical budgets will not allow the use of highly precise and expensive optical elements.

Reflection, Refraction and Diffraction

There are three ways of altering the path of a beam of light not counting those phenomena observed in distant space:

1. Reflection: The path of the light beam is altered by being bounced off a surface.
2. Refraction: The path of the beam is altered by its passage from a medium of one optical density to one of different density.
3. Diffraction: The path of the beam is altered grazing an edge.

Reflection and refraction are constantly used in the engineering of stage lighting luminaires, often both in the same fixture. Diffraction is rarely encountered in stage lighting except when its results are reported in spectrograms of color media.

Reflection

Although reflectors vary widely in their appearance and their effect on light striking them, they all work according to the Law of Specular Reflection: the angle of incidence equals the angle of reflection, and they are in the same plane. The phrase, "and in the same plane," means that the outgoing rays are always on the same plane as the incoming rays, not skewed off at an angle. This law is illustrated in Figures 7.2A and 7.2B. The following terms apply:

Law of specular reflection

Point of incidence: the point on the reflector where the ray of light hits;

Normal: a line perpendicular to the surface at the point of incidence. If the reflector is a plane surface, the normal will be perpendicular to that surface. If the reflector is curved, as it often is in luminaires, the normal will be perpendicular to a tangent at the point of incidence;

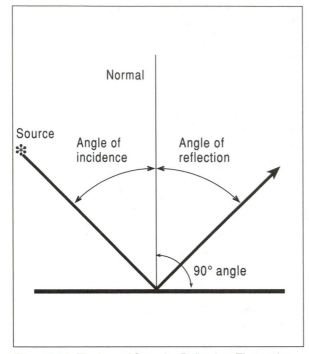

Figure 7.2A. The Law of Specular Reflection. The angles of incidence and reflection are measured from the normal, not the surface which may not be a plane. These angles are equal and the rays are in the same plane.

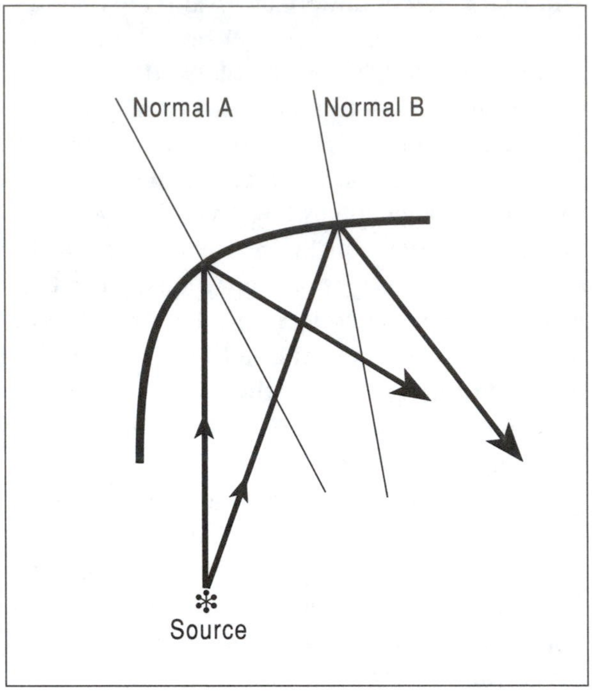

Figure 7.2B. Specular Reflection from an Uneven Surface. Note that a separate Normal is established at each point of incidence. Angles of incidence and reflection are equal as measured from that normal.

Angles of incidence and reflection

Angle of incidence: the angle between the normal and the incoming light ray;
Angle of reflection: the angle between the normal and the outgoing ray.

Specular Reflection

Specular reflection

Reflectors which obviously follow the law of reflection, are often called "specular" reflectors, a term derived from the Latin "speculum," meaning "mirror." Mirrors, highly polished metal surfaces and the surface of a still pond of water are common examples. Specular reflection affords the most precise control over light, For example, it is the basis of the collection and control of light from distant stars caught in astronomical telescopes.

First and second surface mirrors

In the case of mirrors made of glass or plastic, it is important to note that there are two types: first-surface and common or second-surface reflection. First surface mirrors have the reflective metal coating (silver or aluminum) applied to the top surface of the glass plate. The glass in this case becomes a "substrate," merely a support for the working surface. Obviously this arrangement places the delicate metal coating at risk and special steps must be taken to protect it. Common household mirrors avoid this problem by placing the reflective material on the back of the glass and coating its back surface for additional protection. While this

Metal mirrors

makes a durable mirror, it also means that the mirror is capable of producing double reflections, one from the front surface of the glass and the second from the metallic coating on the rear. This can produce unacceptable confusion in precision optical equipment.

Metal mirrors made of highly polished aluminum or other highly reflective materials, avoid this problem completely; they automatically reflect from their front surfaces. Dichroic mirrors, a special class of specular reflectors in which the surface coating selectively reflects various wavelengths of light, will be detailed below.

Diffuse, Spread and Mixed Reflection

Diffuse reflection (Figure 7.3) imparts maximum dispersion to any beam of light striking the surface, however controlled and defined that incident beam may be. The best example of such a reflector, ignoring durability, is a piece of clean white blotting paper. Each point on its surface will reflect whatever light strikes it as though that point were a source of light sending forth spherical radiation. None of the directional quality of the incident beam remains in the reflected light.

Diffuse reflection

Modern diffuse reflectors used on stage are made of specially surfaced aluminum. They are found in many varieties of floodlighting equipment such as in modern borderlights, cyclorama lights and floodlights. If kept clean, these reflectors are highly efficient.

Diffuse reflection also abounds on stage scenery. Most surfaces painted with scene paint are diffuse reflectors as are most fabrics with the exception of satins. Generally stage painters purposely avoid the gloss of enamels and varnishes except where specially required, because varnished or enameled surfaces can produce mixed reflection (below).

Scene paint is a diffuse reflector.

Spread Reflection

After striking a spread reflector, incident light is dispersed over a wide but controllable area, retaining some of its original directional characteristics (Figure 7.4). Spread reflectors are often made by treating an aluminum surface in a manner that leaves fine striations, or lines. Light striking such

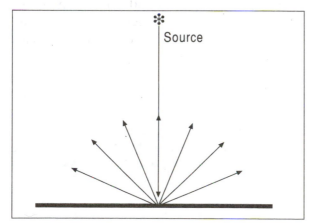

Figure 7.3. Diffuse Reflection. Note that the light is reflected equally along every possible angle from the point of incidence. (The length of the arrows represents the amount of light reflected along each path.)

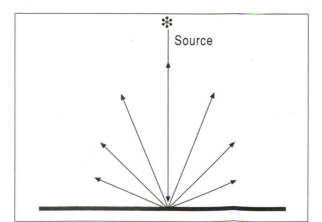
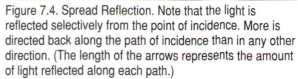

Figure 7.4. Spread Reflection. Note that the light is reflected selectively from the point of incidence. More is directed back along the path of incidence than in any other direction. (The length of the arrows represents the amount of light reflected along each path.)

a surface will disperse more in the plane perpendicular to the striations than that parallel to them. This affords the designer of the reflector quite precise control over the degree of spread and diffusion the reflector causes.

Spread reflectors are found in a variety of lighting equipment where a flood of light is needed but with control over the distribution of that light. For example, cyclorama lighting equipment is usually mounted much closer to the top of the cyclorama than the bottom. Carefully designed spread reflectors provide one way of equalizing the distribution over the cyc from top to bottom. This problem may also be solved by the use of glass roundels molded to have controlled spread characteristics.

Mixed Reflection

Unlike diffuse and spread reflection, which find useful applications on stage, mixed reflection is usually detrimental. It consists of a combination of diffuse and specular reflection usually produced by a highly polished but transparent surface such as a varnished table top. The diffuse portion, which comes from the underlying parts, does not create a problem. The specular portion, which comes from the polished surface, can produce distracting patterns of reflected light on setting walls or other background surfaces. Sometimes these patterns even include upside-down shadows of moving actors. Multiple reflections are likely if more than one light source strikes the offending surface.

One positive application of mixed reflection is found in satin fabrics. The glossy surface of the satin reflects light specularly with its color unchanged. The underlying fabric reflects diffusely altering the color of the reflected light unless the satin is white. The result is the rich shimmer often desired in costumes and in some drapery.

Clearly, mixed reflection from varnished surfaces must be controlled: Assuming that the luminaires cannot be reangled, the solution is to alter or cover the surface causing the reflection. If the offending surface is a desk or table, it may be possible to have the property personnel provide a cover or table spread for it that will "kill" the reflection. In some cases a good coat of flat scene paint will do the job. If, however, the furniture is borrowed or rented, painting will be out of the question and a spread may not always be appropriate. Another possibility is to give the offending surface a heavy coat of a furniture polish that dries into a dull coating. The polish is left in this condition—and even renewed if it begins to produce the reflections again—until the show is over when the furniture is polished back to its original shiny best. If the offending surface is a varnished stage floor, the best solution is to put down a ground cloth, a canvas floor covering, for the duration of the run. Note that proper stage floors are never varnished or otherwise finished with a reflective surface for exactly this reason.

Describing the Efficiency of Reflectors

Reflector efficiency, which can vary from near-zero (black velour) to near-perfect (highly polished aluminum), is usually stated as a simple percentage figure arrived at by comparing the amount of white light incident to

Mixed reflection

Satin

Eliminating mixed reflection

Ground cloth

the reflector to the amount reflected. If, for example only half of the light is reflected, the reflective efficiency would be 50%. Since ordinary aluminum reflectors used in luminaires do not selectively reflect visible wave lengths, efficiency by wave length is seldom a concern. Therefore the reflector's efficiency is simply stated for white light.

Controlling Light: Refraction

Refraction may be simplistically defined as the bending of a ray of light when it passes through a surface separating two different light transmitting materials. For example, light traveling through the surface separating water from air, the surface of a pool, for example, will be bent. This causes the bent appearance of a straight stick thrust partly into the water. Another example of refraction is the bending of light when it passes through a surface separating glass from air. For instance, an imperfect piece of window glass will impart a wavy quality to things viewed through it—the result of refraction. To the lighting artist or technician the most important refraction is that which happens when light passes through a lens. In order to understand this effect more fully, we must use the exact language of the physicist. First, some terms must be defined:

Bending light waves

Medium: any material that will, at least to some degree, transmit light. Note that refraction deals with light that actually passes through the medium, not that which is stopped and absorbed or simply reflected away. Therefore the rules of refraction apply equally to the murkiest piece of glass or plastic that light can pass through or to the finest optical plate.

Optical density: refers indirectly to the speed of light in a medium. You will recall that the speed of light in a vacuum is about 186,200 miles per second. The speed of light when it travels through any matter that will allow its passage is less than that figure. For example, light is minimally slowed when passing through air and slowed considerably when passing through glass. Optical density is expressed by the index of refraction.

Index of refraction: A number which expresses the ratio between the speed of light in a vacuum and its speed in any other medium. Thus the index is 1.000 for a vacuum and a larger number for other media. For example, the index of refraction for air is 1.000293, for water 1.333, for various kinds of glass 1.5 to 1.9, and for diamond, 2.419. Note that this index is always a number greater than 1. This arithmetically expresses the fact that light travels slower in all other media than it does in a vacuum.

Normal: A line drawn perpendicular to the point where the light strikes a surface separating two kinds of media. As with reflection, the normal to a point on a curved surface is the vertical to the tangent at the point of incidence.

Using these terms, it is now possible to cite a more scientifically accurate definition: *Refraction is the bending of light rays caused by their passage through a surface separating a medium of one optical density from one of different optical density, provided that the light rays are not traveling along a normal.*

Refraction is differential by wave length. This means that the bending of the light rays will always be the same for a given wave length and set of media, but will vary as the wave length varies. Differential refraction makes it possible for a prism to sort out light waves according to their length, producing a spectrum. Unfortunately it also causes chromatic aberration, a flaw that puts fringes of color around images formed by simple lenses.

Refraction is of great importance to the lighting designer and technician because it describes the operation of all of the many lenses used in lighting and scenic projection. In the world of physics refraction is evident in a wide variety of cases where light, visible or otherwise, passes from one to another of the many thousands of materials that transmit it. Fortunately theatre designers and technicians can limit their concern to those cases where light passes from air to glass or to certain plastics sometimes used to make lenses and to the reverse of that passage—back to air.

Figure 7.5 illustrates one of the simplest examples of refraction—light passes from air-to-glass-to-air when the sides of the glass are plane and parallel to each other. According to the definition of refraction, as long as the beam strikes the glass plate on any path other than along the normal (or at such an acute angle—the "critical angle"—that none of it penetrates the surface eliminating any consideration of refraction), bending

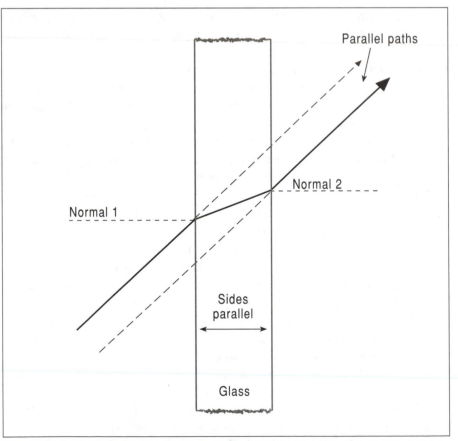

Figure 7.5. Refraction. Diagrams path of a "ray" of light passing through a perfect piece of plate glass. Note that the new path is parallel to the original but offset from it. The normals are also parallel, being perpendiculars to the parallel planes of the glass surfaces.

will take place at the point of entry. A reverse of this bending will occur where the light beam exits the glass The amount and direction of bending depend on the ratio between the two indices of refraction and whether the beam is passing from air to glass or vice-versa. The rule governing the direction of the bending is:

If the beam passes from a medium of low optical density to one of higher optical density (such as from air to glass), the beam will be bent toward the normal. If the passage is from high optical density to low, the bending will be away from the normal.

Note that the normal referred to is the one at the point where the beam enters or leaves the glass. This bending is illustrated in Figure 7.5. Note that the bending (angle D) all takes place at the surface. Once inside the glass, the light travels in a straight line until it encounters the second surface which separates glass from air. Here another bend takes place which is equal to and opposite in direction to the first bend, i.e., the beam will bend away from the normal at the point of exit. The bending is equal to the bend at the entry because the optical densities are the same; only their order is reversed. The only condition under which the second bend will not take place is when the first bend puts the light beam exactly on the normal to its point of exit. In this case there will be no second bend.

Bending takes place at surfaces.

The effect of these bending actions, as long as the sides of the glass plate are plane and parallel, is that the beam is offset but continues on in the same direction from which it entered. The amount of bending may be exactly calculated, if necessary, although this calculation will be beyond the needs of theatre lighting personnel.

Absorption and Surface Reflection

It is important to note that not all of the light striking the surface of a medium which transmits light will be refracted. Even the most perfectly transparent of media will absorb some of the light as it passes through. Also, the amount of light which passes through the separating plane will depend on the angle at which the light approaches the separating surface. If that angle is less than a certain minimum known as the *critical angle*, all of the light will be reflected according to the laws of reflection and remain within the first medium. At angles greater than the critical angle part of the light will penetrate the separating surface following the law of refraction but another part will be reflected. As the angle of incidence approaches perpendicular, most, but still not all, of the light will pass through the surface following the laws of refraction. Note that the surface reflection can take place either when light passes from a medium of low density to one of higher density (air/glass) or the reverse (glass/air). The latter situation is often called *internal reflection*.

Critical angle

Surface reflection

Internal reflection

How Refraction Makes Lenses Work

Prism

Whenever the two sides of a piece of glass or plastic, i.e., a medium of optical density higher than air, are not parallel, bending occurs in the manner illustrated in Figure 7.6. Note how the nonparallel sides have the effect of arranging the normals at the points of entry and exit so that the bending at these two points adds together instead of cancelling as it would if the sides were perfectly parallel. A prism is a piece of glass with plane sides which are intentionally not parallel to each other. Although prisms are seldom used in the theatre, their light-bending function will serve as our introduction to lenses, which are much used.

Three conditions control the amount of bending that takes place when light rays are refracted:

1. *the ratio between the indices of refraction of the two media involved* (The greater the difference between the indices, the greater the deviation. The index of refraction of glass depends on its chemistry.);

2. *the angle between the normal at the point of entry into the denser medium and the normal at the beam's departure* (This is a factor of the geometry of the media, which in theatre comes down to the curvature of the surfaces of the lenses involved.);

3. *the wavelength of the light passing from one medium to the other* (Short wavelengths—blue and violet—will be bent more that long rays—reds and oranges.).

Altering any one or more of these variables will change the amount of refraction. Designers of lenses alter both the shape of the lens and the chemistry of the glass to achieve their goal. However, altering the composition of the glass is limited in applications where heat is involved because only a certain types of glass can withstand heat without cracking. Heat considerations also eliminate the use of many plastics which otherwise have favorable optical characteristics.

From Prisms to Lenses

Lenses as "infinite" prisms

It is but a step from Figure 7.6, which shows the optical effect of prisms, to that of a plano-convex lens. Refer to Figure 7.7. Note how the lens can be considered to be an infinite series of prisms. The effect on each ray of light is the same as it would be if the light were striking a prism at the point of incidence, instead of the curved surface of the lens. Note that lenses and prisms are two-way devices: The effect on a beam of light is the same whichever way it passes through the lens.

Focal length

The light bending (refractive) power of lenses could be described in terms of the curvature of their sides, the composition of the glass and, of course, the wavelength of the light to be bent. This is awkward. Therefore the concept of *focal length* has been developed. This number describes the way in which the lens will bring parallel rays of light into a focus. This is normally done with white light although focal length can also be established for a specific wavelength if this is needed.

Before a formal definition of focal length can be cited, its terms need definition. Note that these definitions, while complete enough for application to theatrical needs, are by no means accurate enough to satisfy the

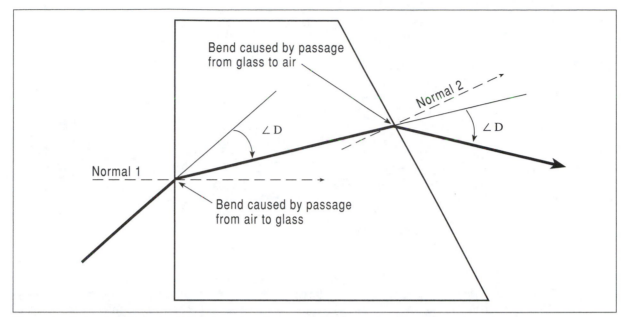

Figure 7.6. Refraction Through a Prism. Note the effect on the light "ray" when the sides of the glass are not parallel. Normals 1 and 2 are perpendicular to their related surface but are not parallel to each other. Angles "D" are also equal and the bending rule—*toward* the normal when the passage is from a medium of low density to one of high density and *away* from the normal when the passage is from high density to low—is the same. However the effect is drastically different. The path of the "ray" is deviated by an amount equal to twice angle "D."

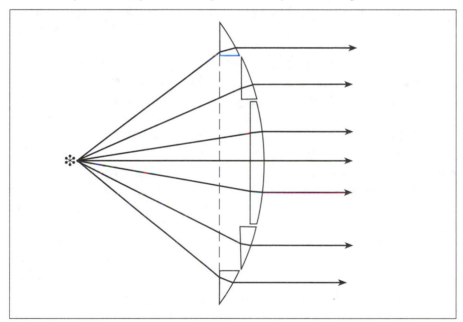

Figure 7.7. Lens as Infinite Prism. A lens may be regarded as an infinite series of prisms which refract light as diagrammed in Figure 7.6. Note that a step lens utilizes this pattern to create a very practical lens.

field of precision optics:

Principal foci: the points on either side of a lens where parallel beams of light are brought to a focus.

Optical center: This is often described as the plane on which the bending performed by a lens seems to take place if the bending from both surfaces were combined. The optical center may be approximately located by setting up the lens on an optical bench, determining the two principal foci and then locating the plane exactly half way between them. In the case of a plano-convex lens, the optical center can

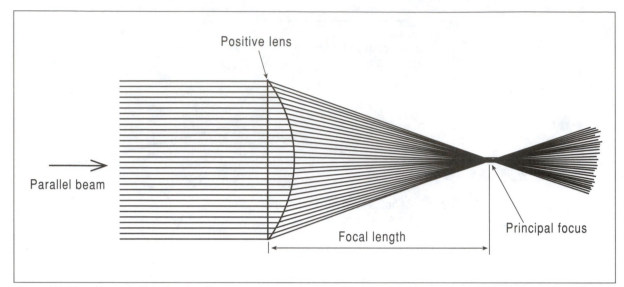

Figure 7.8. Focal Length. This drawing illustrates the standard conditions that determine the focal length of a positive lens. Parallel light is passed through the lens which brings these beams to a focus at the *Principal focus.* The distance from the principal focus to the optical enter of the lens, stated in inches or millimeters, is the focal length. (Note that the optical center of a plano-convex lens such as the one shown can, for stage purposes, be considered to be its plane side.)

generally be considered to be the plane side of the lens.

Optical axis: A line passing through the two principal foci and the center of the lens. All of the elements of an optical system must normally be lined up on the optical axis with the plane representing the optical center perpendicular to it.

Definition of focal length

Figure 7.8 illustrates the standard set of conditions stipulated in the definition of focal length: *The focal length of a lens is the distance from its optical center to either of its principal foci.* This distance can be stated in either inches or centimeters. Optical experts use a precision device known as an optical bench to determine focal length. This is simply a precisely machined, very rigid metal bar upon which various optical devices can be mounted and moved back and forth until they are properly adjusted and measurements can be taken. An optical expert might set up an optical bench to replicate the conditions illustrated in Figure 7.8. A device known as a *collimator*, which produces parallel rays of light would be aimed through the lens onto a target. When the parallel rays are brought to an accurate focus, the distance from the focal point to the flat side of the lens would be measured. This will give the approximate focal length. If greater accuracy is needed or the lens is of a more complex variety (convex-convex or compound lenses in barrels for example), the locations of the collimator and the target can be reversed to find the second principal focal point. One half of the distance between the two principal foci will give a better approximation of the focal length than the single reading taken from one side. While these two readings will suffice for most theatrical purposes, much more accurate measurements are necessary for precision optical work.

Locating the principal focus

Finding the focal length of a PC lens

Fortunately the lighting technician does not need an optical bench to determine the focal length of spotlight lenses which are crude optical devices normally made only in focal lengths measured in even inches. Instead of a collimator, the theatre worker need only find a source of light at a considerable distance away, which will make its rays relatively parallel. A light at the end of a long hallway will do. Simply bring the distant light into focus on a piece of paper and measure the distance from the flat side of the lens to the paper. This can even be done with a fragment of a broken lens, enabling the technician to order a replacement. Note that it makes no difference which way the light is passed through the lens; the distance between the principal focus and the flat side (the approximate optical center) will remain the same.

Efficiency of Lenses

Clearly, the larger the diameter of a lens, the more light it will pass through. The kind and quality of the glass also make a significant difference. The efficiency (and a number of other characteristics mainly of interest to photographers) of photographic and projection lenses is described by an "f" number. This is calculated by dividing the focal length of the lens by its *effective diameter*.

Effective diameter

Photographers select a lens by its focal length, which will determine the size of the image it will make and by the "f" number which determines the brightness of the image it will cast on the film, i.e., its speed. The brighter the image, the faster the shutter speed can be set and the greater the possibility of stopping action in the picture. Smaller f numbers indicate faster lenses.

Spotlight lenses are normally described by their diameter and focal length, not by their f number. Nevertheless is can be instructive to determine the f number of a simple plano-convex lens and discover the effect of reducing its effective diameter. Consider a 6 x 12 lens: It is 6 inches in diameter and has a focal length of 12 inches. Thus its f number is 12 divided by 6 or 2. This would be a rather fast photographic lens. However, if the mounting ring takes one-quarter inch off the radius of the lens (a rather compact mounting), the effective diameter is reduced to 5.5 inches and the f number becomes 12 divided by 5.5 or 2.18. This repre-

"f" number

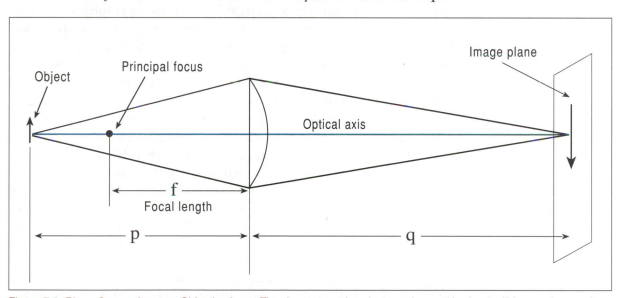

Figure 7.9. Plano-Convex Lens as Objective Lens. The plano-convex lens (or any other positive lens) will form an image of any lighted object located farther from the lens' optical center than the principal focus. Only two rays from a point near the center of the object are traced. Distances "p" and "q" and the focal length "f" are used in the optical formula: 1/p + 1/q = 1/f.

sents a significant reduction in transmitted light.

Objective Lenses

Quality objective lenses

An objective lens is a lens operated in a way that causes it to produce an image (Figure 7.9). While any simple positive lens can form an image and sometimes project a usable picture, most objective lenses, designed for use in cameras or projectors, are highly developed masterpieces of the lens maker's art. They are corrected for distortions inherent in a simple lens, such as chromatic and spherical aberration, treated to reduce surface reflections and made of special optical glasses chosen to transmit the most light possible.

Locating the Image

The distance from the lens to the image will vary, moving toward infinity as the slide approaches the principal focus. This relationship between the distance between the image material and the optical center of the lens (which indirectly describes the distance from the principal focus) can be expressed mathematically as:

Lens formula

$$1/p + 1/q = 1/f$$

In which: p = distance from the optical center of the lens to the image material; q = distance from the lens to the focal plane where the sharpest image appears; and f = the focal length of the lens. This formula will prove useful when working with projection equipment.

Depth of Focus

Although there is always one plane on which the image material can be placed to produce the sharpest image on the projection surface and, conversely, a single plane where the image is the sharpest, there is considerable latitude in the focusing process. On either side of the sharpest focal distance is an area where images may still be formed that are practically as good as that at the exact focal plane. The depth of this space measured along the optical axis is known as the *depth of focus* of the lens. In general, the larger the *f* number of a lens i.e., the slower it is photographically speaking, the greater the depth of focus. Although depth of focus has little relevance to most lighting applications it is important when image projection is the goal. "Doughnuts," disks of metal with holes of various sizes in them, are often added to an ERS to sharpen the image of a gobo. This is the stage equivalent of a photographer "stopping down" the lens (reducing the size of the opening through which the light must pass) and thus increasing its "*f*" number. The doughnut makes the image sharper but dimmer.

The depth of focus of the objective lens in a sophisticated automated luminaire makes it possible for several image controlling devices to operate effectively in the optical train although they obviously cannot all be at the ideal focal plane. Similarly, scenic projectors (Chapter 16) utilize lenses designed to be as fast as possible but with adequate depth of focus to accept bulky image devices.

Chromatic Aberration

As already noted, refraction varies with wave length. While this is useful for the purpose of creating a spectrum with a prism, it turns out to be a problem when simple lenses are in use. If the image cast by the lens is sharply focused, it will display color fringes because it is impossible for the lens to focus all of the wavelengths of the visible spectrum on the same plane at the same time. If the lens is being used as a converging lens, the pool of light it produces will display color fringes. If it is functioning as an objective lens, the image will display color fringes throughout. There is no solution to this problem except to mask it by keeping the whole image or pool of light slightly out of focus or by covering the color fringes with light from other sources.

    In more sophisticated, and expensive, lenses the chromatic aberration problem is solved by the use of multiple lens elements which are designed to cancel out the aberrations. Such lenses are known as achromatic lenses or achromats.

Diffraction

When a beam of light grazes an opaque edge or passes through a slit narrower than its wavelength, it is bent proportional to its wavelength. Thus a surface etched with a series of precisely spaced very fine parallel lines which act as edges, can disperse a beam of light sorting out the beam into its component wavelengths. Such a surface is called a *diffraction grating*.

    Gratings can produce wider dispersion of light beams than prisms producing more detailed spectra. Indeed, most spectrometers utilize gratings for exactly this reason.

    Diffraction gratings, in the form of mass-produced printed or molded plastic are commonly found as ornaments, as a background security images embossed onto credit cards and even as ornamental foils. All of these gratings evidence their presence by the way they reflect light in varied colors as the observer's angle of view changes.

    Theatrical applications of diffraction are presently limited to the use of the ornamental foils for decorative purposes and utilizing spectrograms made by using gratings to analyze the characteristics of theatrical color media.

Chapter 8

STAGE LUMINAIRES

Although it makes little difference to the lighting designer or technician using the equipment, it may be useful for the student to consider three categories of luminaires based on the complexity of their optical systems:

1.   Luminaires using only reflectors;

2.   Luminaires using reflectors and condensing lenses;

3.   Luminaires using reflectors, objective lens systems, and sometimes condensing lenses.

Floodlighting equipment

Simple reflector luminaires seek merely to control the radiation of light from the source by reflecting it toward the stage and cutting off that part which radiates in unwanted directions. These luminaires, usually called floodlighting equipment, produce a broad flood of light, often filling the entire stage. They date back to a period even before the introduction of electricity to the theatre. These first stage lights were rows of oil lamps and later rows of gas burners extending from one side of the stage to the other. The flames were backed up by the simplest of reflectors which helped to direct light toward the stage and prevented scenery from swinging directly into the flames. Later rows of electric lamps were substituted for the gas lights much improving the safety of theatres but making little change in the broad flood of light striking the actors. These

Borderlights

Footlights

rows of lights, termed *borderlights* and *footlights*, still persist on stages although there are a number of other, more controllable, ways of creating a flood of light when one is needed.

Borderlights were so named because they were hung directly upstage of pieces of scenery used to mask off the area over the stage called "borders." Border/borderlight pairs were usually hung at intervals of about 6 feet from the proscenium to the cyclorama or sky drop. The borders extended beyond the limits of sight lines stage right and left and the border-lights behind them were only slightly shorter. These heavy units, considered a permanent part of the stage equipment, consisted of long sheet metal troughs equipped with a row of sockets for general service lamps. In the early units, these lamps were colored by dipping them while hot into special heat-resistant colored lacquers (lamp dip). The troughs were painted flat white, which soon deteriorated to a dirty grey. Later, as lamps were improved by filling with inert gas to increase efficiency, bulbs became too hot for lamp dip and border and footlights were made up with individual compartments arranged so that gelatin filters could be installed over each lamp. Still later the compartments were replaced by spun aluminum reflectors, each capable of being fitted with glass filters known as *roundels*. Such border and footlights are still sold today. Many roundels are cast into lens-like shapes to assist in controlling the distribution of light.

Roundels

Color in Borderlights

The earliest colored borderlights utilized dipped lamps in red, white and blue. Each color was circuited and dimmed separately. This choice of color had little to do with patriotism but much to do with the needs of musical theatre where the colors used were warm white, pink or blue ("moonlight"). As the more efficient roundel-type borderlights came into use and as lighting designers came to use colors over a wider range, particularly on cycloramas, the color filter arrangement changed to red, green and blue, from which all other colors can be mixed. In some of the best installations a double circuit of blue was supplied to improve the effectiveness of this hard-to-produce color. Roundels in pink and straw are also available if these colors are needed. The red-green-blue (RGB) color scheme still persists along with the problem of producing blue light in sufficient quantity and purity.

RGB borderlights

Portable Borderlights

Full-stage-width borderlights (Figure 8.1) are huge units seldom dismounted once installed. They weigh hundreds of pounds, may be over 60 feet long and, if a "full set" is installed, completely occupy a counterweight set approximately every six feet from the proscenium wall to the cyclorama. Until spotlights became the main tool for lighting actors, borderlights were automatically specified for every stage from high school theatres to opera houses. Modern dramatic lighting seldom requires borderlights except for cyclorama lighting or for blending acting areas. These purposes can be easily served by two borderlight rows at most— one just upstage of the main curtain (the concert borderlight) and another properly situated to light the cyclorama.

Footlights have been retained in some installations but in much reduced power being used mainly to reduce shadows on faces, particularly those shaded by hat brims. Often only troughs for footlights are built into the building. A few portable striplight units can be installed when needed for shadow control or for the stylistic effect of early footlight lighting.

Footlight trough

There is still occasional need for general stage illumination for concerts, lectures and the like. Borderlights may still be the first choice for this task because they are effective and reasonably cheap to operate. However, on many modern stages the space-consuming full-stage-width units are often replaced by sectional borderlights (Figure 8.2). These can be easily moved about the stage, stored when not needed, and are equally as effective for general stage lighting. They are simply short sections of borderlight equipped with electrical connectors to allow them to be daisy-chained together. These units can be easily handled by two persons and are useful for other purposes such as back lighting an area outside of a window or in an alcove. Although the larger types of these units are often sold as "portable borderlights" and the smaller, more compact ones as "striplights," there is little except minor size and power differences to distinguish them. Both produce a somewhat controllable flood of light and can be used in three-color mixing or any other color application needed.

Striplights

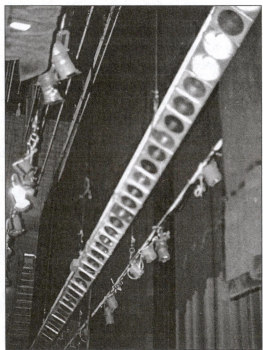

Figure 8.1. Full-Stage Borderlights. Photo shows a typical full-stage-width installation of borderlights. This arrangement is typical of many older theatres which were equipped in the l940s through 1970s or even later. These units were rarely removed thus permanently occupying an entire line set. The earliest were simply metal troughs with sockets closely spaced. Later they were equipped with individual spun aluminum reflectors and roundels and still later many were made to take "R" lamps. Wattages ran from 100-500 (or more) watts per socket. Courtesy UCLA Department of Theatre Arts.

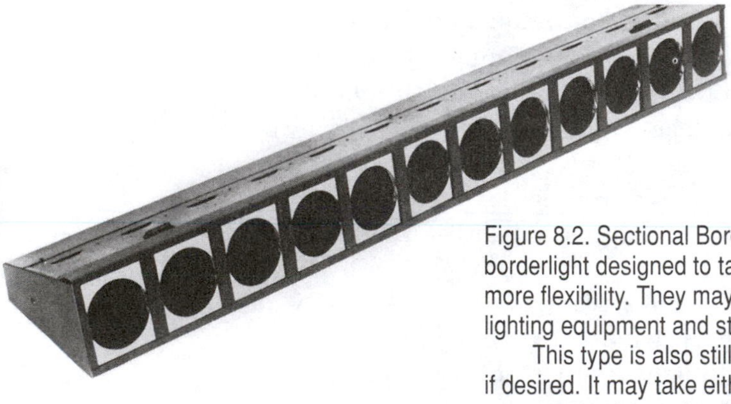

Figure 8.2. Sectional Borderlights. This photo shows a modern sectional borderlight designed to take "R" lamps. These units offer the designer more flexibility. They may be dismounted to make space for other lighting equipment and stored or utilized as striplights wherever needed.

This type is also still available on custom order at full-stage lengths, if desired. It may take either color frames or roundels, is rated up to 300 watts per socket and weighs about 7.5 pounds per foot of length. Photo courtesy Altman Stage Lighting Co. Inc.

Figure 8.3. Scoop Floodlight. This photo shows a generic version of the type. Scoops are available in a variety of sizes up to about 18 inches in diameter and can be had with or without the color frame holder. The reflective surface is almost always matte finish aluminum producing a diffuse spread of light. Wattages range up to as high as 2000 W using general service lamps.

However, borderlights are not always necessary on a modern stage, even for lighting an onstage orchestra or other utility purposes. A number of other, lighter weight, more compact types of floodlights are available which can serve these same purposes, take up much less space and also have other uses when not needed for general stage illumination.

The simplest of these is the *scoop* (Figure 8.3), a one-piece floodlight in which the reflector itself is the body of the unit. Its shape may be ellipsoidal, parabolic or spherical depending on manufacturer. Actually the shape is of little consequence since the reflective surface is diffuse surfaced aluminum. The unpainted but specially treated surface of the aluminum forms the reflector. Scoops may be had with or without demountable color frame holders.

Light from scoops is only moderately controllable but evenly distributed. A row of scoops mounted on a batten over the acting area can serve most of the purposes of a borderlight without the weight and without permanently occupying a line set. Scoops may also be used to light cycloramas and sky drops if circuited in three colors and carefully angled to achieve even coverage for each color.

Scoops for cyc lighting

Cyclorama Lighting Units

These are essentially floodlighting units especially designed to produce an even flood of light over a cyclorama when mounted near the top or bottom of the cyc. Since the luminaire may easily be 4-5 times closer to the top of the cyc than the bottom (if it is the top lighting unit), the even light distribution from an ordinary flood unit would result in the top of the cyc being much brighter than the bottom. This is often the reverse of what the designer would like. Manufacturers have remedied this problem with the skillful use of spread reflection and shaping of the reflective

Cyc floodlights

surface. Tubular T-H lamps are usually the source (Figure 8.4). The results are very effective cyc lighting. Some of these units consist of four floodlights built into one housing, one each for red and green and two for blue, making control over blue light much easier. Although these rather bulky units tend to remain in position near the cyc, they are adaptable to other uses if needed.

Reflector Lamp Floodlighting

"R" and "PAR" lamps

Reflector lamps (types "R" and "PAR"), which incorporate the functions of both a light source and the reflector needed to gather and direct the light output, are perhaps the most efficient of luminaires using an incandescent source. This efficiency is achieved by the use of a carefully shaped highly efficient aluminum reflector deposited on the inside surface of the lamp. They come in two general categories. The less expensive thin-glass-bulb variety, known as type "R" is fragile and cannot be

Figure 8.4A. The Far Cyc. This luminaire is designed to produce an even top-to-bottom distribution of light over a cyc as much as 7.5 meters high from as close as 2.5 meters from its top when the units are spaced 2.5 meters apart. Tubular T-H lamps may be 1.0, 1.5 or 2.0 kW. Units may be hung singly, in pairs, triplets or a group of four as shown, connected by means of special latches. Courtesy Colortran.

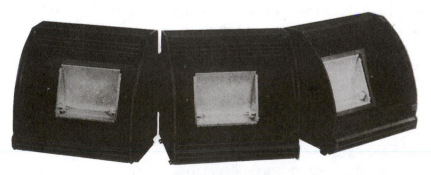

Figure 8.4B. Cyclorama Floodlights. This luminaire is designed with a moveable reflector allowing changes in light distribution to compensate for being very close to the top of the cyc and distant from its bottom. It uses tubular double-ended T-H lamps in wattages up to 1500 watts. Photo courtesy Altman Stage Lighting Co. Inc.

Figure 8.5. PAR Can. This unit accepts a wide variety of PAR lamps providing a wide range of brightness and beam sizes. The highest wattage rating is 1000 watts.

It is supplied in either an all-steel flat black finish both inside and out or an aluminum type, flat black inside and finished aluminum outside. The latter version is supplied for locations where the equipment is exposed to the view of the audience. The steel fixture weighs about 11 lbs. and the aluminum one about 8 lbs. Both types are equipped with metal mesh safety screens to trap flying glass if the lamp should break.

The high efficiency of these units plus their light weight makes them highly desirable for touring. A variety of auxiliary devices is also available, such as barn doors, snoots and color wheels. Courtesy Altman Stage Lighting Co. Inc.

used places where they may be subject to splashing with water or to bumping. Type "PAR" (parabolic aluminum reflector) lamps, on the other hand, are rugged and resistant to splashing or hard knocks. Both types, particularly in high wattages, have been adopted by the pop concert world as a major source of lighting.

Reflector lamps come in a considerable variety of "spot" and "flood" variations. All produce considerable spill light outside the beam and many produce back spill where light leaks around the edges of the reflective surface near the base. All operate at high glass temperatures which can cause fire if flammables touch or come too close to the envelope. Beam temperatures within a foot or so of these lamps may also be capable of causing fire or burning anyone unwary enough to intercept the beam. Obviously, all of these lamps are prone to shattering if struck. Type R lamps are also subject to dangerous shattering if they contact a cool object such as a metal batten or if water is spilled on them while they are on.

Although these lamps may often be seen operating unenclosed in store display windows, it is dangerous and usually illegal to operate them on a stage without being enclosed. Housings designed for stage and concert use, often termed PAR cans (Figure 8.5), hold the lamp securely in place allowing angling, protect nearby flammables from the heat of the lamp and protect the lamp from touching objects that might harm it. PAR cans also control spill light and may allow the installation of color medium far enough in front of the bulb to avoid burning it out. Nevertheless, heat resistant color medium is required. Examination of the catalogue of any major lamp supplier will reveal that reflector flood lamps are available in

Hazards of reflector lamps

PAR cans

conventional incandescent and T-H types in a wide variety of wattages and beam spreads. Some specialized types even use an HID arc tube as their source. Socket arrangements vary from screw base to screw terminals and special pin types.

Designers of theatrical lighting will find these lamps a very useful addition to their list of controllable floodlighting apparatus, but always with the caution that they are potentially dangerous because of their high temperature and fragility.

Users facing a shortage of theatrical spotlights should be cautioned that the "spot" variety of reflector lamps is *not* the equivalent of a regular spotlight. Instead, these lamps are best treated as a special, high efficiency luminaire whose beam is not adjustable except by altering the throw distance. These lamps produce a very intense beam center with the remainder of the beam tapering off to a blurry edge accompanied by considerable spill light.

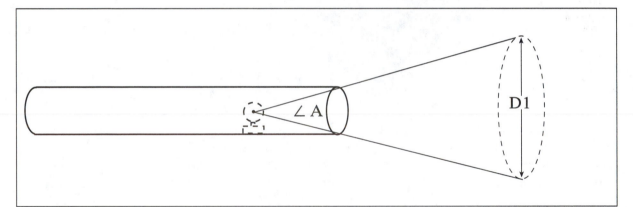

Figure 8.6A. Stovepipe Spotlight. Drawing shows the source located near the front of the pipe. This results in a large, not very useful pool of light and relatively high efficiency as represented by angle A.

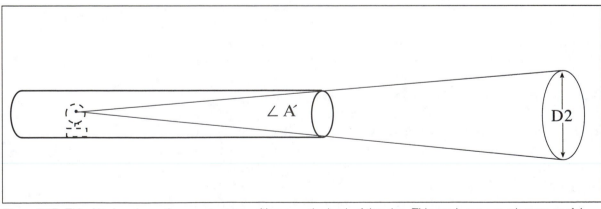

Figure 8.6B. This drawing shows the source at a position near the back of the pipe. This produces a much more useful pool of light, but at the expense of severely reduced efficiency as shown by angle A'.

Sophisticated Floodlight Units

Many developments in lighting equipment have been motivated by the rock music industry, whose budgets inspire manufacturers to develop new equipment at costs exceeding those most legitimate theatres are willing or able to pay. One such recent development is a line of remotely controlled floodlights equipped with color scrollers, positioning motors to allow them to be angled remotely and a powerful HID source.

Reflectors and Condensers in Spotlights

The simplest of all spotlights has no lens at all. It is the "stovepipe spotlight," the last resort of the totally impoverished lighting technician. It consists of a sheet metal tube, the "stovepipe," large enough to house the concentrated filament lamp and its socket, these being arranged so that they can be moved back and forth within the pipe with the filament on the centerline. One end is closed to prevent light leakage and the inside is painted black. When the lamp is on, a cone of light will be emitted from the open end of the tube whose size will vary depending on how close the source is to the opening (Figures 8.6A and 8.6B). Efficiency may be measured by the vertex angle of the cone of light; the wider the angle, the greater portion of the total output of the lamp is being used, and the greater the efficiency. In practice, efficiency will be dismally low at any location of the source that will produce a usable pool of light at any reasonable throw distance. Moving the source toward the open end will

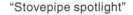
"Stovepipe spotlight"

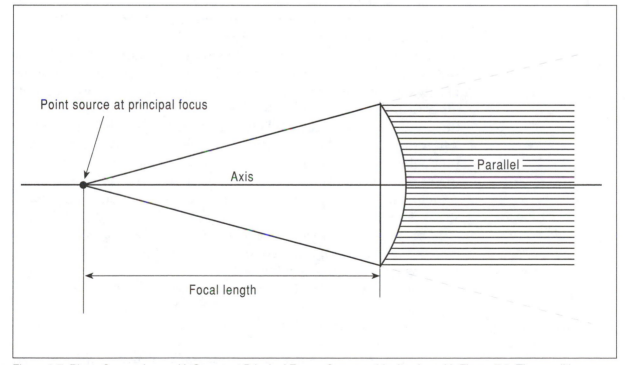

Figure 8.7. Plano-Convex Lens with Source at Principal Focus. Compare this drawing with Figure 7.8. The conditions are the same except that the direction of travel of the light is reversed. In practice the parallel beam will never occur because no light source is really a mathematical point and no lens is free of distortion. Instead, the result will be a very narrow beam of light mottled by the out-of-focus details of the filament.

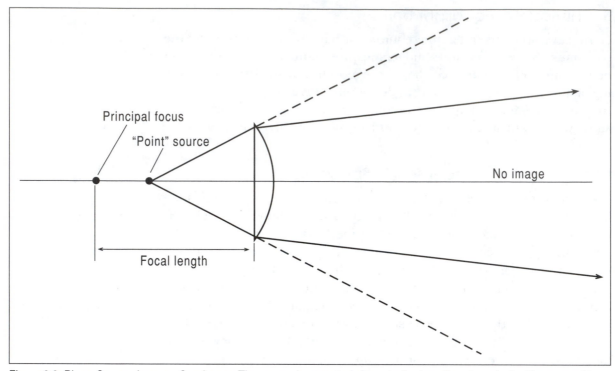

Figure 8.8. Plano-Convex Lens as Condenser. The source is operated closer to the lens than the principal focus resulting in no image, but the beam is narrowed (condensed) to form a useful pool of light with good optical efficiency.

improve efficiency but at the expense of producing a pool of light too wide to be useful.

What is needed is a way of gathering up the light from a wide-angle beam into a useful beam. A converging lens, i.e., a *positive* lens that bends light rays toward the optical axis, is the solution; the addition of a spherical reflector (see below) will also improve efficiency significantly. To understand how such a lens can improve this situation, we must know more about how converging lenses handle light other than in parallel beams. Refer to Figure 8.7 which simply reverses the direction of travel of the light beams as they are shown in Figure 7.8. A point source has been placed at one of the two principal foci, producing parallel rays as the light passes through the lens. Note that the same result would occur if the source were placed at the other principal focus, except that the light would be traveling in the opposite direction.

The distinguishing factor that determines how a positive lens is being used (and the name applied to it) is the location of the source with relationship to the principal focus:

- If the source lies between the principal focus and the optical center of the lens, the lens is operating as a *condensing lens*. It will converge light rays passing through it, but cannot produce an image(Figure 8.8)
- If the source lies farther from the optical center of the lens than the principal focus, it is operating as an *objective lens* and will produce an image. If the source is the filament of the lamp, it will be imaged, if it is an illuminated slide, an image of the slide will be produced. (Figure 7.9)

Converging lens

Condensing lens

Objective lens

Note that these functions depend on *how the positive lens is used*, not on the nature of the lens itself despite the fact that most of the efforts of optical specialists go into making objective lenses into precision masterpieces because sharp, perfectly colored pictures are highly treasured. We will examine the use of positive lenses as condensers first to discover how such a lens can improve the efficiency of the crude stovepipe spotlight.

Application determines how lens is named

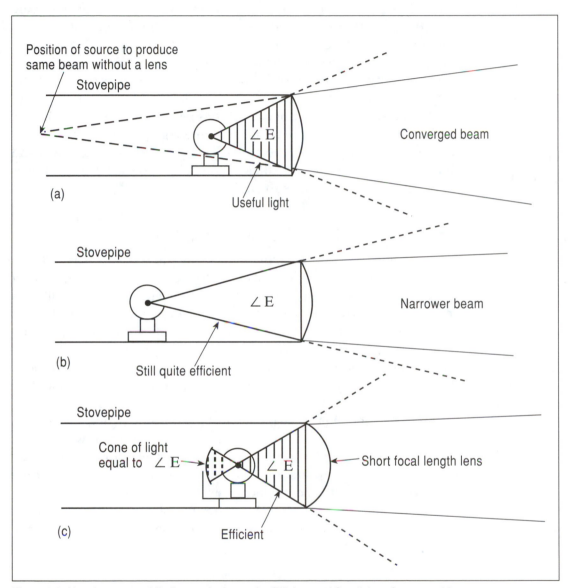

Figure 8.9. How Lenses and Reflectors Increase the Efficiency of Spotlights. Compare this figure with Figures 8.6A and 8.6B. Efficiency is indicated by angle "E" which represents the apex angle of the cone of light collected by the lens and directed towards the stage. Note how the addition of a positive lens increases this angle and thus the efficiency of the spotlight. However the beam is still too wide for many applications. It can be narrowed by moving the source back from the lens (b) but at the expense of reduced efficiency. Or a shorter focal length (greater converging power) lens can be installed (c), maintaining the efficiency but narrowing the beam.

Figure (c) also shows the effect of adding a spherical reflector which intercepts a cone of light equal to that caught by the lens and returns it past the filament toward the lens. This increases efficiency still more.

Condensing Lenses

Converging effect of lens

If a compact light source is placed on the optical axis of a converging lens at any point between the principal focus and the lens itself, the light passing through the lens will be *converged* to form a narrower cone of light than would be produced if the light simply passed through a hole the same diameter as the lens. If the source is moved back and forth along the optical axis, but always closer to the lens than the principal focus, the cone of light produced will be made larger or smaller, efficiency varying according to the diameter of the cone of light intersected by the lens (Figure 8.9 a, b and c). A lens used in this manner is a condensing lens. Its converging power is exactly what is needed to improve the efficiency of the stovepipe spotlight. Note that the terms "condensing" and "converging" are synonymous as far as this discussion of lenses is concerned.

Short focal length equals great converging power.

The converging power of a lens is described by its focal length. The shorter the focal length, the greater the converging power. Thus a short focal length lens of large diameter will have great converging power and potentially will make a very efficient spotlight. We shall see that this is what makes the fresnel lens so effective.

Applying Condensing Lenses and Reflectors

Note in Figure 8.9 how the addition of a lens and reflector makes it possible for the lamp to be operated closer to the opening thus capturing a much larger cone of illumination (angle E in Figure 8.9). Installing a spherical mirror capable of returning a cone of illumination equal to the largest cone collectible by the lens yields a significant increment of efficiency. The result is a luminaire that produces a very useful pool of light which can be adjusted over a considerable range of diameters. In short, the stovepipe spotlight has become a simple plano-convex lens spotlight (PC spotlight).

Plano-convex lens spotlight

Most PC spotlights are made with a long housing to accommodate a variety of lens focal lengths. When such a luminaire is fitted with a short focal length lens, it will be possible to move the source towards the back to points beyond the principal focus. This will cause the lens to form a blurry image of the filament which is useless for spotlighting purposes. This movement of the source, called "back focusing" from the days when it was used to reduce the brightness of carbon arc follow spotlights, should be avoided.

Back focusing

Limitations of Plano-Convex Optics

The lens, the reflector and the lamp in theatrical luminaires are not perfect optical devices. The glass surfaces of the lens will reflect and waste about ten percent of the light that strikes the lens. The glass itself will absorb yet more. The reflector will also lose about ten percent of the light that strikes it. The lamp filament obstructs a significant share of the light returned from the reflector. In spite of these handicaps, a plano-convex lens spotlight is a very useful luminaire much used in European theatres although it is rarely found in USA theatres.

Limitations of the PC optics

Lens changes are common where PC spotlights are in use. The rule for choice of lenses is: short throw—short focal length; long throw—long focal length. Following this rule will allow the throw to be most efficiently matched to the needed beam sizes.

Limitations of the Plano-Convex Lens

Up to a certain point, the obvious way to improve the efficiency of a plano-convex lens spotlight is to operate the lamp as close to the lens as possible, increase the diameter of the lens and reflector, and use the shortest possible focal length lens to get the desired beam convergence. However, large diameter, short focal length PC lenses are so thick at the center that they are subject to breakage from heat stress, transmit light poorly, and are very heavy. Furthermore, as the diameter of the lens increases, light rays from the outer part of the cone of illumination from the source strike the surface of the lens at angles approaching the critical angle, causing more and more light to be reflected off the surface of the lens thus reducing the efficiency of the outer part of the lens to near zero. Thus there is a limit beyond which the PC lens system cannot be improved by increasing lens diameter.

Limitations of large
PC lenses

The Fresnel Lens

The fresnel lens represents a breakthrough. Its basic principle depends on the fact that refractive bending of light rays take place at the surface between the two media of different densities. Once it has entered, light travels through the medium itself in a straight line. This means that light entering the first side of a plano-convex lens is bent at that entry point, travels in a straight line until it exits on the other side where it is once again bent, assuming that neither entry or exit follows a normal.

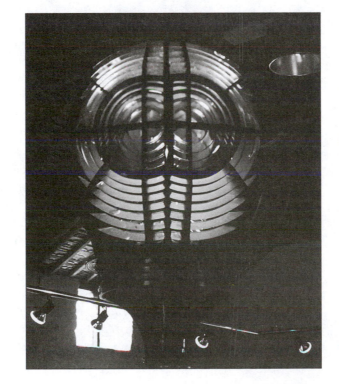

Figure 8.10. Fresnel Lens in Lighthouse. This photo shows a fresnel lens once installed in an Oregon Coast lighthouse. The complete assembly consists of several lenses which rotate around the light source to create a flashing light visible far out to sea. Each lens consists of a number of elements that work together to make up a complete fresnel lens. These parts are optically polished and precisely positioned, making up a very expensive but efficient lens. Photo by author.

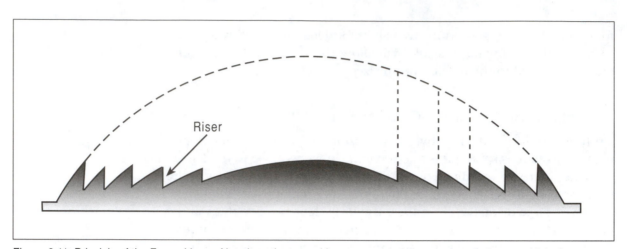

Figure 8.11. Principle of the Fresnel Lens. Note how the curved lens segments follow the curve of a very thick plano-convex lens. The risers contribute to the soft-focus quality of these lenses.

Figure 8.12. Fresnel Lens Applied to the Theatre. This photo shows a typical theatrical fresnel lens. Note that it is a one-piece lens cast of glass. Its cross section follows the outline shown in Figure 8.11. Optically it is a very crude lens which has been modified by adding a dimpled surface to its flat side and, in the case of this particular lens, also shaping the flat side to form a cylindrical fresnel lens to make it produce a very soft-edge oval beam. This makes it ideal for acting area lighting.

Note that this figure also illustrates the method of removing/installing a lens in a spotlight using a lens ring to hold the lens in place. Photo by author.

Around 1800 Augustin Fresnel, a French physicist was concerned with making a better light houses, not with stage lighting equipment, but he was confronted by basically the same problem: how to gather the most light from a source and send it outward where it would be useful. He reasoned from the above fact about refraction that most of the intervening glass could be removed without changing the effect of the lens. To this end, he devised a segmented lens whose curvature maintained that of a very short focal length plano-convex lens but which avoided the huge amount of glass that only added weight, absorbed light, and was subject to heat breakage. Since a lighthouse lens is a custom device, M. Fresnel could afford to have each segment of the lens especially ground to optical perfection and carefully set in a frame to hold the entire unit together to make up the lens. The result was a very efficient large diameter, short focal length lens and that was resistant to heat damage and avoided large glass losses. Clearly, this was expensive, but the need was great and a lighthouse is a long-term investment. A number of these lenses are still extant, one is shown in Figure 8.10.

Fresnel's geometry was simple: He stepped back the curve of his basic lens outline whenever the glass became too thick for effective operation. This produced a series of rings of glass, each representing part of the curvature of a large, thick plano-convex lens plus a much smaller diameter lens of the same curvature at the center.

In the 1930s theatrical lighting equipment manufacturers adopted the same principle to create a crude, effective and economical adaptation of M. Fresnel's precise and expensive lens. See Figure 8.11. Note the curve dotted in to represent the outline of a very short focal length plano-convex lens. To make up the fresnel lens, this curve has been broken into segments which have the same converging power as the dotted-in lens. Unlike M. Fresnel's optical masterpiece, these lenses, which are still very much in use, are cast into one piece of glass with minimal precision. Nevertheless, they are efficient light gathering devices.

One of the drawbacks of the cast fresnel lens is that it produces much more spill light than a plano-convex lens. This comes from the edges of the segments of the curvature and from the vertical parts of the glass where the curve is stepped back (see Figure 8.11). The result is that the ordinary fresnel lens is a soft edge device which cannot produce a sharply defined pool like that from a PC lens spotlight. A soft edge can be advantageous for acting area lighting, but the spill makes fresnel lens spotlights useless for front-of-house purposes. In an attempt to convert a flaw into an advantage, many fresnel lenses are made with purposely dappled or bumpy backs. These lenses produce a very soft edge beam ideal for acting area applications.

Although it adds to their cost, fresnel lenses can be made that produce minimal spill or flare. One step in this direction is *flatted risers*. Risers cause much of the spill light produced by cheap lenses. They are flatted by coating them with flat black ceramic enamel which cuts off the spill by absorbing the light, but this makes the lens run hotter. Another way of improving the performance of fresnel lenses is more precise casting of the glass or even grinding the curved surfaces to make them more optically effective.

Cast fresnel lenses for the stage

Spill from fresnel lenses

Fresnel lenses for acting area lighting

Flatted risers

Oval Beam Fresnel Lens

Another variation on the fresnel principle is the oval beam lens. It is specifically adapted for acting area applications or other needs where an oval, soft-edged pool of light will be advantageous. Oval beam lenses are cast with a fresnel lens on one side and a fresnel adaptation of a cylindrical lens on the other (Figure 8.12). The cylindrical portion resembles the cast lens of some automobile headlamps. The cylindrical side may also be lightly dappled for a softer beam edge. In use, the oval beam lens is rotated in the luminaire until the oval beam is oriented as needed. Focal length for stock fresnel spotlight lenses is standardized in the USA where the focal length is generally equal to the lens radius.

Step Lenses

Although M. Fresnel himself made his lenses by stepping back the curved side of a plano-convex lens, his principle applies equally well if the curved surface is left intact and the glass is stepped back from the plane side. The result is a *step lens* which is easier to grind precisely than a fresnel lens.

From the simple step lens, it is but a small move to shape the stepped side to also serve as a lens, increasing the converging power with minimum glass. Such lenses are often used in ellipsoidal reflector spotlights (see below). They produce little spill or flare and weigh much less than the pairs of plano-convex lenses they replace. Note that the focal length of these specialty fresnel-type lenses is determined by the luminaire manufacturer, not standardized.

Fresnel Lens Spotlights

Any plano-convex lens spotlight can be equipped with a fresnel lens, if it will fit the lens opening, and probably become more efficient. However, most of the back part of the housing will turn out to be useless because the fresnel lens will have a shorter focal length than any plano-convex lens available. Also, the size of the lens opening will be too small to take advantage of the larger diameter fresnel lenses available and the lamp base probably will not allow the lamp to operates as close to the lens as needed.

To take advantage of the special qualities of fresnel lenses a whole new family of luminaires was developed. These have been so successful that, along with the ellipsoidal reflector spotlight, they have almost completely crowded the plano-convex lens spotlight off the market in the USA. These luminaires have short housings, large lens openings and are designed to operate with the lamp very close to the lens thus collecting a large cone of light. Originally special type "T" lamps were designed for

Figure 8.13A. General Purpose Fresnel Spotlight. This 6-inch fresnel is typical of thousands in use. At a throw distance of 20 feet it produces a 5.6 ft. dia. pool of light (231 fc) in spot focus or a 28 ft. dia. pool (39 fc) in flood focus using conventional incandescent lamps. Maximum wattage is 750. It is somewhat more efficient in the T-H lamp version. These data make it a convenient luminaire for acting area lighting. Courtesy Altman Stage Lighting Co., Inc.

Figure 8.13B. Six-inch Theatre Fresnel. This efficient luminaire weighs about 11 lbs. It produces an intense beam and a smoothly tapered field. At 15 feet throw, spot focus, the beam angle is 6.1°, at flood focus the field angle is 64.5°. It may be lamped with 500W (BTL), 750W (BTN) or 1000W (BTR) lamps or their 3200 K equivalents. Photo courtesy Colortran.

use in these luminaires. Their narrow, elongated bulb made it possible to operate the lamp closer to the back of the fresnel lens than a "G" type lamp. The more recent introduction of T-H lamps which are smaller still, has reduced the demand for type "T" lamps, but they are still in use in older equipment.

Fresnel lenses can be increased in diameter until the angle of the light striking the outer edges is so great that most of the light is reflected. At that point, there is no advantage in making the lens larger. Since spherical reflectors can be made to collect any cone of light needed by making them small but with great curvature and placing them close to the source, it is possible to make very efficient fresnel lens spotlights. Indeed, under ideal circumstances, they can be more efficient than comparable ellipsoidal reflector spotlights. See Figure 8.13 for some modern fresnel lens spotlights.

Handling Fresnel Luminaires

A well-constructed fresnel spotlight is a rugged device that should serve for a long time on stage. It requires little maintenance except for occasional dusting, including the reflector, and relamping when needed. If the unit is a modern spotlight made for use with T-H lamps, it can be mounted in any position without regard for the lamp's operating position. If it is an earlier model using a type "T" lamp or such a spotlight that has been upgraded by installing a T-H lamp, base-down-to-horizontal mounting precautions should be followed. Otherwise the ventilation system,

Figure 8.13C. Theatre Fresnel. This luminaire is available in a variety of wattages, all using T-H lamps. It is highly efficient, particularly at wide beam settings. Courtesy Strand Lighting.

Figure 8.13D. Daylight Fresnel. This powerful luminaire is designed for motion picture and television but applicable to the stage where a high-powered, high-color-temperature beam is needed. Its 2500-watt HMI lamp, color temperature 5600 K, produces a 6° beam 3.2 ft. diameter, 1309 fc at 30 feet. Courtesy Strand Lighting.

which was originally designed for this kind of operation, may not function properly.

Other than lamp outages, the principal malfunction of a fresnel spotlight will be misalignment of the reflector. This can be caused by accidentally pushing the reflector out of position while relamping or cleaning or, in some types of luminaires, by set screws working loose and allowing the reflector to move.

Symptoms of poor reflector alignment

Symptoms of a misaligned reflector are poor light output, two overlapping pools of light or two pools of differing diameters atop one another. The solution is to wait until the housing is cool, then aim the luminaire toward a plain surface such as the back of the safety curtain, and bring it up on dimmer just enough to allow the technician to see the pool(s) of light. Then, wearing gloves to protect against the already very warm lamp, the technician moves the reflector back into position while observing the pools of light. Many fresnel lighting fixtures have the reflector mounted on a pliable support which can simply be bent back into place. However some will have the reflector mounted on a post and held in place by means of a setscrew. In this case the screw must be loosened, the reflector moved into position and the screw retightened.

Damage from badly misaligned reflector

The most damaging type of misalignment occurs when the reflector leans toward the lamp until it touches it usually causing the lamp to fail and almost certainly damaging the surface of the reflector. If the lamp does not fail, it will usually bulge from the extra heat concentrated on the bulb. In either case, both lamp and reflector should be replaced and the reflector carefully aligned and locked into place.

Luminaires Using Objective Lens Systems

The fresnel spotlight is incapable of producing an essentially spill- and flare-free beam of light. Indeed, most fresnels produce so much spill they cannot be used as front-of-house equipment. Thus a new category of luminaires was developed in the late 1930s, the ellipsoidal reflector spotlights (ERSs). These devices are really projectors with all of the basic optics of a slide or motion picture projector—a light-collecting system, an aperture containing image material (a "slide"), and an objective lens system that projects an image on stage.

An ERS is a projector

When first developed and for many years following, ERSs were the most sophisticated luminaires found on the legitimate stage. However, more recently a whole new line of projection type luminaires has been developed, first for the concert industry, which can afford their high cost, and now for the theatre as a whole. These "automated luminaires" are still basically projectors but with a wide variety of features, including the ability to be remotely reangled, have their beam characteristics altered along with several other new and very useful variables. They are the new "top of the line." They will be discussed after the workhorse of the live stage, the ERS, has been explained.

As just noted, the ERS is a projector. Its lens or lenses operate as objectives projecting its light output onto the stage as an image. As Figure 8.14 shows, the reflector serves as a very efficient light collector which focuses an intense cone of light onto an adjustable

Aperture

opening called the aperture. This lighted aperture functions as a "slide"; its image focused on stage by the objective lens. Shape of the image depends on adjustments made in the shape of the aperture by means of moveable shutters or sometimes by an iris mechanism. Although the size of the image can be adjusted over a fairly narrow range by changing the size of the aperture, major size alterations must be done by changing the focal length of the objective lens, just as image size is adjusted in a slide projector. Modern "zoom" ERSs can be adjusted over a wide range of beam sizes by means of a variable focal length lens. Earlier and simpler models have fixed focus lenses, although some of these can be changed between shows. Sharpness of the image is determined by adjusting the aperture-to-lens distance. This adjustment also causes minor changes in the size of the pool of light produced.

Zoom ERSs

Fixed focus ERSs

Although it is a projector and can form an image of whatever is placed in the aperture, the ellipsoidal reflector spotlight is designed for maximum light gathering and focusing efficiency and only secondarily for the production of a quality image. The high efficiency of the reflector-lamp combination makes the operating temperature at the aperture so high that only a few heat-resistant materials can survive there. Nevertheless the aperture is often used for image projection purposes by inserting image producing *gobos* made of etched sheet metal or very heat resistant glass. ("Gobo" is a term whose derivation is mysterious—some say it is a shortened form of the word "go-between" once used in film lighting—but it has become standard in the lighting industry.) See Figure 8.15 for examples of some of the many commercially produced gobos that are available.

Gobos

When the ellipsoidal reflector spotlight was developed, a special line of base-up type "T" lamp was developed to go with it. In early ellipsoidal reflector spotlights, the lamp socket was mounted at roughly a 45° angle to the housing. This caused the lamp to operate near vertical, base

Base-up operation of early ERSs

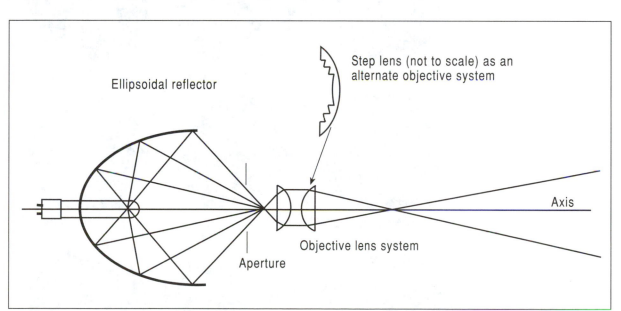

Figure 8.14. Optical System of the Ellipsoidal Reflector Spotlight. Note that the reflector collects a large share of the light from the source and directs it to the lens system. The lens(es) function as an objective system, producing an image of the aperture on the stage. Many modern ERSs utilize a one-piece step lens with curvature designed into both sides. Note the axially mounted lamp which is standard in most modern ERSs.

Figure 8.15. Gobos. Illustrated here are a few of the wide variety of commercially prepared gobos (templates) available from various manufacturers. Sizes have been somewhat standardized but gobos may still need trimming (use scissors) to make a gobo by one manufacturer fit into the carrier by another manufacturer. The metal gobo may sometimes be simply inserted into the slot built into the spotlight, but a better method is to install the gobo in a special metal carrier which fits into the gobo slot. This protects the thin metal gobo.

In addition to metal gobos, which can only produce silhouette images on stage, glass gobos are available which can produce images in multiple colors. Some of these are made using dichroic coatings which makes them much more efficient. Gobos are used in ERSs and in intelligent luminaires. One can often achieve artistically satisfying effects by superimposing one gobo over another in an ERS and/or by superimposing two images on the same surface. When used in intelligent luminaires, movement of the gobo(s) is possible making spectacular, if usually unsubtle effects.

Figure 8.15A. The gobos pictured here are but a small assortment of the many offered by several manufacturers. These are designed for use in ellipsoidal reflector spotlights. Courtesy GAMPRODUCTS (G) and Rosco (R).

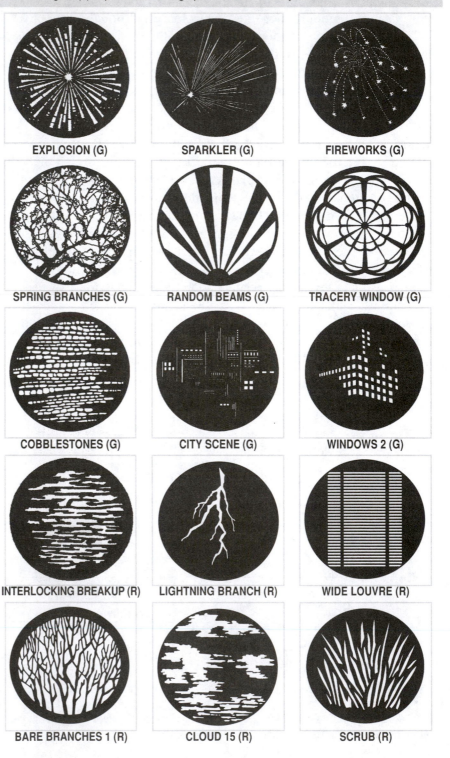

EXPLOSION (G)   SPARKLER (G)   FIREWORKS (G)

SPRING BRANCHES (G)   RANDOM BEAMS (G)   TRACERY WINDOW (G)

COBBLESTONES (G)   CITY SCENE (G)   WINDOWS 2 (G)

INTERLOCKING BREAKUP (R)   LIGHTNING BRANCH (R)   WIDE LOUVRE (R)

BARE BRANCHES 1 (R)   CLOUD 15 (R)   SCRUB (R)

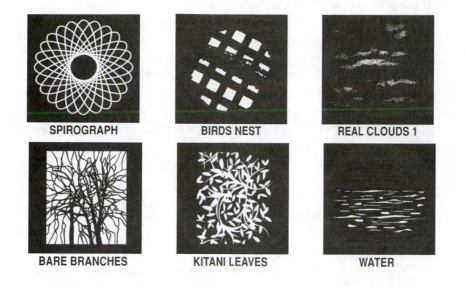

SPIROGRAPH   BIRDS NEST   REAL CLOUDS 1

BARE BRANCHES   KITANI LEAVES   WATER

Figure 8.15B. Gobos for use in automated luminaires. Courtesy Vari-Lite, Inc.

up when the luminaires was aimed downward in a typical light beam or batten mounting location. Users were cautioned to be sure that, whatever the mounting location, the lamp should only be operated at or near to base-up. If the lamp were operated in any other position it might fail prematurely because of filament sagging. Also the base-up position of the lamp increased efficiency by causing sublimated tungsten from the filament to condense in the vicinity of the socket, an area not in the path of any usable light. However the introduction of the T-H lamp changed all of this. T-H lamps can be operated in any position and do not have the sublimated tungsten problem. This allowed luminaire designers to develop ellipsoidal reflector spotlights with the lamp mounted axially and to eliminate the caution that the lamp must be operated near to base-up. (See Figure 8.14.) Axially mounted lamps are now standard in these luminaires.

Axially mounted lamps in modern ERS luminaires

Lens Systems for Ellipsoidal Reflector Spotlights

The objective lens or lens system for an ellipsoidal reflector spotlight must efficiently transfer the light from the reflector to the stage. Ideally it should also be capable of focusing a sharp image of a gobo in the aperture and should produce an evenly distributed pool of light when the luminaire is adjusted for this purpose. Two types of lens systems are commonly in use. One utilizes two plano-convex lenses spaced some distance apart to make up a compound lens of short focal length capable of handling the heat load from the lamp. The other system uses a single lens, usually convex on its front and stepped on the back, often the steps are also shaped according to the fresnel principle to further shorten the focal length. In some instances a double, stepped fresnel lens is used. Whatever their optical configuration, ERS lenses are best made of high transmission heat resistant glass such as borosilicate. Note that there are some ellipsoidal reflector spotlights in use with two-lens objectives in which only the rear lens (closest to the aperture) is made of heat resistant glass. Workers who remove the lenses while working on these luminaires should be cautioned that they must replace the lenses in their

Double plano-convex lenses

Stepped lenses

proper location to avoid destroying the non-heat-resistant lens.

A large share of the ellipsoidal reflector spotlights now being sold have zoom lenses. In its simplest form zooming is accomplished by altering the distance between two lenses and also moving the entire lens unit to keep focus. More elaborate systems may move several lenses in different amounts and directions as the zoom handle is moved. Lenses for these luminaires must meet the same heat resistance requirements as fixed focal length units.

Efficient Operation of ERS and Fresnel Spotlights

Both the fresnel lens spotlight and the ellipsoidal reflector spotlight can be very efficient devices—much more efficient than the plano-convex lens spotlights they have largely replaced. However efficiency varies drastically with application. Any application which requires that a fresnel spotlight

Figure 8.16. Modern Ellipsoidal Reflector Spotlights. These figures illustrate some of the many varieties of ERSs now available. Most manufacturers supply them in a variety of wattages and beam configurations. Although the acceptance of zoom luminaires has theoretically reduced the need for stocking a wide variety of luminaires to satisfy various throw needs, the greater efficiency of fixed-focus ERSs, their lower cost and lighter weight causes most theatres to continue with fixed-focus luminaires designed for easy lens changes.

Better lenses, dichroic reflectors and specially configured lamp filaments have all increased the efficiency of ERSs significantly. Thus several manufacturers are able to offer luminaires that run at considerably reduced wattages and still produce as much or more light then their inefficient predecessors. However, light output specifications are not always comparable. Potential buyers should study them carefully and be prepared to make (or hire) tests of their own if a large number of luminaires is to be purchased.

Figure 8.16A. Source Four. This modern ERS has been engineered for efficiency, making it one of the strongest competitors in the field. It uses specially efficient lenses, a special 575-watt HPL T-H lamp, and a dichroic reflector. A combination claimed to produce the output of a conventional 1000-watt luminaire with 40% less power. The same housing is engineered to take lens tubes with lenses that produce 5° to 50° field angles. The lens barrel rotates making it possible to orient the "cut" of the aperture to any angle. With special 77-volt lamps, these luminaires support "dimmer doubling" technology used by ETC. Photo courtesy ETC.

have its beam narrowed by moving the lamp toward the back of the housing or that requires an ERS to be shuttered down to a narrow aperture will reduce efficiency. Zooming a zoom ERS to get a small pool of light also reduces the total light output. If a very small, intense pool of light is needed, the best solution is to install an ellipsoidal reflector luminaire specially designed for that service, i.e., one designed for "long throw."

However light handling efficiency is not the only consideration in the choice of a particular spotlight; flexibility and adaptability to the specific use are also important. We have already noted that the fresnel spotlight is particularly well adapted to acting area lighting from onstage positions. Its soft edge beam makes it easy to blend the areas to avoid dark spots or hot spots. However it is not suited to front of house applications because of its spill. This is where the ellipsoidal reflector spotlight comes into its own. It produces very little spill light and can be framed to fit the sides of a proscenium opening or any other odd shaped space. It can be adjusted to a sharp-edged beam or unfocused to give its pool of light a soft edge. Modern zoom ERSs make a wide variety of mounting positions possible for the same luminaire. If zoom luminaires are not available, the designer should take care to see that the ellipsoidal reflector spotlights are selected to match their application. Thus balcony spotlights, for example, should have a throw characteristic that enables them to operate efficiently, i.e., with the least possible shuttering. Refer to Figure 8.17 for various typical field angles of common ERSs.

Narrowing the beam reduces efficiency.

Match the luminaire to its application.

Figure 8.16B. This ERS is equipped with interchangeable lens tubes providing beam angles from 5° to 50° in 10° increments. The shutter assembly rotates 180°. It uses standard T-H lamps up to 750-watt. Courtesy Altman Stage Lighting, Inc.

Handling Ellipsoidal Reflector Spotlights

Like the fresnel, these luminaires are basically very rugged devices that should give long, efficient service on stage. Their lamps are, however, fragile. The filaments are so tightly packed that vibration from jarring or bumping the luminaire, particularly when it is on, can cause the filament parts to contact each other shorting and destroying the filament.

When in storage ERSs should always have their shutters pushed into the housing as far as they will go. This will prevent accidental bending of the thin metal shutters during handling. However it should also be standard procedure that the shutters are pulled into their open position as soon as a luminaire is installed. This will prevent destruction of the luminaire when it is turned on because all of the heat from the lamp is trapped in the housing.

Users should take care that ellipsoidal reflector spotlights are not operated for long periods of time with their shutters nearly closed, a situation that may occur if the luminaire is framed down to cover a special small area. Such operation may warp the shutters, reduce lamp life and even damage the reflector. Select a very long throw luminaire that can be operated with its shutters open to a reasonable degree when this situation arises.

If the theatre is still using the old "burn base up only" ellipsoidals, care should be taken to observe this caution even if the lamp has been replaced with a T-H lamp. The ventilation system in these older luminaires is not adapted to operation in other positions and overheating is likely to occur.

Close shutters for storage

Open shutters immediately after mounting.

Figure 8.16C. Colortran 5/50 Ellipsoidal Reflector Spotlight. This luminaire has a peak/flat field adjustment by means of a heat resistant knob on the back of the housing. It accommodates 500-watt to 1000-watt regular spotlight service T-H lamps and is equipped with an Alzak double-flatted ellipsoidal reflector. The lens(es) are low-expansion borosilicate glass. The gate assembly is designed to allow the shutters each plus or minus 30° of rotation. Photo courtesy Colortran.

Alignment

Although there is no chance that a lamp will somehow touch the reflector, as can happen in a fresnel luminaire, misalignment can still produce poor light output and an uneven field. Most ERSs are designed to give the user the option of setting the alignment to produce a relatively even field (flat) or to produce a peaked field with the peak centered. The flat field is best for projecting gobos and the peaked field aids blending when the luminaire is used for acting area lighting. Alignment adjustments, whether to correct for poor light distribution or the change from flat field to peak or vice versa, are made on modern ERSs by moving a single handle at the rear of the lamp housing. Earlier types may require the adjusting of three screws on the lamp housing

Flat field or peaked?

Figure 8.16D. Fixed Focus Ellipsoidal Reflector Spotlight. Although the focal length of its lens is fixed, lens tubes are interchangeable: 19°, 26°, 36° and 50° lenses are available. The optical system is designed around the GLC T-H lamp for high efficiency. A glass dichroic reflector and aspheric lenses are standard. The body may be rotated 360° to aid in aligning gobos or shutter cutoffs. Courtesy Strand Lighting.

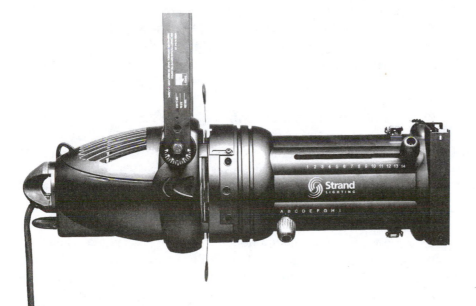

Figure 8.16E. Zoom Ellipsoidal Reflector Spotlight. This luminaire has all of the optical and mechanical features of the luminaire described in Figure 8.16D but offers a zoom lens tube instead of the interchangeable tubes. It is available in two zoom ranges: 15° to 32° and 23° to 50°. Courtesy Strand Lighting.

An unavoidable cause of luminaires going out of alignment is the aging changes that take place in lamps. Filaments warp, moving out of their manufactured position. Thus a luminaire that functioned well a few performances back will suddenly display poor light output. Realigning should be tried before replacing the lamp.

Figure 8.17. Typical Field Angles

The field angle is derived from the field area. The following table gives averages of some standard equipment. Beam angles are not included since they vary enormously depending on instrument brand, lamp alignment and lamp type. Roughly, however, the beam area is 2/3 of the field area.

Ellipsoidal Reflector Spotlight (ERS)	Field Angle	Field Diameter* (per 1 ft. of throw)
4-1/2 x 6-1/2	50°	.9326 ft.
6 x 9	37°	.6692 ft.
6 x 12	27°	.4802 ft.
6 x 16	17°	.2989 ft.
6 x 22	10°	.1750 ft.
8 x 8	20°	.3527 ft.
8 x 11	16°	.2811 ft.
8 x 14	10°	.1750 ft.
6″ and 8″ fresnels		
spot focus:	20°	.3527 ft.
flood focus:	50°	.9326 ft.

* When the field angle and throw distance are known, the field diameter can be calculated using the following formula: diameter = 2 x (distance x tangent of half of the field angle).

Source: *Backstage Handbook* by Paul Carter

Color Changers

Although remotely controlled color changing devices have been available for many years, they were relatively crude, often noisy devices used either on follow spotlights (below) or on luminaires that were inaccessible except with the use of very high ladders or special scaffoldings. Recently, with the advent of digital control, color changers have become standard equipment for large-budget shows and are now becoming common in any theatrical situation. Recently, one type has acquired a new name: *scrollers*.

Scrollers mount on the front of the luminaire and move a band made up of various panels of color media, called a color string or color scroll, in front of the lens (see Figure 8.18). They are usually operated remotely by a digital signal (e.g., DMX512) from a control console although some can be set to cycle automatically. Since the color medium is outside of the housing of the luminaire, it runs cooler and lasts longer than media mounted inside the luminaire (below). Custom-made color bands are available from a number of suppliers.

Well-made scrollers are nearly silent. A number of them may be ganged together to control the color of a front-of-balcony wash, for example, or to change acting area colors from scene to scene. Clearly, a scroller can make one luminaire serve the purpose of several if color change is the only reason for adding luminaires.

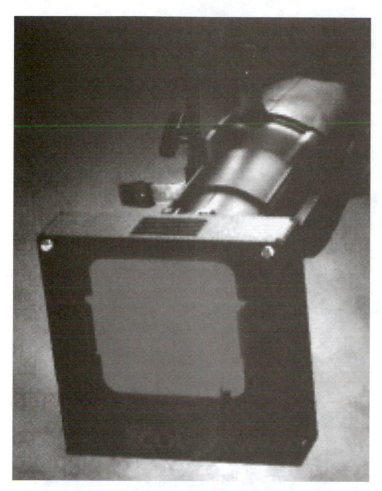

Figure 8.18. Wybron Scroller. This color changer features quiet, reliable operation and comes in sizes to fit all major luminaires. A weatherproof version is also available. Handles 2-32 colors (2-24 colors in the 10-inch model). Speed varies with model; e.g., the 7.5-inch model moves end-to-end in 2.5 seconds. Can be operated at slower speeds for color cross-fades. Powered by 24-volt DC control via DMX512 signal from console. Diagnostics data feeds back to power supply. Photo courtesy Wybron, Inc.

Color changes in follow spotlights are often made by using a "boomerang," a set of internally mounted color frames carrying color media that can be moved to bring one or more pieces of media into the beam. These are hand-operated by the follow spot operator, not remotely controlled. Although regular color media (preferably polycarbonate) will endure the heat inside the follow spotlight, for some time, dichroic filters with glass substrates are better.

Automated Luminaires

These are also called, robot lights, servo-operated instruments, intelligent luminaires, wiggle lights, and other names in addition to their trade names. They all have in common the ability to be remotely angled, focused, have their color medium changed and in many cases make a number of other changes even including movement of gobos and operation as a strobe effect.

Such luminaires, because of their complexity, are expensive. Indeed one well-known brand is only rented, not for sale at all. However their flexibility makes one such luminaire the equivalent of several conventional ones not counting the addition of various effects not even possible with conventional spotlights. Whether this flexibility can make up for the high cost of this equipment is a matter that can only be worked out on the basis of each individual show.

Figure 8.19. Scanning automated luminaires move their beams by means of a motor driven mirror mounted just in front of the lens. The body of the luminaire remains fixed. Movement is sufficient to allow any reasonable aim of the luminaire once its body is positioned towards the center of the desired range of movement. The mirror is driven by a precision stepping motor that enables the luminaire to place the beam with great accuracy and to return it exactly to a previous position. In addition to the moving beam, scanning automated luminaires are equipped with a diversity of "attributes," such as beam focusing, color changing, insertion and movement of gobos and more.

Figure 8.19A. High End Technobeam automated luminaire. Courtesy High End.

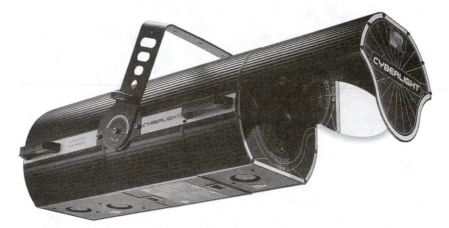

Figure 8.19B. High End Cyberlight. Courtesy High End.

Figure 8.19C. Martin Roboscan R98. Courtesy Martin.

There are two general categories of automated spotlight luminaires, those which use moving mirrors (scanners) to direct the beam and those which move the entire luminaire with a motor-driven yoke that affects both tilt and pan. Additionally there is automated flood lighting (wash) equipment and, although not much used in the legitimate theatre, a number of special effects devices commonly found in discos.

Scanners

Motor-driven yoke

The mirror moves to direct the light.

Scanning Luminaires

Scanning automated luminaires (Figure 8.19) are sometimes simply referred to as "scanners," although that term also refers to the small, much more rapidly moving mirrors used to direct laser beams. They consist of rather large housings which are mounted in a fixed position for the run of a show (unless mounted on a remotely controlled moveable batten in which case changeable location is added to the variables list). A powerful light beam produced by projection optics is directed to a moveable mirror immediately in front of the lens which directs the beam toward the stage. This mirror is moved by a precision device called a stepping motor which is controlled by digital circuitry. The best of these luminaires can be counted on to return to a previous position and focus time after time. The range of movement of the mirror allows pan and tilt sufficient for almost any situation.

Stepping motors

Moving Yoke Luminaires

Tilt and pan are effected in moving yoke luminaires (Figure 8.20) by means of special motor driven yokes which can pan and tilt the entire fixture over a wide range. This makes it possible to make units in which the housing can be moved from yoke to yoke changing, for example, from spotlight to floodlight. Moreover, the range of tilt and pan is even greater than that offered by the scanning type.

Both types of these devices are basically high-quality projectors. Light, usually from a high-efficiency HID source, is collected by a combination of mirror and lenses and passed through an image plane where an assortment of devices such as an iris, and a moveable set of gobos produce an image on the stage. An assortment of color filters, usually dichroic, provides anywhere from a few dozen to literally thousands of colors, depending on the complexity of the unit. A mechanical dimmer is included in the optical train when an arc source is used. The many variables produced by the optical equipment are controlled by digital signals that originate at the control console. As many as eight channels of control per luminaire may be used.

Sophisticated projectors

Automated Wash Luminaires

Wash luminaires (Figure 8.21), essentially controllable floodlights utilizing the same digital control, are also available. In at least one case these devices are interchangeable on the same automated yoke with spot type equipment. One type is also provided in a weatherproof housing for use

Figure 8.20. Panning Automated Luminaires. These luminaires achieve their movement by means of a motorized yoke that adjusts tilt and pan, moving the entire body of the luminaire. Focus, color changing, etc., are adjusted from within the housing. Range of movement is exceedingly wide, almost 360° both horizontally and vertically. Like the scanning luminaires, these movements are achieved by means of precision stepping motors. The luminaires shown here have a diversity of attributes making them adaptable at the sending of a cue to movements and changes that it would require several conventional luminaires to achieve, plus some changes, such as movement of the beam while on and change of focus of a gobo *a vista* that are impossible with conventional spotlights.

Figure 8.20A. High End Studio Spot. Courtesy High End.

Figure 8.20B. Martin Mac 250. Courtesy Martin.

outside as an architectural lighting device.

Controlling Automated Luminaires

Control problem remains unresolved

As noted in Chapter 4, consoles for controlling these devices are still in their infancy as far as the subtlety of control needed for the dramatic stage is concerned. This is no simple problem because of the many control channels needed for each luminaire and the need to make their subtle control intuitive for the operator. Some modern consoles are now being offered with a "moving lights control section" that purports to give the operator the kind of control needed for dramatic lighting. Nevertheless much remains to be done if the full potential of these luminaires is to be open to the dramatic stage. Computer-assisted position control, described below, represents a major development toward the solution of this problem.

Remote Control of Follow Spotlights

To an operator working from a spotting booth or any other commonly used position on stage, aiming a follow spotlight is intuitive—he or she simply points the beam wherever it should go. The geometry that determines the aim of the beam is automatic. However, that same simple ma-

Figure 8.21. Automated Wash Luminaires. Wash luminaires are the modern version of what once were stationary, unadjustable floodlights. These units are also adapted to architectural lighting needs where they become an essential part of colored light displays on buildings, bridges, etc. For greater flexibility the same automated yoke can accommodate either a wash luminaire or a spot type. Photo by Lewis Lee, courtesy Vari-Lite, Inc.

neuver becomes complicated when the luminaire is operated remotely by an operator with a perspective different from that viewed when the operator is at the luminaire. Angles representing the proper direction of the beam must be consciously adjusted. This problem occurs during calibration sessions when remotely controlled luminaires are being set up to be operated from the console but becomes acute when the automated luminaires are being used as follow spotlights.

If a number of luminaires, in several locations, are to be used to follow a performer—such as following a skater in an ice arena—a single operator, remote from the luminaires, cannot make the many angle adjustments on the console needed to keep each luminaire properly angled.

The conventional solution to this problem in the concert world has been to preset the movements of the remotely located luminaires inputting the information, luminaire by luminaire, via track ball or joy stick devices which adjust x, y, and z coordinates as needed. Very complicated movements of large numbers of luminaires can be handled in this manner to create spectacular light effects. However this presetting does not satisfy the need for live follow of a performer who may move about randomly with timing that differs with each performance.

Three-D Position Control

This is a system that uses a computer to do the geometry involved in follows fast enough to enable the follow spotlights to be remotely operated in real time. The follow point is determined by the operator or is automatically located by a radio locating system. If the follow point is manually located, this may be done using a joy stick or track ball on the console or, much better, a telescope-like pointing device which the operator keeps aimed at the proper point. The angle of the pointer determines the direction to the follow point; a radar system determines the distance. Such devices may even be equipped with night vision apparatus enabling the operator to pick up a performer on a dark stage or arena. Systems using this method offer to control as many as 64 luminaires. (Additional equipment may be added to increase the number to 128!) The performance area over which follow control may be applied is practically limited only by the sight lines of the operator. The scope device also provides the operator control over the other variables available on the automated luminaire.

The ultimate in automated follow control is achieved by equipping the performer(s) with a radio transmitter that allows a system of receivers to locate the performer over a defined amount of performing space. This "automated space" is more limited than the range of the operator-assisted telescope device, but affords total automation throughout that space.

These aiming systems, while clearly very expensive, offer the console operator relief from one of the tasks common to live theatre—the proper location of the focus point of the lighting. This can enable the operator to concentrate on the many other variables at his or her disposal when using automated luminaires. However real time (not preset) control over these many variables remains difficult with consoles available today, the only solution being limiting the designer to specifying control over only one or two variables at a time and providing multiple operators at the console.

Economics of Automated Luminaires

Automated luminaires are expensive even without the added cost of the follow controls discussed above. Most legitimate theatres will probably decide at first glance that these modern wonders are far beyond their means. This will be true in many cases, but equipment buyers should not dismiss these luminaires out of hand. The economics of purchase can be complicated: For instance, an automated luminaire needs no dimmer—it has one built it. It seldom needs color media—its dichroic filters have a very long life and can usually mix almost any color the designer specifies. Most important, the luminaire can reangle itself, refocus its beam, alter the beam spread, add or remove gobos. Thus, depending on the needs of the show, it may serve the functions of a number of conventional luminaires while also offering the dramatic impact of making any of the listed changes live before the audience. Furthermore, many of these luminaires use lamps with life ratings many times those of T-H lamps. All of these factors affect the ultimate cost of equipment and its operation. Because each theatrical situation will be different from all others, it is impossible to suggest a ratio indicating how many conventional luminaires can be replaced by one automated luminaire. Nevertheless, it is obvious that the number replaced may, in many shows, be large enough to justify purchase of automated luminaires.

Another option may also be pursued: Manufacturers and dealers may be on the lookout for new markets because the previously lucrative concert market is becoming sold to saturation. They may sometimes be willing to rent automated luminaire systems at reasonable rates to introduce their equipment and to allow new users to realistically test the economics discussed above.

Rental may be a way to try out these luminaires

LIGHT AND COLOR

What Is Color?

Color is a human phenomenon. To the physicist, the only difference between light with a wavelength of 400 nanometers and that of 700 nm is wavelength and amount of energy. However a normal human eye will see another very significant difference: The shorter wavelength light will cause the eye to see blue-violet and the longer, deep red. *Thus color is the response of the normal eye to certain wavelengths of light.* It is necessary to include the qualifier "normal" because some eyes have abnormalities which makes it impossible for them to distinguish between certain colors, red and green, for example.

Note that "color" is something that happens in the human seeing apparatus—when the eye perceives certain wavelengths of light. There is no mention of paint, pigment, ink, colored cloth or anything except light itself. Clear understanding of this point is vital to the forthcoming discussion.

Colorants by themselves cannot produce sensations of color. If the proper light waves are not present, colorants are helpless to produce a sensation of color. Thus color resides in the eye, actually in the retina-optic-nerve-brain combination which teams up to provide our color sensations. How this system works has been a matter of study for many years and recent investigations, many of them based on the availability of new brain scanning machines, have made important discoveries. These discoveries have made it evident that the workings of color sensation, indeed, all elements of seeing, are even more complicated than previously thought. Nevertheless, after taking these new-found complications into consideration, it appears that the basic three-color theory based on three kinds of receptors in the eye still holds. The manner in which nerve impulses from these receptors are processed however is complex indeed. Fortunately, the lighting designer or technician need not be involved in this complexity.

Different wavelengths cause the eye to see different colors.

Only light itself causes sensations of color.

Color vision is complex and not completely understood.

To be accurate, any reference to sensations of color should be attributed to the eye-optic-nerve-brain complex. This terminology is awkward. Therefore henceforth in this text references to the eye should be read to include the entire eye-optic-nerve-brain complex.

Eye = eye-optic-nerve-brain

Color vision is probably the most precise determination that our senses make. The wavelength difference between one color sensation and another is only a few hundred-millionths of a centimeter, yet the trained eye of a color expert can perceive millions of hues and never mistake one for another. Anyone with normal vision can do almost as well.

Readers may wish to refer to Chapter 5 where physical nature of light is detailed. As noted there, a number of kinds of spectra are commonly discussed by physicists, astronomers and other scientists. However "the spectrum" to artists, including lighting designers, refers to that part of the vast radiant energy spectrum that the normal eye can see, with occasional references to those wavelengths just longer or just shorter than visible light, i.e., infrared and ultraviolet. In the past the spectrum has, for artists and lighting technicians, referred to a continuous spectrum, often compared to the rainbow. This is still applicable but with the caveat that some modern light sources produce line spectra and the technician and artist must deal with the way these affect color mixing.

The spectrum

Continuous spectrum

Labeling Colors

The spectrum provides the physicist with a catalogue of all of the individual wavelengths the normal human eye can see. Wavelength, as displayed by spectral analysis, is still the most accurate way to describe the potential capacity of a beam of light to affect the eye or to react physically. However there are color sensations called *nonspectral hues* some of which are not represented by individual wavelengths of the spectrum. These are sensations produced by mixtures of red and blue light; there are no single wavelengths which can elicit them. They are commonly identified scientifically by referring them to their complements, which do lie on the spectrum and can be identified by a single wavelength. Thus a purple-magenta might be referred to as the "complement of 530 nm green." However artists are apt to leave this scientific notation to the laboratory and depend on more artistically friendly ways of organizing colors for reference. Perhaps the most universal of these is the color wheel.

Identifying nonspectral hues

Color Identification: the Color Wheel

The color wheel shown in Plate VI is, in effect, the spectrum simplified into samples of color and curled around on itself to allow for the inclusion of the red-blue mixtures. Thus the color wheel can be said to be a simplified map of all the colors the eye can see. However it is important to note that most color wheels are labeled according to the subtractive system because they refer to colorants. Therefore the primaries are identified as red, yellow, and blue, and secondaries as purple, green and orange. *Primaries* are colors which cannot be made by mixing other colors within the system, *secondaries* are equal mixes of primaries.

Primaries and secondaries

The color wheel tends to be a tool for those who work with pigments instead of light. It is particularly useful for working out color harmonies. A number of other color labeling systems are also in use. One of the most complex and comprehensive is the Munsell system which arranges all pigment colors into a "color solid." Yet another, much used in printing and graphic arts, is the Pantone color system which is a catalogue of color samples together with formulae for producing the colors using printing inks. All of these systems relate mainly to color in dyes, inks and paints. Their ability to represent colors in light is limited because of limited brightness. In lighting, there is, theoretically, no brightness limit and, indeed, the practical limits far exceed anything possible with pigments or dyes. Therefore lighting artists often find the C.I.E. Chromaticity Diagram (hereafter, C.I.E. Diagram) (Plate I) more useful because it deals directly with the way wavelength mixtures affect the eye. While the C.I.E. Diagram also has its limits as far as brightness is concerned, it is so arranged that one can extrapolate brightness outside of the range of its printed version. The color triangle, discussed in detail below, is a simplification of the C.I.E. Diagram often used by lighting artists to estimate the effects of mixing colored light and/or the use of colored light on colored objects.

Spectroanalysis for Color Identification

In the scientific world, spectroanalysis (analyzing light by breaking it into a spectrum and measuring the amount of each wavelength present) is a highly precise tool used, for example, to identify the presence of even exceedingly minute amounts of elements in a sample and by astronomers to determine the composition of distant stars by analyzing their light. The theatre takes advantage of this major scientific procedure to accurately describe color media—a much less precise but very useful procedure. Practically every manufacturer of color media provides sample books of its product accompanied by simple spectroanalysis charts (i.e., spectrograms) of the transmissivity of each sample. These spectrograms are simplified versions of graphs created by a spectrophotometer set to plot the sample against a known standard such as equal energy white light. Although Plate III shows such a spectrogram superimposed over a spectrum in color, no color medium booklet will provide this much assistance. The user must picture the spectrum from the numbers (usually stated in nanometers) arranged across the bottom of the graph.

A major advantage of a spectrogram is that the user can closely estimate the amount of light being transmitted by the filter at any wavelength and can estimate from this what the effect of this light will be on any pigment illuminated by it. A resourceful lighting artist or technician can also mentally sum up the transmission from two media to find out what the effect will be on objects lit by the combination in, for example, a cross-spotting situation.

An additional bit of information accompanying most theatrical spectrograms is the inclusion of an overall transmission figure. This sums up the light from all visible wavelengths transmitted and gives the user some idea of the brightness that an instrument equipped with this medium will contribute to the stage, ignoring color. Just as important, it tells the user

Munsell system

C.I.E. Chromaticity Diagram

Spectroanalysis

Spectrograms of color media

Overall transmission

what percentage of the light striking the medium will be absorbed into the filter and converted into heat, which will ultimately destroy most media.

Those lucky enough to be using very sophisticated luminaires equipped with dichroic filters (see below) should note that these filters can be evaluated by the amount of each wavelength they transmit but that, instead of absorbing the rest, usually including the infrared, they reflect it elsewhere.

Sources of Colored Light on Stage

Even with all of the recent advances in lamp technology and the development of new, more efficient, light sources, most colored light used on stage is made in the old-fashioned, highly wasteful way: an inefficient (by modern standards) incandescent lamp is used to make white light which is then filtered to get the color(s) wanted. The remainder of the white light plus an unavoidable and often large portion of the light sought, is absorbed by the color media and turned into heat which can degrade many filter materials and harm equipment.

Making colored light by absorption is wasteful.

Some more efficient alternatives to this method are now available but have yet to find widespread use in the theatre because of high initial cost and, more complicated electrical and optical arrangements. These will be discussed later.

Stage color filters: absorption

The filters discussed below all work the same way: They screen out the unwanted wavelengths, plus a share of those wanted and pass the remainder on to the stage.

Lamp dip

Early vacuum lamps ran cool enough to allow the use of colored lacquers as colorant. These lamp dips were applied by dipping the bulb into the lacquer while it was on and allowing the heat to dry the lacquer. The lamps were then used in early borderlights and footlights.

This process was no longer practical when gas-filled lamps were developed because their bulbs ran at temperatures high enough to char the dip. Presently lamp dips are occasionally listed in supply catalogues to be used with very small vacuum lamps in property devices such as artificial "fires" or for painting projection slides.

Glass

Colored glass has been made for centuries and was used as a light colorant even before electrical lighting entered the theatre. It was and still is expensive, heavy, and breakable, not only if dropped but also by heat stress. However, barring breakage, it is practically permanent. Pieces of colored glass many hundreds of years old still retain their color. However, as lamps became more powerful and the heat became greater, glass soon became obsolete, with the exception of colored glass roundels used in footlights and borderlights. These persist to the present. They are available in primary red, green and blue, pink, white and sometimes other

Glass is "permanent."

Roundels

colors. Roundels are usually molded to perform lens functions as well as serving as a colorant. Many are shaped into a crude fresnel cylindrical lens which aids in controlling light distribution, others are shaped with a bumpy or mottled surface to even out light distribution.

Gelatin

The first replacement for glass and lamp dip was gelatin. This was simply the food material that had been dyed, poured out in sheets and allowed to dry. It was fragile, dried out to even greater fragility, faded rapidly and, if it encountered dampness returned to its original gelatinous state as a lump of gluey uselessness. Nevertheless, it served the theatre's needs for a number of years and gave its name to the process of installing color media in equipment: *gelling*. The term now applies to all color media and to the process of installing them: Whatever its composition, it was and is called gel. The name has persisted through several "generations" of color media, each an improvement over the predecessor. Presently, many technicians would be hard-put to explain where the name originated and might not recognize a sample of gelatin color medium if presented with one.

"Gel" has become part of the theatre vocabulary.

Plastics

Acetate media

After gelatin came a series of plastics beginning with cellulose acetate. It faded, warped and was flammable. Later came other plastics until presently proprietary formulations of polyester, polyvinyl acetate, polycarbonate, or similar high-heat-resistant materials are in use. Dyes have improved as well, making many color media almost as durable as glass. The best is so durable, and expensive that some manufacturers offer differing grades of medium depending on the amount of heat the user expects it to encounter. Failure, when it finally comes, may be a progressive deterioration of the surface of the medium accompanied by warping which ultimately makes it unusable. Even then, fading may not occur.

Plastic color medium is the "standard" in the theatre, being available in a very wide variety of colors and in several brands. Sample color books are part of every lighting designer's or technician's equipment. Most designers can cite the brand names and numbers of their "favorite" colors from memory. Plastic media are also available in frost which disperses the beam and in a variety of striated forms that spread the light beam at right angles to the striations leaving it unchanged (except for some diffusion) parallel to the striations.

Media that also control distribution of light

However plastic color media suffer from another handicap besides their ultimate failure from heating. In the case of saturated colors, particularly blue and green primaries, they are inefficient both as to the amount of the desired light transmitted and as to the transmission of unwanted wavelengths. Primary blue is notorious in this regard. Some blue primaries transmit only 50-60 percent of the wanted blue light and still leak significant amounts of deep red. When this problem is added to the fact that incandescent light is already deficient in blue, it is clear that producing a pure blue field, say on a cyclorama, is a costly, power consuming process. Efficiency, as measured from the input of electrical energy through to the blue light delivered on stage, may be as low as one per-

Inefficiency in saturated cool colors

cent. Other hues in the blue and green range are also inefficient, more so as they become more saturated. Therefore the arrival of a kind of filter that produces pure blue or green efficiently and with few impurities is good news even at much higher cost.

Dichroics

Unlike all other filters used in the theatre, dichroics do not work by absorbing light and dissipating the energy, mostly as heat. Instead, they utilize a phenomenon known as *interference*, one of the classic proofs of the wave theory of light. An effect of interference is often seen when a thin film of oil is somehow dispersed over a still pool of water. Light striking the pool is broken into colors that depend on the thickness of the oil film and the angle at which the light strikes. Dichroics separate out various wavelengths by precisely controlling the thickness of layers of materials carried on a glass substrate. This makes them capable of sorting out wavelengths, reflecting some and allowing others to pass through producing beams of colored light of great purity and with relatively little loss of the wavelengths wanted. Note the sharp cutoff and high efficiency of the spectrogram of the dichroic filter in Figure 9.1.

Dichroic materials are made by placing a substrate (a foundation material, usually heat resistant glass) in a vacuum chamber. Various materials are then vaporized in the chamber and deposited on the substrates to form very thin (molecule thick), layers whose thickness is adjusted to under half of the wave length of the light to be controlled. A variety of materials is used by various manufacturers to make up dichroic coatings including aluminum, silver, gold and oxides of silicon and titanium. These filters have several applications for the theatre:

Interference

Dichroics are a high-efficiency means of sorting light waves.

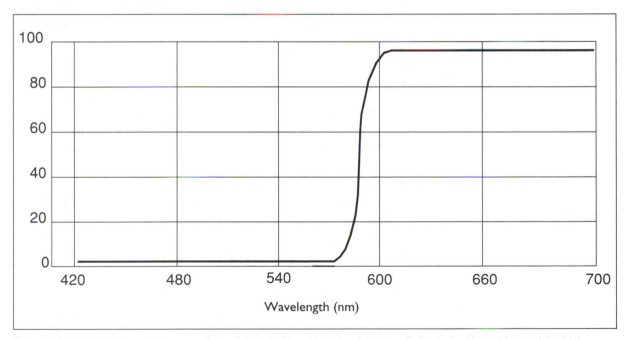

Figure 9.1. Approximate spectrogram of a red dichroic filter. Note the sharp cutoff, the lack of impurities and the high level of transmission of wanted light.

- *High quality light filters:* The dichroic material can become a filter of very high efficiency which produces light of exceptional purity, including pure blue.
- *Heat control mirrors:* The material can be used to make reflective surfaces that can sort heat wavelengths (infrared) from visible light thereby controlling the path of waste heat in a luminaire
- *Multicolored gobos:* Multicolored gobos can be made up displaying images created by controlling the deposition of the material on the substrate. Such gobos produce colors of high purity and efficiency and are very durable because they absorb little heat.
- *Anti-reflection coatings for high-quality lenses:* Projection lenses and camera lenses can be treated with dichroic coatings to reduce surface reflection, thereby increasing the efficiency of the lens. This process is too expensive for use in most theatrical spotlight lenses, but not for the more sophisticated lenses used in scenic projection or in automated luminaires.

Dichroic filters

These can be made to pass a wide variety of wavelengths, but the most useful are those that produce the primary colors, (RGB) from white light making three-color mixing a much more efficient process than when absorption filters are in use.

Dichroic primary filters are commonly installed in modern automated luminaires where they are used to produce a huge variety of colors. Since they are normally left installed in these luminaires, they are not subject to the kind of handling that might cause breakage. Although they are expensive, they have a very long life. Dichroic glass is also available (albeit expensive) in sheet form for installation in other equipment.

Dichroic mirrors

Although not a color medium itself, the dichroic mirror is a development that contributes much to the life of color media. It consists of a different application of the dichroic principle: Instead of sorting white light to produce colored light, the material is used to sort infrared from visible light, i.e., dichroic mirrors are heat control filters. There are two types: cold mirrors and hot mirrors. A *cold mirror* will transmit a major part of the system's heat and reflect the visible light (Figure 9.2B). For example an ellipsoidal cold mirror will allow the IR to pass through into the rear of the luminaire but reflect the visible light forward into the lens system. A *hot mirror* does the opposite—it reflects the heat and transmits the visible light (Figure 9.2A). Such a mirror might be mounted just before the slide in a projector, protecting the slide from IR heat. A system utilizing both a cold and hot mirror can remove as much as 99% of the IR heat from an optical system while transmitting about 90% of the visible light. Operators must remember that the back of such luminaires will get much hotter than that of a conventional luminaire of the same type.

Plate I. The C.I.E. Chromaticity Diagram. This diagram is the most practical color map for the lighting designer or technician. Within the limits of the color printing process, it displays all of the color mixes possible using the RGB light primaries.

The perimeter of this diagram displays the spectral colors wrapped around the curved portion and nonspectral mixes of red and blue at the bottom along the straight line.

Plotting Colors and Mixes on the C.I.E. Diagram. Note that the diagram includes a curved line near its center. This line, the "black body locus," delineates the visible light output of a standard black body as it is heated from the deepest visible red through white to pale blue. Along this line are plotted key points (color temperatures) vital to plotting information about color filters. The IES standard for "white light" produced by general service incandescent lamps is **2848 K**. This is the point most commonly used to plot complimentary colors. It also approximates the "white" produced by 3200 K theatre lamps under conditions of reduced line voltage typically found at the lighting positions in a theatre. The nominal temperature agreed upon for "outdoor" illumination is **5400 K**. (Note: outdoor light can vary from the dimmest red of sunrise to the deep blue of a northern sky at noon, approximately 25,000 K.) The 5400 K point is used to determine complementary colors when using high-color-temperature lamps such as HID. "Equal energy white" (not plotted), lies very close to 5400 K and is often cited in the place of 5400 K for color plotting purposes.

As a sample of the application of the C.I.E. Diagram to predicting color mixes, two typical gel colors, labeled GAMColor 570 (light yellow-green; x=0.40, y=0.52) and GAMColor 990 (dark lavender; x=0.45, y=0.28) have been plotted using data from Gelfile. A line drawn between the locations of the colors will include all of the possible mixes of these two tints. The midpoint of that line, which in this case is in the cool white area, indicates the result of an equal intensity mix. Note that this mix is dependent on the sources operating at full intensity. If the lamps are dimmed, the colors would have to be replotted indicating their red shift. It is also possible, but with less accuracy, to "eyeball" plotting colors by comparing what can be seen by holding a sample of the color to be plotted up to a source of the proper color temperature and searching out a spot on the C.I.E. Diagram that matches. Note that one must be sure

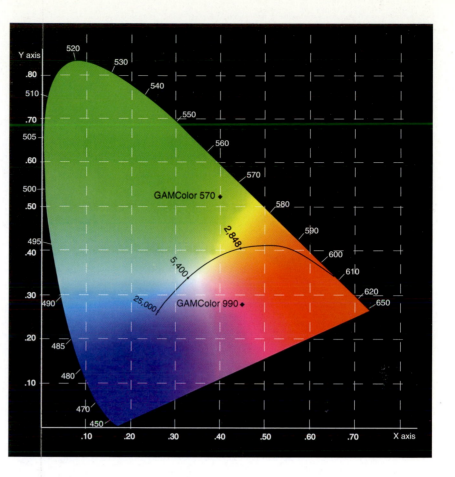

that light transmission is viewed (only one pass of the light through the medium.) Viewing the color medium lying on a white surface makes the light pass through it twice.

Fully saturated complementaries can be located by drawing a line from one perimeter of the diagram through either 2848 K or 5400 K (or the point representing the color temperature of the source in use) to the opposite perimeter. The ends of the line mark the most contrasting pair of complementaries possible using those two hues. Other pairs located equidistant from the 2848 K or 5400 K mark will also be complimentary, but with less saturation.

Complimentary tint pairs for acting area lighting may be determined by choosing one tint of the proposed pair and drawing a line from its location on the diagram through either 2848 K or 5400 K to a point equidistant on the other side. Actually all pairs of tints located equidistantly on lines passing through the point marking whichever source is in use will be complimentary, but not all will be practically useful for acting area lighting.

Three-color mixes can be plotted on the C.I.E. Diagram by locating the three colors and drawing a triangle with these points at the vertices. Any color included within that triangle can be mixed by adjusting the proportions of the three colors chosen. Colors outside of the triangle cannot be made with this mix.

(Plate I was developed with the assistance of GAMPRODUCTS, Inc.)

THE ELECTROMAGNETIC SPECTRUM

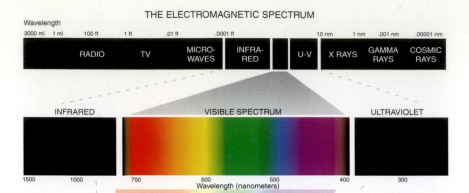

Wavelength

3000 mi	1 mi	100 ft	1 ft	.01 ft	.0001 ft		10 nm	1 nm	.001 nm	.00001 nm

| RADIO | TV | MICRO-WAVES | INFRA-RED | | U-V | X RAYS | GAMMA RAYS | COSMIC RAYS |

INFRARED   VISIBLE SPECTRUM   ULTRAVIOLET

| 1500 | 1000 | 700 | 600 | 500 | 400 | 300 |

Wavelength (nanometers)

INFRARED

ULTRAVIOLET

PRISIM

WHITE LIGHT

Plate II. The Electromagnetic Spectrum. This diagram shows schematically how white light from an incandescent source can be separated into its component wave lengths by a prism, and how this visible spectrum fits into the complete electromagnetic spectrum. Within the limits of the printing process it displays all of the wavelengths visible to the human eye and thus all of the color sensations that can be produced by exposing the eye to individual wave lengths. Note that there are a number of color sensations that are not on the spectrum that can only be produced by exposing the eye to mixtures of wave lengths. The color magenta, an equal mixture of red and blue, is one example.

The top part of the plate shows schematically the arrangement of the entire electromagnetic spectrum. Note that the actual portion of that spectrum occupied by visible light is much smaller than diagrammed. Adapted from Human Information Processing. Peter H. Lindsey and Donald E. Norman. Academic Press. New York and London, 1972

Plate III. Color Medium Spectrogram. This plate graphically illustrates the information in color medium spectrograms commonly distributed by dealers. A representation of the visual spectrum has been superimposed over the spectrogram. The areas under the curve indicate the relative amount of each wavelength transmitted by this particular medium. For example, the spectrogram indicates that this Pale Blue color medium transmits considerably more light in the blue wavelengths (over 80% transmission at 450 nanometers) than in the orange and red wavelengths (less than 20% transmission at 600 nanometers).

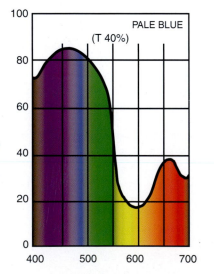

PALE BLUE
(T 40%)

100			
80			
60			
40			
20			
0	400	500	600	700

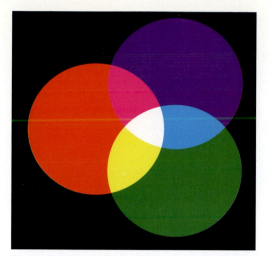

Plate IV. Additive Color Mixing. This figure illustrates what would be seen if three spotlights of equal brightness and color temperature producing "white" light were equipped with pure primary red, blue and green media and focused to overlap on a white surface. Where all three colors are present, the result will appear to the normal eye as white; where only two of the three colors (primaries) overlap, the result will be the secondary colors, yellow, magenta and cyan (blue-green).

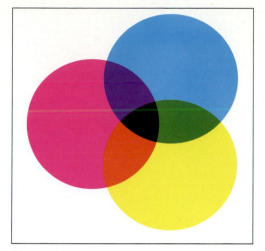

Plate V. Subtractive Color Mixing. This diagram shows three circles of pure secondary color medium overlapped as shown and viewed with white light source behind them. Note how the secondary colors of one color system match the primary colors of the other system.

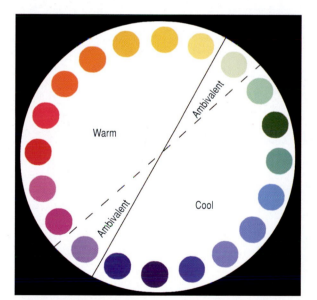

Plate VI. The Color Wheel. This plate reproduces a color wheel made with stage-quality color media of moderate saturation. Acting area colors derived from these samples would be even less saturated. Note the categories of "warm" and "cool" and how tints of yellow-green and red-purple are ambivalent, being either warm or cool depending on the color to which they are contrasted.

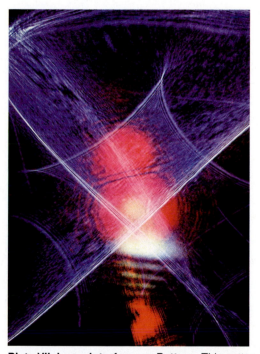

Plate VII. Laser Interference Pattern. This pattern was produced by one of the earliest laser projectors devised for stage use. Josef Svoboda worked with the Siemens Co. of Germany to produce laser images that could flood the stage including dancers. The laser beam is dispersed and sent through an irregular piece of glass which produces an infinity of random patterns. While the patterns vary with distance from the projector, they are in focus from the projector to infinity. Interference patterns remain to be a feature of laser displays today although laser scanning has added many other possibilities. Courtesy Siemens, Germany.

Plate VIII. Wedding scene, *A Midsummer Night's Dream*, Shakespeare. Performed at the Colorado Shakespeare Festival. Director, Robert Cohen; set design, Douglas Scott Goheen; costumes, Chuck Goheen; lighting, Richard Devin. Note the focus on the figure downstage with secondary foci on the other figures. This lighting coordinates with the blocking to unify the scene. Photo Richard Devin.

Plate IX. *Le Bourgeois Gentilhomme* (Molière). Staged at ACT. Adaptation by Charles Hallihan; directed by William Ball; scenery, Richard Seger; costumes, Robert Fletcher; lighting Richard Devin. Note the strong but realistic use of directional light coordinated with the facing of the actors. Photo Richard Devin.

Plate X. *Orféo.* This plate, and Figure 15.1, illustrate the effectiveness of close integration of projection techniques into a production. Scenic projection and video techniques are used in this production of *Orféo* in a way that allows the actors to appear to interact with the projected images, not merely playing in front or behind them.

Orféo, an adaptation of the Orpheus legend, is a one-hour music/dance/multimedia presentation co-produced by Theatre Français du Centre Nationale des Arts, Ottawa, the John F. Kennedy Centre, Washington D.C. and l'Usine C., Montreal. Creative concept/ theatrical direction by Michael Lemieux and Victor Pilon; associate director, Ginette Prévost; music, Michael Lemieux; costume designers, Gabriel Tsampalieros and Carole Courtois; stage projections design, Victor Pilon with the assistance of Marc Bilodeau. Photo courtesy Victor Pilon.

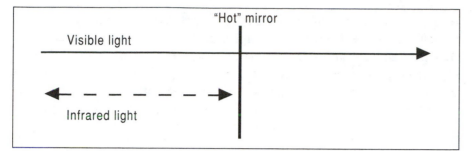

Figure 9.2A. "Hot" Mirror. Note that the dichroic coating transmits the useful light toward the stage but the infrared light is reflected by the mirror and dissipated away from the heat-sensitive slide or effects device.

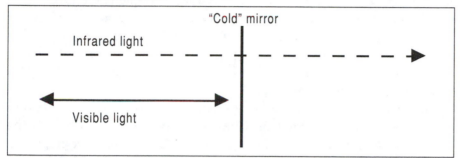

Figure 9.2B. "Cold" Mirror. This mirror allows the infrared light to pass and reflects the visible light. It is often formed into a spherical, ellipsoidal or parabolic mirror which collects useful light and passes the infrared to the back of the luminaire where it is dissipated.

Dichroic gobos

Conventional gobos are made from heat resisting metal and can project a silhouette onto the stage when installed in an ellipsoidal reflector spotlight or a modern automated luminaire. A single color may be added to the lighted parts of the silhouette by adding a color filter.

More sophisticated gobos are available, although at a price. One type of these is made of dichroic-coated glass and may be had in a single color or multicolored. In addition to providing a colored image, these gobos operate with the same efficiency and low heat absorption characteristics as regular dichroic filters.

Colored gobos

Other Sources of Colored Light on Stage

It is clear that the incandescent lamp is a poor source of visible light and an even poorer source of cool colored light. HID lamps, for example, operate much more efficiently than incandescent lamps, particularly at the blue end of the spectrum. Thus even with no change in the quality of the filters used, overall efficiency can be raised substantially by using HID lamps. Using dichroic filters further increases efficiency.

The ideal light source would be one that could be tuned to produce any wavelength or combination of wavelengths needed as a point source without filtration, dimmable, and without wasting energy. This goal remains elusive although there are available a number of sources that produce single wavelengths or narrow bands of wavelengths. These include lasers, long arc discharge lamps, such as sodium vapor lamps and "neon" sign tubes, and fluorescent lamps with special phosphors to produce "pure" colors. Unfortunately none of these meet the remainder of the specifications for the "perfect light source." They all need extra equipment such as ballasts, are far from point sources, usually cannot be dimmed other than mechanically and still waste a sizeable portion of their output as heat or unwanted non-visible light. Thus, for the present, the theatre must make do with the inefficiency of the incandescent lamp or, only somewhat better, the complications of short-arc gaseous discharge lamps.

Color by Reflection

A commonly overlooked source of colored light is the colored light reflected from colored objects. An aggravating example is the green light that bounces off a grassy lawn and lights up the lower parts of faces in photos taken of people standing on the grass. The eye ordinarily learns to ignore this effect, which, although present most of the time, is usually unnoticed. However when a photo is taken, the green "footlighting" is suddenly very evident and disliked.

Bounce light

    Bounce light on stage can act the same way, producing sometimes distracting colored shadows on faces and flooding parts of the setting with unwanted color. The solution is to track down the offending luminaires and reangle or re-gel them or to remove or cover the surface causing the reflection.

Color Mixing

Since all sensations of color, with the exception of those few induced in laboratory experimental situations, originate when light enters the human seeing apparatus, we begin our discussion of color and color mixing with an examination of that apparatus. Be sure to keep in mind that, for the purposes of our discussion, the word "eye" will be shorthand for "the eye-optic-nerve-brain complex" that creates and interprets our color sensations. As our discussion proceeds we will find evidence that there appear to be two "systems" that describe color mixing: the *additive system* and the *subtractive system*. It will eventually be apparent that these two are really interlocking parts of a single comprehensive explanation of color. This problem is further complicated by semantic confusion. Color names refer to entirely different colors as the discussion moves from one "system" to the other. This too will need to be dispelled as we proceed.

Additive and subtractive systems

    The study of the physiology of color vision has progressed over the years but its original concept, the Young-Helmholtz theory remains intact. Thomas Young's assertion in the late 1800s that the eye contains three types of sensors, one for each of the three fundamental color sensations, has since been verified by examining the chemicals in each of the three types of sensors thereby verifying their responses to light of specific wavelengths.

Three sensors for red, green and blue

    However continuing research into the remainder of the seeing apparatus has brought both more understanding and more confusion about the details of the chain of nerves that moves the signals from the eyes to the brain and, in the process, makes major changes in their nature. Indeed, the safest comment on the whole process is that it seems to be considerably more complicated than was earlier thought and that we do not yet have all of the answers.

Rods and Cones

The retina of the eye is the layer of sensitive cells on which the image formed by the lens is focused. Its surface layer is made up of the sensitive ends of special cells, many of which are shaped like minuscule rods and other like cones, their flat ends toward the image. The rods are sensitive to light of all visible wavelengths but do not distinguish between wavelengths, although their sensitivity tapers off at either end of the visible spectrum. Therefore rods do not contribute to color vision. They do, however, have greater sensitivity to light than the cones and function in very low light situations that the cones cannot handle. Thus in very low light we are all color blind.

Rods are "color blind" but function in very low light levels.

The cones are the focus of our attention; they are responsible for our color vision. There are three types, each containing a unique chemical that is sensitive to a part of the visible spectrum. When light of proper wavelength strikes these chemicals, they change and the body immediately strives to return them to their original state. In this process, messages start on their way through the optical nerve to ultimately arrive at the brain where they are interpreted as color sensations. If a single-color stimulus is presented over the entire visual field for an extended period of time, the strength of the sensation generated diminishes. This visual fatigue reduces the attention value of the stimulus and leads to the saying: "All of a color is none of a color." The design problem this phenomenon generates will be dealt with later.

Cones provide color vision.

Visual fatigue

Also, when a strong color stimulus is presented for a period of time, the chemical reaction in the cones tends to overshoot. Then when the original stimulus is removed, the eye produces the sensation of the complement to the one originally presented. This effect is called an after image which will usually alternate between the color of the stimulus and its complementary.

Adaptation

The pupils of our eyes adjust to protect the eyes from too-bright light. This is known as *adaptation* and is done by the iris, the colored circle of tissue that surrounds the pupils, contracting to make a small size opening when exposed to bright light. Closing down happens very rapidly when bright light strikes the eyes but the reverse, opening up when the light is dim, happens much more slowly. This slow adaptation to dim light after exposure to bright light is what makes us nearly blind upon entering a dark room such as a movie theatre from the bright, sunny outdoors. This phenomenon must be taken into account when changing from brightly lit to dark scenes on stage and can also be exploited to accomplish open-curtain scene changes in near darkness. If the crews await the end of a brightly lit scene with their eyes closed, they will be able to see to make the shift while the audience is still bright-adapted and thus

Adapting to dark scenes

nearly "blind." However speed is necessary, the audience' eyes will soon begin to adapt.

Persistence of Visual Images

The sensing process that takes place in the eye-optic-nerve-brain complex is not instantaneous. It takes a small but measurable amount of time to develop and, more important, a longer time to diminish after the stimulus is removed. Thus still pictures presented at more than about sixteen frames per second are seen as continuous movement, i.e., as motion pictures. Visual persistence also makes possible one type of color mixing discussed below.

Motion pictures

Contrast and Brightness Changes

Contrast depends on the overall brightness of the stage.

Contrast is the apparent difference in intensity between two parts of the visual field. At very low light levels, even low degrees of contrast are apparent; as the overall brightness of the field increases the eye becomes less sensitive to contrast differences. At very high brightness levels it takes a much higher contrast difference to be apparent to the observer. Thus a small change, say, one half point on a dimmer, will be very apparent on an otherwise almost dark stage. Such a change will not even be noticeable when the stage is brighter.

Color Stimulus Mixing

Response to mixed stimuli involves much of the optical chain.

As we have indicated, various wavelengths presented to the eye will produce sensations representing a synthesis of the stimuli presented. This synthesis does not take place, or at least is not completed at the retina, a fact which can be demonstrated by holding a piece of color medium, say a light straw, over one eye and a piece of, say, light steel blue, over the other. This will produce two separate color sensations, one in each eye. If one closes an eye, one sees the color covering the other eye, etc. When both eyes are open and the viewer is looking at a white surface, he or she will see the mixture of the two colors, sometimes, depending on the individual, as a stable mix and sometimes alternating between the mix and the individual colors. Clearly, the mixing is taking place somewhere along the optical chain beyond the individual eyes. Complex research in the laboratory also confirms what this simple test reveals: The mixing of color sensations is indeed a complicated process.

Primaries are defined by the peaks of the sensitivity curves.

The peak of sensitivity for each type of cone encompasses a band of closely spaced wavelengths any or all of which can produce essentially the same sensation. These three peaks define the three primary colors, red, green and blue, which will be discussed in detail below.

How We Control the Color Sensations We Experience

Except in the laboratory where some visual effects can be created from within the seeing apparatus, all the visual sensations we experience, including color, are caused by stimuli from outside of the body. Thus "seeing colors" is the result of the entry of various wavelengths into the eye.

Terminology

- *Color sensation*: as noted above, this is a response to the entry of light into the human seeing apparatus (assuming that the subject is not blind or color blind). This response may be verbalized as "pink," "blue" or any color name.
- A *colorant* is any material that has the property of absorbing some wavelengths of light and reflecting others. Note that colorants cannot generate light; they can only affect light already present.

Color mixing: two definitions

1. The mixture of color sensations in the eye. This can be done in any of the several ways discussed below, but the result is always the direct stimulation of the seeing apparatus.
2. Mixing colorants. This is done by mixing paints, dyes, pigments and the like. The result is a combination of pigments that reflects any wave lengths reflected by all of the ingredients. No stimulus to the eye results unless the proper wave lengths of light are used to illuminate the mixture.

Unfortunately these two definitions get used indiscriminately adding confusion to the understanding of the art and science of color.

We will first study color mixing as defined according to definition 1 above. It can be done in several ways:

1. Different wavelengths or bands of wavelengths of light can be presented to the eyes at the same time. This is the common theatrical method: For example, specific wavelengths are filtered from white light and directed toward a cyclorama from which they are reflected to the eye where they elicit color sensations.
2. Various sets of wavelengths may be presented to the eye in rapid succession. If this is done rapidly enough, the persistence of vision will cause the sensations to blend together producing the same effect as if all of the wavelengths were presented at once. This is the method of color television which presents red, green and blue images in such rapid succession that the eyes see them as one full-color picture.
3. Color sensations can be divided into tiny parts of the visual field, so tiny that the eyes see them as blended together. This is the basis of pointillage, a painting technique developed by the impressionists and also the basis of much color printing where tiny dots of color are laid down on the page in a way that causes the eyes to see them blended together.

Note that each of these methods has the effect of adding together stimuli in the eye. Thus they are called additive color mixing or the *additive system*. In contrast, the mixing of colorants is termed the *subtractive system*. It will be detailed presently. To understand additive color mixing more completely we must examine the way the three kinds of color sensors in the eye respond. The groups of wave lengths at the peak of each of the three curves are called *the primary colors*. "Primary" means that combinations of these colors can be used to mix

The three primary colors

any other color but that no mixture of other colors within the system can produce the sensations of the primaries. *Secondary colors* are equal-brightness mixes of two primaries.

Confusion caused by the two definitions of color mixing begins here: The terms, "primary" and "secondary" are also applied to the mixing of colorants (color mixing definition number two) which refers to a different set of colors and produces very different results. The first step in eliminating this confusion is to clarify exactly what the additive primary colors are. This is best done by reference to their wavelengths:

WAVELENGTHS OF ADDITIVE PRIMARY COLORS	
Color Name	**Approximate Wavelengths**
red	780 nanometers
green	520 nanometers
blue	480 nanometers

Still more confusion must be resolved: color names. The names *blue* and *red* refer to very different colors depending on whether one is talking about color sensations in the eye or mixing colorants. Therefore, it is important to note the actual hues as they are reproduced on Plate I or, better still, on a computer reproduction of the *Commission Internationale de l'Eclairage* Chromaticity Diagram (C.I.E. Diagram) mentioned below as displayed on a well-calibrated color monitor.

Secondary colors are yellow, cyan (blue-green) and magenta. They can be evoked by equal-brightness mixtures of the primaries:

$$R + G = Yellow$$
$$G + B = Cyan$$
$$B + R = Magenta$$

The C.I.E. Diagram

Although there are a number of ways of organizing color relationships, most of them concerned with relationships between colorants, the one most useful to lighting artists and technicians is the C.I.E. Diagram (Plate I). It shows the way the primaries, red, green and blue intermix to produce sensations of all of the colors on the spectrum and also those nonspectral colors that are mixtures of blue and red. Moreover, it is precise if the user has the proper data to exactly locate colors on it. Until the development of Gelfile, a software catalogue of color media that locates almost every color medium available on the C.I.E. Diagram, the designer was reduced to making an educated guess as to the exact location of a color to be referenced. This reduced the precision of the diagram and left many designers with a preference for the color triangle (below) although it is far less accurate. Gelfile is available on the Internet from GAMPRODUCTS.

Once colors have been located on the map, two-color additive mixes are easily worked out by joining the two colors with a line. All mixes will be located on that line, their position depending on the relative bright-

(margin note, left:) Primary colors

(margin note, left:) Secondary colors

ness of the two sources. Thus the designer will have available the entire array of mixes between the two colors he or she has under consideration. One can even attempt an estimate of dimmer ratios apt to produce the color sought. However there is a catch: dimming shifts the color temperature of incandescent sources toward red and throws off the calculations based on the diagram. Most designers simply depend on their experience instead of attempting to reach a quantitative answer.

Red shift throws off color calculations.

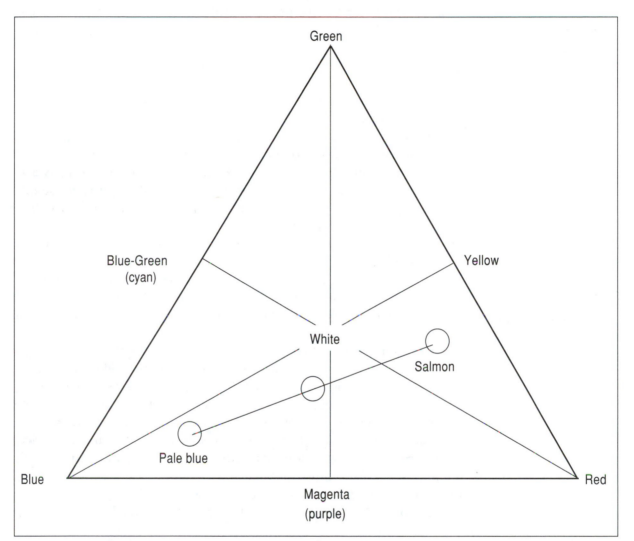

Figure 9.3. Color Triangle. Essentially the C.I.E. Diagram (Plate I) simplified by reducing it to an equilateral triangle with the three light primaries located at the apexes, this diagram is useful for quick estimates of additive color mixing. A sample mix of salmon and pale blue has been plotted to illustrate its application:

1. Locate the approximate position of the two hues on the triangle using eyeball estimates or by referring to the Gelfile version of the C.I.E. Diagram (available on the Internet) and transposing this information to the triangle. Note that some manufacturers of color media may include the C.I.E. coordinates of their media in their spectrogram booklets.

2. Draw a line between the two points located. This line will be the locus of all additive mixes of the two hues, the position of the resultants depending on the relative amounts of the two hues. If the amounts are equal (as estimated by brightness to the eye), the resultant will be at the midpoint of the line, as shown. Other proportions can be estimated by moving the resultant point toward the color which predominates in the mix.

Those using either system should keep in mind that mixes worked out apply *only to luminaires at "full."* Any dimming will shift the mix toward red.

The Color Triangle

While the C.I.E. Diagram has increased in usefulness with the publication of the locations of all available color media, the color triangle (Figure 9.3) remains a very useful tool for working out color problems. It is a simplification of the color diagram in the form of an equilateral triangle with the three additive primary colors located at the three corners. Secondaries are located at the three halfway points and "white" is placed in the center. Colors may be located on the triangle in the same manner as the C.I.E. Diagram and mixes may be predicted, although less accurately. It can also be adapted to aid in predicting subtractive mixes.

"White" Light

Sensations of white light may be evoked by presenting the eye with any of the following:

- An equal brightness combination of all visible wavelengths such as light from the sun or from an incandescent lamp
- A combination of many line spectra which contains enough wavelengths to stimulate the three sensors in the eye to a roughly equal degree. HID sources frequently appear white because their light is so composed.
- An equal brightness mixture of red, blue and green sensations (RGB) produced by mixing the narrow bands of wavelengths at the peaks of the three sensitivity curves of the eye. This is the method often used to light a theatrical cyclorama.

White light is always a mixture.

There is no single wavelength or narrow band of wavelengths that produces the sensation *white*.

The "white" central area of the C.I.E. Diagram or the color triangle encompasses a wide variety of very pale colors which when viewed by themselves will be identified as white by most observers. Nevertheless, there are important and noticeable differences between these very pale colors which will be apparent if several of them are viewed side by side. For example, the "white" light produced by incandescent lamps is noticeably warmer than that produced by HID lamps or the white displayed on a computer screen. Although the eye will adapt in a short time to whatever "white" is presented to it, neutralizing any sensation of "warm" or "cool," the ability of these whites to subtly accent pigment colors will remain.

As discussed in Chapter 6, the white light produced by various light sources is often described by the color temperature (kelvin) system. However this terminology is only rarely used to describe white light created by mixing the primaries or by the mixing of complementary tints.

All Additive Mixes Tend Toward White

Adding wave lengths moves an additive mixture toward white.

Both the C.I.E. Diagram and the color triangle reflect the tendency of wavelength mixing to move toward white, i.e., the more wavelengths added to the mix, the closer the resulting color sensation will be to white. Therefore "adding color to the stage" cannot be effective if more colors of light are simply superimposed upon one upon the other—the result will move closer to white. A "more colorful stage" will result only if carefully separated and contrasted areas of color are created.

Combining equal brightness portions of red, blue and green primaries is a very inefficient process on stage where the primaries are made by filtering already white light Nevertheless RGB mixing is much used because of its flexibility; any of a wide variety of colors may be had in short order. Note that this same primary-mixing process is very efficient when applied to a color TV screen. The difference is that the phosphors on the TV screen produce only the red, green and blue needed—no wasteful filtering is required.

Spectral and Nonspectral Hues

As noted near the beginning of this chapter, color sensations produced by a single wave length or, more likely, narrow bands of wavelengths adjacent to each other on the spectrum, are termed *spectral hues*. There are also many *nonspectral hues*, which are the result of mixing disparate wavelengths, for example, red and green which create the sensation of yellow, or blue and red, which create the sensation of magenta. Many other combinations are possible and when the mixtures are in the form of tints, they form the basis of a major kind of lighting for acting areas.

Spectral and nonspectral hues

While many nonspectral hues can be matched on the spectrum, yellow, for instance, the entire array of colors ranging from primary blue to primary red across the bottom of the C.I.E. Diagram has no single-wavelength equivalents. These sensations are often identified by referring to their complements, as already noted.

There are also many nonspectral hues that do have spectral counterparts. Spectral and nonspectral hues that produce the same sensation, such as spectral and nonspectral yellow, cannot be differentiated by the unaided eye although they produce drastically different results when used to illuminate colorants.

Pure spectral hues are typically produced by narrow band sources such as gaseous discharge lamps and lasers. They can also be produced by filtering using dichroics or special pure absorptive filters. Note that conventional plastic filters pass both spectral and nonspectral colors whenever this is possible. For example, ordinary yellow color medium passes red, spectral yellow and green (the red and green comprising nonspectral yellow). This makes for greater efficiency and avoids the color distortion that pure spectral colors create. While most pigments reflect both spectral and nonspectral hues when these are present, some are made to reflect only spectral colors.

When spectral colors are being used, for example spectral yellow from a low pressure sodium vapor lamp, it is important for the designer to remember that these colors contain only a narrow band of wavelengths. Therefore red and green pigments will appear black or grey under spectral yellow although they would retain their original colors if illuminated by nonspectral yellow or by light containing both spectral and nonspectral yellow.

Complementary Colors

The term, *contrast* describes the tendency of colors displayed adjacent to each other to stand out from each other and to increase each other's apparent brightness. *Complementary* describes pairs of colored light which display maximum contrast when placed next to each other and which, when mixed in equal proportions as sensations, produce the sensation of white. Complementary colors can be found on the C.I.E. Diagram by passing a line from any color mapped at the edge of the diagram, through the point on the black body locus that represents the color temperature of the light to be used, usually 2848 K, and continuing to the other side of the diagram. Any two colors on that line and equidistant from 2848 K will be complimentary but those at the ends of the line will display the most contrast. Complementary colors may also be defined on the color triangle in a similar, but less accurate manner.

After Images

When the cones in the retina, say those sensitive to red, are stimulated by red light entering the eye, and the stimulus is removed, there is a lag before the cones return to their non-stimulated state. The more powerful the stimulation, the greater the lag. Moreover, if the stimulus is sufficiently powerful, it will cause the cones to overshoot the quiescent state and send a nerve signal indicating the complement of the color that just stimulated them, In our example, the red light would cause the cones to signal cyan, the complement of red. These sensations, known as *afterimages*, are a common experience for anyone who has fixed his or her vision on a brightly lighted object for a period of time and then looks at some other object. If the first stimulus is white, instead of a colored afterimage, a flare of white light will appear which alternates with a black afterimage until the cones re-stabilize. If the original stimulus is colored, the after image will display the complement of that color, often alternating with a display of the original color.

Colored after images contribute to the contrast between complementary fields of color by creating a fringe of complimentary afterimage around the color fields. This effect, which heightens the apparent brightness of the colors is called *simultaneous contrast*.

Since afterimages tend to appear in the complementary to the stimulus which created them, they offer a means of determining with considerable accuracy what the complementary of a given color may be. Simply stare at the color for a period of time and then at a white surface. The color of the afterimage is the complementary.

Subtractive Color Mixing

Although there are rather exotic ways of producing monochromatic light such as lasers, gaseous discharge tubes and some fluorescent lamps, almost all of the colored light used on stage is produced by filtering. Light containing a broad mixture of wavelengths is produced and passed through a filter to get the wavelengths needed.

It is now our purpose to study these filters and the ways they interact. This filtering process is known as the *subtractive color system* for the obvious reason that filters subtract from the beam of light which passes through them. The result is always less light than was in the beam before filtering. The fundamental rule of the following discussion is this:

Absorptive filters

> *Filters never add anything to a beam of light, they can only subtract.*

Ironically, this rule appears to contradict the common notion: "Pop in a gel to add color to the light." The filter can indeed cause color to appear where only white was evident before, but the amount of light is diminished.

Filters, with the exception of those that work on the dichroic principle, do their job by absorbing some of the wavelengths that strike them. This absorbed light is usually converted into heat which must be somehow dissipated, often at the expense of damaging the filter. Dichroic filters are also subtractive; they sort out the wave lengths they are designed to control, allowing some of them to pass through and sending the others off in another direction instead of absorbing them.

Filters sort wave lengths.

Opaque, Translucent and Transparent Filters.

All filtering of light involves the light passing through the colorant. It may pass through in a straight line coming out filtered (a transparent filter), it may pass through coming out diffused (a translucent filter), or it may penetrate into the colorant, pass through parts of it and then be reflected back toward its source (an opaque filter—see Figure 9.4). Actually, many filter materials allow two or even all three of these processes to happen at the same time. Moreover, a filter may also display surface reflection: light that only strikes the surface of the filter and is reflected without passing though anything.

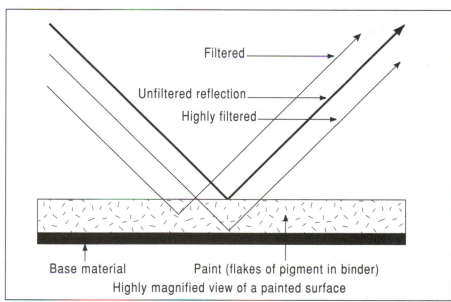

Figure 9.4. How Opaque Filters Work. Note that the light must pass through some of the colorant if it is affected by the filter.

Traditional Color Mixing: the Subtractive System

Mixing colorants is
not the same as
mixing light.

Mixing filters, i.e., causing light to pass through more than one of them, is the common color mixing method of the painter, the printer and the photographer. It is what we all learned at an early age with finger paints: mix the primaries, red, yellow and blue, to "get all the other colors."

It must be made clear as we continue: we are discussing the mixing of the absorptive capabilities of colorants, not beams of light causing sensations in the eye. Of course, when the results of these mixtures of colorants are illuminated and the resulting colors transmitted to the eye they act upon it additively. The eye will respond the same to any beams of light, whether they are the result of being reflected from or transmitted through a complex mixing of colorants or directly produced colors such as those that appear on a color television tube.

Subtractive Primaries and Secondaries

These are the all-too-familiar red, yellow and blue of the paint box; the secondaries are green orange and purple. Clearly, the names, "red" and "blue" must mean something different than the same names when used in the additive system. A careful matching of colors, not names, reveals that the "red" primary in the subtractive system colorant is a match for magenta on the C.I.E. Diagram (Plate I), the "blue" a match for the cyan, and the yellow a match for secondary yellow. Semantics is our undoing, along with the fact that many so-called pigment primaries are so impure that they cannot be trusted to produce anything like the results that theory would predict. If high quality color printers' inks or even top quality theatrical paint colors are compared with colors on the color diagram, it will confirm that, names ignored, the primaries of the subtractive system are color matches for the secondaries of the additive system. Again, if high quality colorants are used, it can be shown that the reverse in also true: the secondaries of the colorant (subtractive) system match the primaries of the additive system. The following table is another way of interrelating the color names:

COLOR NAMES IN ADDITIVE AND SUBTRACTIVE SYSTEMS

Names used in additive system	Names used for the same colors in subtractive system
Red	Red-orange or orange
Green	Green
Blue	Blue-purple
Magenta	Red
Yellow	Yellow
Cyan	Blue

Mixing Colorants

The general principle of mixing colorants is completely different from that which governs the additive mixture of sensations. Each colorant in the mix must be analyzed to determine which wavelengths are passed and which are absorbed. Once this is done the process is arithmetical: Begin with the complete list of wavelengths in the light striking the colorant mix and subtract any wavelength that is absorbed by any colorant in the mix. The remainder will be what is seen by the eye as an additive mix. Where the incident light is white, it may be represented by samples in the form of the primaries and secondaries instead of an impossibly complicated list of all wave lengths. This is done in the diagrams below.

The following diagrams illustrate this process by clarifying why blue colorant added to yellow colorant results in green colorant:

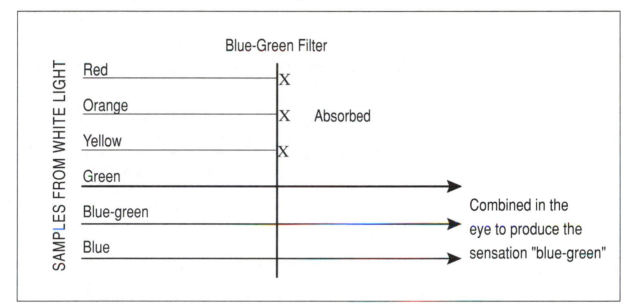

Figure 9.5A. This diagram summarizes the absorption/transmission characteristics of a hypothetically perfect blue-green colorant which would be named "blue" in the subtractive system.

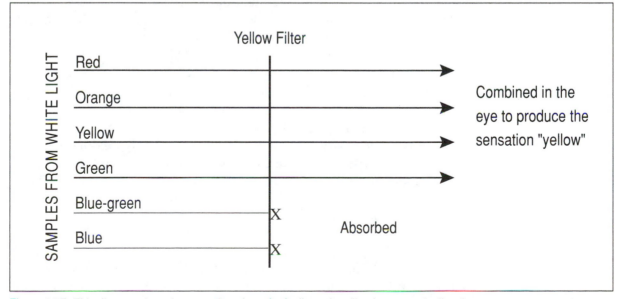

Figure 9.5B. This diagram does the same for a hypothetically perfect filter known as "yellow."

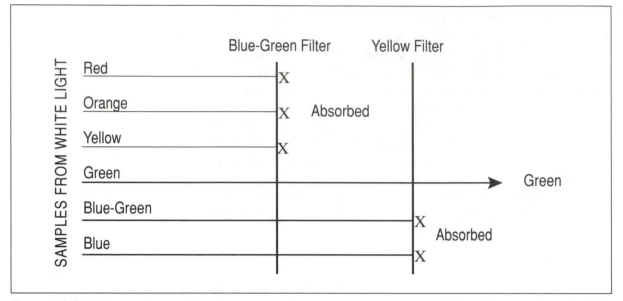

Figure 9.5C. This diagram illustrates how the filtering characteristics are combined when the two colorants are combined.

Note that it makes no difference which filter the light passes through first. It also makes no difference whether the filter is transparent, translucent or opaque. Light that actually passes through the filtering material, whether it continues onward or is reflected back, is altered in the same way.

Colored Light on Colored Objects

In most non-theatrical situations, colored objects are viewed in white light, either daylight at about 6000 K or incandescent light at about 2900 K Under either of these sources, colored objects will be rendered with acceptable accuracy in most cases, although professionally accurate color matching will usually require light nearer to equal energy white than the 2900 K light of the typical general service lamp. The theatre is another matter. Highly filtered light is often used, usually with no ambient light from daylight or general room illumination. Under this condition, the effect of colored light can be drastic. Colors of pigments can be completely changed, reduced to near black or ugly brown or blended together. Therefore it is important that the lighting artist be able to predict what the effect of colored light will be on each colored object on stage.

This requires a two-step process. The steps may be done in either order: 1) The designer determines which wave lengths are available in the colored light to be used. If highly saturated primaries or secondaries are to be used, their wave length content should be already known to the designer. If other colors are to be used, their spectrograms will provide this information. 2) The designer then determines what wavelengths the colored object will reflect. The wavelengths common to both lists will be added to make up the resultant color. If, for example, an object colored magenta (red-blue) is illuminated only with cyan (blue-green) light, the reasoning will be:

Available wavelengths: **blue + green**
Object can reflect: **red + blue**
Object will appear: **blue**

Note that this is theoretical—it assumes that all of the colorants are completely pure, which is seldom the case. After making the theoretical determination, the designer or technician must use his or her experience with the colorants involved, possibly consulting the spectrograms again, to determine what the practical result will be. In this example there is a high probability that the spectrogram of the cyan color medium will reveal that it leaks a significant quantity of red light. If this is the case, the result will be a dulled-down bluish magenta instead of blue. If the magenta object must be made to appear blue, another filter will have to be chosen, one that transmits less red.

The chart below lists the results of illuminating saturated colorants which match the primaries and secondaries of the subtractive system with pure light in the primary and secondary colors of the additive system. In a real-world situation, unless high quality dichroic filters are in use, most of the "black" results will turn out to be dull and unpleasant remainders of red. This is because it is difficult to make absorptive colorants that do not leak red light.

COLORS RESULTING FROM COLORED LIGHT ON COLORED PIGMENT

INCIDENT LIGHT COLORS	RED	GREEN	BLUE	YELLOW	MAGENTA	CYAN
PIGMENT COLORS						
RED	red	black	black	red	red	black
GREEN	black	green	black	green	black	green
BLUE	black	black	blue	black	blue	blue
YELLOW	red	green	black	yellow	red	green
MAGENTA	red	black	blue	red	magenta	blue
CYAN	black	green	blue	green	blue	cyan

Colored Light and Color Contrast

Color contrast is a major factor in stage design. Most of the factors controlling it are fixed relatively early in the process of finishing the staging as paints are applied and fabrics chosen and worked into drapery, costumes, and properties. Once set, changing these elements is difficult and expensive, and sometimes impossible. In some cases and to a limited extent, lighting can ameliorate color contrast problems by exploiting the capability of colored light to emphasize or de-emphasize colors.

Lighting may be able to correct one color problem at a time.

Generally, only one contrast problem can be solved at a time and that only to the extent that other colors on stage can withstand the sometimes color-distorting effect of colored light chosen to adjust contrast instead of for the best lighting of the actors and the staging as a whole. Note that these adjustments may also affect the makeup which, fortunately, can usually be changed very late in the production process. Obviously, if a color is emphasized or de-emphasized by these techniques all objects of this color will be effected that are within the specially illuminated stage space.

Contrasts between colors can be altered by choosing lighting that will separate the colors or bring them together. The methods are these:

Increasing contrast

1. To increase the contrast between a color and the background, provide an abundance of the wavelength the color reflects best plus enough white or near-white light to make the background appear normal.

   Example: To bring up a green costume from the background add green to the acting area illumination while keeping the general color of the stage near the same as it was before. An additional luminaire gelled with light green and brought up just far enough to get the effect wanted may do the trick. Check makeup for over-emphasis of any green shadows or liners.

De-emphasizing
a color

2. To de-emphasize a color, deprive it of the wavelengths it reflects best.

   Example: To "take down" a blue sofa, use light with less blue in it for the acting areas and reduce blue in any blending or effects lighting that strikes the sofa. Acting area tints of orange instead of rose will do this, but makeup may have to be adjusted.

Separating two tints

3. To separate two tints that appear too much alike, decide which is to receive emphasis and determine which wavelengths it reflects better than the other color. Provide more of those wavelengths and, if possible, less of the wavelengths best reflected by the other color.

   Example: To separate a rose-pink from an orange-pink (assuming you have decided to emphasize the rose pink) add pale magenta to the acting area lighting and reduce any straw or light amber. Adjust makeup as needed.

4. To bring together two tints that don't quite match: choose wavelengths they both reflect equally well and reduce any color favoring one or the other as much as possible.

   Example: To bring together the two pinks in example three, choose tints of true red while reducing the amount of blue-pink or orange-pink. Makeup may need adjusting.

Chapter 10

APPLYING COLOR THEORY TO THE STAGE

Color of Lighting as "Master Color" on Stage

The apparent color of things seen on stage ultimately depends on the color of the lighting. This power over color places a great responsibility on the lighting designer and can, if abused, result in antagonism from the other designers who may feel that, "The lighting is sucking all of the color out of my design!" Moreover, it is possible that they may have cause to gripe. The power of lighting can easily overwhelm all of the other aspects of design.

Clearly, the goal of the lighting designer should be to work with the other designers, preferably from very early in the design process, not only to avoid color conflicts, but to heighten all design elements by bringing them into a scenographic unity. This works best if not only the lighting designer but the set designer, costume designer, makeup designer, and particularly the director, all have a knowledge of the way light and color work on stage, what lighting can and cannot do, and when in the design process various decisions are ideally made.

Lighting can be destructive of other designs.

Collaboration is the key.

Lighting the Actors

The chapters on design emphasize the importance of controlling the focus of the audience' attention. The key artist effecting this control is the director who works with the actors using blocking, movement, and the lines of the play to cause the audience to place the focus where he or she wishes. However lighting can controvert all of these efforts. A character shrouded in near darkness, even though moving, gesturing, and speaking, will have great difficulty holding attention over a brightly lit but stationary and silent one. This power makes the lighting of the actors one of the most important parts of the art of stage lighting.

Lighting controls focus of attention.

Plasticity

Not only must the actor be well lit to command attention, he or she must be lit with concern for the audience's ability to respond to characterization. A large part of characterization is communicated via the actors' facial expressions which, in turn, depend on the lighting if they are to be seen by the audience. "Body language" may also contribute much to characterization. If this is an important part of the production, as it is in dance, lighting must be arranged to make body language visible.

Plasticity

Good facial lighting is a matter of achieving *plasticity*, the modeling of the face by light and shadow which brings out its three dimensional quality. Except in the smallest of theatres where everyone in the audience is within about twenty feet of the farthest actor, three dimensionality of faces depends on shadow detail. Shadows reveal the shape of the face, its protruding and receding parts and particularly the facial expressions which reveal characterization. (Note that the traditional shapes of the comedy and tragedy masks are a stylization of this very theatrical fact.) Shadows are produced by directional light arranged to cause them to appear within sight of the audience. The lighting that produces these shadow patterns is referred to as *key* and *fill*, terms borrowed from photography. *Key light* is the light that produces the highlights on any object, including faces. In "normal" stage lighting situations, the key light will strike the actor from above and in front, either to his/her left or right (See Figures 10.1A and 10.1B) If "normal" is not the designer's purpose, key light can be angled to strike the actor's face at any angle.

Key and fill light

In nature, shadows are seldom dead black; instead they have color and their contents can be seen. This is usually the result of skylight or reflected light from nearby objects. In the theatre, fill light is *designed*. Shadows may range from dead black to any degree of brightness up to that of the key light. They may be any color and the light filling them may be angled from any direction.

Thus the color pattern on a face lit by key and fill will consist of three kinds of areas:

1. Those parts of the face lit by both key and fill and have the color of the additive mixture of these two sources. Obviously, these are the brightest parts of the face.
2. Those parts of the actor's face lit only by the key light. This will be the second brightest part and its color will be that of the key light.

   These two areas constitute the "highlight" part of the face.
3. Those parts illuminated only by the fill light. This will be the least bright part and will have the color of the fill light. It is the "shadow" part of the face.

Three areas of illumination on the face

These three areas of brightness and color on the actor's face will be visible to the audience if the brightness difference between key and fill is sufficient and the intensity of the fill light great enough to add visibly to the key light. Color differences between key and fill can improve the visibility of these facial areas (see below). The effectiveness of key and fill light (K/F) depends on several factors including the following:

1. *The background lighting*. If the background is dim, the apparent contrast ratio between highlight and shadow will be increased.
2. *The sharpness of the shadow edges*. If either the key light or the fill or both come from wide or multiple sources, e.g., multiple spotlights used to build up a large lighting area or from large floodlights or fluorescent "pans," the edges of the shadow patterns on the actors' faces will be less distinct. The key/fill lighting will be less effective.
3. *Makeup*. If the painted facial shadows are heavy and applied in a way that contradicts the real shadows cast by the key/fill light, the result will be confusing to the audience.

Key/Fill Lighting Using Acting Areas

Key/fill lighting may be produced on stage by a variety of means but is most commonly created by spotlights because they allow the designer to individually control the lighting over relatively small parts of the stage. This method of control began with McCandless' *A Method of Lighting the Stage* (1932) and has been in use ever since. McCandless' original concept for lighting acting space was taken from nature. He noted that a person standing outside about mid-morning or mid-afternoon on a clear day and facing generally south (for the northern hemisphere) would be lit by directionless sky light plus light from the sun which might come from a wide variety of horizontal angles but whose vertical angle would range in the vicinity of 38° to 45°. This sunlight was the original key light.

Seeking to emulate nature to comply with the style of naturalism which predominated on stage in the 1930s, McCandless developed the idea that the actors' faces should be lit with fill light coming from "general illumination" equipment, mostly border lights, and that the faces should be keyed with light from spotlights whose vertical angle was between 38° and 45° and which should strike the actor at about 45° to his or her left or right. The light from each spotlight constituted an acting area.

Realistic lighting of the 1930s

The Modern McCandless Lighting

The modern version of McCandless lighting is done entirely with spotlights, usually ellipsoidal reflector luminaires, mounted in pairs so that one strikes the actor at about 45 degrees to the left of a line intersecting the actor's face and perpendicular to the curtain line, and the second at 45 degrees to the right. Both luminaires should be at a vertical angle of 38° to 45° measured to a horizontal plane intersecting the actor's face (See Figures 10.1A and 10.1B). The stage is divided into a number of discrete areas, known as *acting areas*, each capable of being lit by a pair of spotlights whose beam edges are diffused to blend into adjacent areas. Although any size area desired by the designer can be created, the most common size varies from about 6 x 9 feet to 12 x 15 feet, corresponding to the capabilities of typical spotlights used for this purpose. The larger dimension normally runs roughly parallel to the curtain line. Note that acting areas have roughly elliptical shapes, the result of the intersection

Modern realistic area lighting

Acting area size

of the two cones of light from the luminaires. They exist at head level of the actors, not as pools of light on the stage floor.

Ideally, each luminaire in each pair should be separately controllable. If this is possible, it will make key and fill roles interchangeable, something the early general-illumination fill lighting could not accomplish.

In most dramatic productions, the acting area lighting is done entirely with spotlights, the ellipsoidal reflector spotlight being most used. However areas lit from behind the proscenium, if a proscenium theatre is in use, may advantageously be lit with fresnel equipment which is easier to blend and may, under these conditions actually be more efficient than the ellipsoidal reflector luminaires. It may also be more economical.

Acting areas for large stages/auditoriums

It is common practice, particularly on large stages serving large auditoriums, to create much larger and more brightly lit acting areas by using groups of luminaires angled and operated as though they were one.

Obviously, if the designer is not interested in naturalistic actor lighting, the angles of the luminaires can be adjusted to any arrangement that suits his or her design concept and that the architecture of the building will allow.

Architectural Limitations

Unfortunately, the architecture of many theatres will not allow any acting areas except those located near the center of the stage to meet the

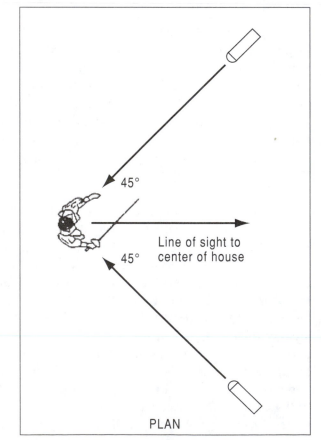

Figure 10.1A. Standard Acting Area, Plan View. Note that the angles are measured from the actor's sightline to the center of the house. Luminaires are located 45° left and right of this line. See Figure 10.1B for vertical angles.

45°

45°

Line of sight to center of house

PLAN

ideal angling requirements. Offstage sides of areas towards the sides of the stage will necessarily be lit by luminaires lighting the actor nearly head-on, unless the theatre is exceptionally well equipped with sidewall lighting ports. Vertical angles may also be restricted. Despite these limitations, the basic concept of area lighting, i.e., numerous individually controlled areas, remains one of the fundamental design concepts of modern dramatic lighting.

Color Media for Acting Area Luminaires

The color of the acting space is a major determinant of mood when the curtain opens. Although this effect soon dwindles, leaving the control of mood to other production elements, designers must remember that the color persists and will continue to affect set, costume and makeup colors throughout the scene.

Until recently, designers were faced with a dilemma: They could settle on an acting area color scheme for the entire production and work within it for whatever variety it would allow, or they could, if budget and mounting space allowed, double hang (or, rarely, triple-hang) the show with additional acting area luminaires gelled in different colors to increase the variety of acting area environments that could be created. The availability of scrollers has changed this; now designers can have the luxury of changing acting area color schemes for each scene. Thus the following acting area color schemes need not be looked upon as mutually exclusive options if the designer is working in a well equipped theatre:

Scrollers add new flexibility to area lighting.

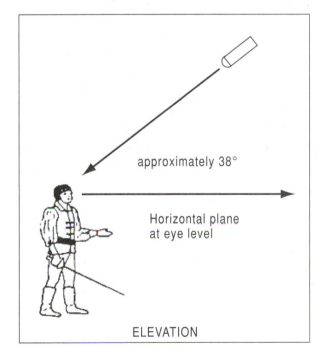

approximately 38°

Horizontal plane
at eye level

ELEVATION

Figure 10.1B. Standard Acting Area, Elevation. Note that the vertical angle is measured from a horizontal plane at the actor's eye level. The angle will be approximately 38° if the two luminaires are exactly 45° to the actor's left and right.

Single-Tint Acting Area Color

This is by far the simplest and most economical of these three choices. All luminaires are equipped with the same tint, usually a pale lavender, pink or straw.

Advantages

1. Simplicity. All luminaires get the same color filters
2. Color adjustments for costume and makeup are simple. Only one color of light need be taken into consideration. Furthermore, that single color can sometimes be chosen to ameliorate minor mismatches in costume or property colors. (See Chapter 9.)
3. Dimming will produce the same color shift for all luminaires dimmed the same amount.
4. Single-luminaire areas are possible if the theatre is short of equipment, although they will lack the plasticity of two-luminaire areas. Such areas should be lit directly from the front but at the same vertical angle as the rest of the areas and, of course, equipped with the same color filter.
5. If the show has a long run, any deterioration in the color filter will be consistent. This problem is lessened with modern, long-life color filters, but may still occur with certain colors, some of which are popular acting area colors.
6. The entire upstage wall of the setting will be lit by the same color spill light from the acting areas.

Disadvantages

1. Monotony is the biggest problem. The effect of whatever color is installed will rapidly diminish because of visual fatigue and the single color cannot be changed by adjusting dimmers, except to whatever degree dimming shifts the color toward warm.
2. Plasticity depends exclusively on the angles of the luminaires and on intensity differences set up in the cueing. Dimming one side of areas to increase the key/fill ratio will cause the fill to become warmer. Interchanging the key/fill roles by changing dimmer settings will cause the color on the sides of the actors' faces to change. While this is not always a disadvantage, it is a consideration for the designer.
3. Those colors favored by the single color will continue to be accented during the entire production and those diminished by it will remain in their lessened condition.

Although the list of advantages runs longer than the list of disadvantages, the three disadvantages are weighty, particularly the first two. Most designers will not opt for single color acting area lighting for an entire show without long and careful consideration.

Obviously, if scrollers are in use, the single-tint system can be but one of several available color schemes that may be used during the show. Given this chance to make in-show changes, monotony and limited plasticity need no longer be a concern and the system can be exploited for its powerful, but short lived, mood setting potential and its color control ability.

The Related Tint System

In this system the two luminaires dedicated to each acting area are equipped with different but similar tints that lie fairly close to each other on the color wheel and are favorable to skin tones. For example, a pale rose-lavender and pale salmon might be paired. Normally the designer will want all of one color to strike the stage left side of the actors' faces and all of the other color to come from the right.

Related tints offer both more potentialities and more possible difficulties for the designer:

Advantages

1. The greatest advantage is the improvement in the plasticity of the lighting over the single-tint system. The color differences between highlight and shadow enhance the audience' perception of the shadow patterns on characters' faces. Since one of the two tints, usually the paler of the pair, will be more efficient than its mate, it will predominate when dimmer readings are equal, making it the key. However subtle dimmer adjustments can shift the roles of key and fill as needed, but at the expense of the usual red shift as lamps are dimmed.

2. Possibilities for controlling the mood via lighting are increased. Color variations can be subtly introduced by altering left/right ratios to sustain the control of color over mood.

3. Costume colors can be subtly emphasized or de-emphasized as the scene progresses by adjusting the brightness of one or the other of the two colors.

Disadvantages

1. Because the two colors are usually consistently directed from opposite sides of all of the acting areas, there will be a tendency for the tints to color the upstage corners of the setting with spill light. In the above example this would result in one upstage corner tending toward lavender and the other toward salmon. This can disturb the color harmonies designed into the setting and should be taken into consideration early in the design process so that the scene designer can compensate by paint changes or can design the setting to make the color difference invisible.

2. The more complex highlight/shadow patterns on actors' faces make it much harder to get by in some less-used areas using only one luminaire.

3. Cues will need to be carefully devised to account for the deterioration of plasticity that will occur when dimming causes both colors shift toward warm and toward each other. Severe dimming may even reduce the color scheme to the status of single-color.

Complementary Tint Acting Area Lighting

This system of lighting actors dates back to the early days of lighting the stage with spotlights. Its complete name is: "Complementary Tint Acting Area Cross-Spotting." Although wordy, this name completely describes the system: It uses pale tints of complementary colors installed in luminaires mounted so that their beams cross as they illuminate the actor. The complementary tints add to make white on those parts of the actor lit by both sources. This system has been adapted to modern equipment, and still finds broad application in modern dramatic lighting and occasionally in television lighting.

There are many tint pairs that can be identified on the C.I.E. Diagram that will add together to make white. Not all of these are useful for acting areas, for example, tints of green are seldom satisfactory. The tints most used are those that flatter skin colors such as pinks, lavenders, pale yellows and ambers. Most always tints used to light actors are very unsaturated, making them efficient light transmitters.

Normally colors are chosen that flatter skin tones.

Clearly, a variety of tint pairs will produce an equal variety of whites. Thus the designer must take into consideration the color of the "white" highlights being created. This color will predominate over much of the stage and affect every pigment or dye on stage. Moreover, this color will change, sometimes quite drastically, as the acting area lighting is dimmed. For example, a cool stage created for its mood value, say for a play by Ibsen, may shift to warm with only moderate dimming, setting a completely different mood.

Advantages

1. Plasticity is increased heightening the audience' perception of facial changes. This aids the actor's characterization.
2. A wide variety of color combinations is made possible which results in the possibility of the extended use of color to control mood.
3. Color values of costumes and makeup are enhanced because the additive result of the two tints is a near-white light containing all visible wave lengths.

Disadvantages

1. As noted above, the system deteriorates toward the single-color system when dimmed. This is not necessarily a crippling disadvantage, but it must be taken into account when designing the lighting. If plasticity is to be maintained while acting areas are dimmed to below about 6 on a 10-point dimmer scale, key light may need to be supplemented using extra equipment and special cues may have to be written.
2. Single-luminaire areas which blend into the overall lighting pattern are nearly impossible to create. Even if the near-white of the combined tints is matched, the shadow patterns will be so different that they reveal the ruse anyway.
3. The tendency for acting area colors to visibly pile up in the up left and right corners of the setting is greater than when related tints are being used. The set designer should take this into consideration when designing and painting the set.

Control of Acting Areas

This should be as flexible as possible, preferably a dimmer per luminaire. Either preset or pattern control may be used to organize the lighting although pattern control will best reflect the interrelationships between the elements of this lighting setup. For example, the area keys can become a pattern, the area fills another and warm and cool sidelights (see below) stage left and right four more. These six patterns, properly mastered, plus the possibility of picking any luminaire or combination of luminaires out for special control, may provide almost all of the lighting setup many shows will require.

Combining Acting Area Lighting with Side Lighting

An unusually flexible and useful combination of acting space lighting can be devised by creating a complete set of acting area lighting using any of the three color schemes and then adding to it front/side lights in colors related to those used in the acting areas. Normally the designer will arrange the side lighting so that the key lighting from the sidelights comes from the same side of the stage as that from the acting area lighting.

Colors for side lighting should normally be related to the acting area colors. In some cases the same colors may be appropriate if the style is naturalistic and the side lighting is related to the direction of key and fill determined by a motivating source such as a window or a lamp onstage. If naturalism is not the style, it may be advantageous to gel the sidelights with colors slightly more saturated but of the same hue as those in the acting areas thus allowing the designer to increase color intensity on stage. A third possibility it to leave the side lights, or at least one set ungelled. This will provide a very bright key light when needed. If scrollers are available, the number of variations on these basic patterns will be awesome.

Key/Fill Lighting Using Wash and Key

Another way to achieve the effect of key/fill lighting over a wide area of the stage is *wash and key* (sometimes known as flood and key), a technique commonly used in large professional theatres. This is done by setting up a strong but carefully shaped wash of light from spotlights mounted on a balcony rail at a level such that their beams strike the stage at a low vertical angle. This wash produces no shadows visible to the audience. Then key light is added produced by banks of strong front/side lights mounted down right and down left of the proscenium opening, sometimes supplemented by a second set mounted upstage of the proscenium arch. Furthermore, the "ultimate" key light, a powerful follow spotlight, is often added (see below). While this system without the follow spotlight, affords no area-to-area control, it can produce very effective key/fill lighting that is particularly useful for chorus and dance numbers in musicals, large chorus scenes in operas, and other such mass stagings.

Since many theatres are not equipped with a balcony front rail at the ideal height to produce a wash without spilling objectionably onto the back of the setting, scene designers are often at pains to conceal the spill. Obviously, relatively flat, blank surfaces are the worst choice. Breaking up the back of the setting by designing in such items as archways, cabinets, or draperies will often hide most of the spill. Dark colors will also help.

Balcony front lighting

Figure 10.2A. Roadie Follow Spotlight.
Courtesy Strong Entertainment Lighting.

Figure 10.2B. Lycian Model 1275
Follow Spotlight. Courtesy Lycian.

Follow Spotlights As Key Light

The lack of individual area control when using wash and key lighting may be overcome by the use of a powerful follow spotlight operated from the rear of the house. Although follow spotlights were once powered by carbon arc sources, these are now obsolete although some are still in use. High wattage HID lamps are now the standard (Figure 10.2B). These luminaires, among the most powerful available, are sometimes called light cannons. At throws of 300 to 600 feet and more, they can produce a brilliant, sharply defined pool of light that can reduce even the most powerful wash and key lighting to the status of fill light. Their angle from an upper balcony level is usually not conducive to producing useful shadow patterns on actors' faces, but their powerful directionality, the fact that they move to follow the performers and that their beam is frequently visible, makes them one of the most powerful attention focusing devices available.

Light cannons

Unfortunately light cannons lack the subtlety necessary to blend with good dramatic lighting. Therefore they are almost exclusively used in musicals, extravaganzas and spectacles where subtly is not important and their power can be openly displayed.

European Follow Spotting

The American theatre has, for the most part, adopted the light cannon approach to follow spotting and relied on other techniques for control of focus of attention when this turns out to be too blatant. The European theatre, particularly for the production of opera, has taken a different approach. Special follow spotlights, usually soft edged luminaires of moderate power (compared to a light cannon), are installed in FOH beams, on the light bridge and even high in the wings, always with space for an operator. These are used to follow principal performers, the following task being passed from one spotlight operator to another as the performers move about on stage. The ideal, seldom really achieved, is to create a sort of halo of light around the performer that moves as though it were part of that person and attracts little attention to itself.

European lighting designers almost always condemn the use of these spotlights, but they also generally use them because they offer a solution to the problem of accenting performers that is nearly impossible to solve otherwise, given the pace of repertory production in most European opera houses. There is neither the time nor the equipment to set up, cue, and operate area lighting control. Nevertheless, designers pay a rather high price for this compromise: They give up any precise control over the angle of the key light on their major performers. Instead, this angle is determined by the location of the performer on the stage relevant to the follow spotlight position that is able to pick up and follow him or her. Worse, the angle may change quite radically as the performer moves out of range of one follow spotlight and into that of another.

Lack of control over lighting angle

On occasion designers, both in the USA and abroad, have even tried to use two soft edge follow spotlights on a single performer to produce the complete key/fill pattern on the performers' faces. This can get complicated and still encounters the problem of artistically uncontrolled

Double follows for key/fill.

angles of illumination. Of course, multiple follow spotlights, often from all sides of the performer, are the standard for spectacles such as ice skating shows.

Color for Wash and Key

The availability of scrollers has opened a large array of possibilities to the lighting designer using wash and key lighting. He or she is no longer restricted to only one or two colors of wash for the entire production. However, when limited to one or two choices of colors by the lack of scrollers, the designer will take care to choose colors that favor skin tones and costumes, usually warm tints, usually slightly more saturated than the key lighting from the sidelights.

Obviously the side lighting will be the key light unless a follow spotlight is in use. A useful technique that affords the designer the chance to build to a climax with brightness is to leave one set of sidelights without gel (or one frame of the scroller color strings clear). This provides an exceedingly bright, sharp edged set of highlights.

When the wash and key lighting is being used to supplement scenes keyed by a follow spotlight, colors may be chosen that heighten costume and setting colors and that harmonize with the colors anticipated to be used in the follow spot. Since colors can be changed at will in the follow spotlight(s), the choice of colors for them is almost unlimited. However designers should note that the higher color temperature of the follow spotlight source will result in much different colors on the actors and setting than when the same color medium is used with an incandescent source. In the unlikely event that it is necessary to match the color output of the high-color-temperature follow spotlight to that of the incandescent wash and key, the designer will need to choose a tint significantly warmer than that used in the incandescent equipment. Another way to adjust the color to achieve a balance between the follow spotlight and the incandescent luminaires is to add a special color temperature adjusting color medium to the regular medium being used in the follow spot. These color temperature adjusting media are commonly used in the film work and are listed in special color media booklets prepared for that industry. They may also be found in some general color media booklets.

Matching color temperatures

Adjusting color temperature with special media

Color for the Cyclorama and Entire Stage

Cyclorama lighting and, when used, general washes over the setting, can be handled variously. For maximum variety in available color, three primary colors (RGB) may be used. Although this is one of the most inefficient ways to produce color, it is by far the most flexible. A good three-color setup for cycloramas will actually require four circuits, each separately controlled. There should be one red, one green and two blue. This provides the extra power in the blue circuit to make up for the lack of blue in incandescent lamps and makes it possible to dim part of the blue without subjecting the entire blue system to red shift.

In those rare instances where the proper equipment is available, it is possible to improve the efficiency of a RGB color wash by substituting fluorescent lamps in red, green and blue for the incandescent cyc lighting, or by using gaseous discharge lamps which will produce blue light much more efficiently. Additionally, dichroic filters may be used to get the maximum and purest blue output to the stage.

If the flexibility of the three color primary system is not needed, there are a number of possibilities. The most efficient, but least flexible, will be to gel the cyclorama luminaires with the single color needed. Of course, this eliminates all color change except whatever may occur when the system is dimmed. If more variety is needed it is possible to gel the three or four cyclorama circuits with secondary colors or to go back to the traditional red, white and blue system much used in early vaudeville.

An old but effective special wash technique deserves mention: When the set is lit only with pure saturated blue or blue-green, for example in a stylized "moonlight" scene, all red and orange pigments on stage, including those in the makeup, will be reduced to either black or an unpleasant grey-brown. However, the addition of a wash of the deepest available purple at a reading just high enough to provide some red light for the red and orange pigments will bring things back into balance. Usually the purple need not be bright enough to significantly change the effect of the predominating blue or blue-green.

Improving all-blue lighting

Chapter 11

ELECTRICITY

The history of stage lighting is much older than the history of electricity in the theatre. For example, the Greek plays, now thousands of years old, were played out of doors. However this does not indicate a lack of concern for lighting conditions. Historians report that some of the plays whose action begins at dawn (e.g., the *Agamemnon*) did begin at dawn. Hours later in the dramatic festival the end of the tragedy may have actually happened at sunset. Even if these speculations are not true, it is apparent that the authors of the Greek tragedies were well aware of the effect on an audience of changes in natural lighting. They often used these changes as images in their writing.

Much later, when the theatre moved indoors, artificial lighting became necessary for visibility if not for dramatic purposes. Soon experimenters were devising special oil lamps with reflectors and even color media in the form of bottles filled with colored liquid (wine, perhaps?) Still later, the Elizabethans again depended on natural light which entered their partially indoor theatre through a hole in the roof.

Early lighting During the eighteenth century when scene painting reached monumental heights with the work of the Bibbiena family, stage lighting was dedicated to the illumination of painted illusion. To this end, the lighting was made as shadowless as possible to avoid revealing any imperfections in the surface of the fabric on which the painting was done. Shadows in the setting were the province of the painter. This lighting was not only flat, but also dim and at very low color temperature—it came from candles and oil lamps. Actors performed in the same kind of light at only slightly brighter levels. One source describes the lighting "equipment" over the actors as a "candle hoop" which "hung in dripping radiance." Concentrating on one's characterization must have been a challenge on **Limelight** that stage.

More recently, the limelight was invented. It consisted of a piece of limestone heated to incandescence by means of a gas flame from a blow-pipe. The gas was usually acetylene which, when mixed with air in the proper proportions produces a hot clean flame. In other proportions the mix can be highly explosive. Later oxygen was substituted for air, making an even more explosive mixture possible. Leaky piping leveled more than one theatre of the era. At about the same time, gas lighting replaced the candle and oil lamp "borderlights" which hung in the flies not far from highly flammable wing and drop scenery—a situation that would give a modern fire marshal nightmares. Theatre fires were common and often deadly. When, in the nineteenth century, the electric lamp was introduced into the theatre to replace the highly dangerous gas lamps, it was greeted with enthusiasm. However the electrical source offered as a substitute for the limelight did not fare as well. It was the electric arc, a spark set up between two pieces of carbon. The light most resembled that often observed today when an electric welder is in use. It was cold in color, flickering and noisy. On the other hand, the limelight produced a complexion-flattering warm white light that was steady and practically noiseless. Therefore the shift to the arc light was resisted in spite of the explosive danger of the limelight. However, as better electric arcs were developed, the arc light became the standard source for follow spotlights and remained so until quite recently when it has been replaced by the powerful enclosed arcs of high intensity discharge lamps.

> **Theatre fires**

> **Carbon arc follow spotlight**

Sadly, the introduction of the incandescent lamp did little for the development of an incandescent-source spotlight because the early lamps were ill-suited for use with a lens. The incandescent spotlight had to await the development of the concentrated filament lamp in the 1920s. Today the incandescent lamp is being seriously challenged by more efficient discharge sources.

> **Early incandescent lamps**

Electrical current is the energy source for almost every aspect of modern stage lighting. Therefore designers and technicians must understand electrical current to use it effectively and safely.

The Nature of Electrical Current

Early experimenters discovered that there were apparently two kinds of electricity. One could be produced by rubbing amber with cat fur and the other by rubbing glass with silk. These were first termed "resinous" and "vitreous" electricity. Later, Benjamin Franklin suggested that vitreous electricity be called "positive" and resinous "negative. These terms still persist although, as we shall shortly see, they cause some confusion.

> **"Positive" and "negative" electricity**

Modern experimenters have established that there are indeed two kinds of subatomic particles associated with electrical phenomena. The electron, moves about when electricity flows and the proton which provides the attraction that makes the electrons flow.

Electricity and Electrical Current

Although common discourse refers to almost every kind of electrical phenomena as "electricity," scientific accuracy requires that we distinguish between *electricity* and *electrical current*. Therefore the following definitions will prevail in this text:

Electricity refers to electrical charges created when a surplus of electrons is built up on some object while a matching deficiency is created elsewhere. No flow takes place until a circuit is completed that allows the electrons to flow and almost instantaneously restores the balance. Such charges are often called static electricity.

The most spectacular electrical charge phenomenon is lightning. Lightning bolts are the evidence of a huge unbalance being eliminated by passage of electrons from cloud to cloud or from the earth to a cloud. Man-made charges, minuscule compared to lightning, are often stored in devices known as capacitors. These are essential parts of electronic apparatus such as television sets and strobe lights. Electrical charges can also be unintentionally built up by friction such as those encountered when you scuff over a carpet on a dry day and suddenly discover that a charge has been built up on your body when it is unpleasantly discharged upon grasping a doorknob.

Electrical current is a flow of electrons that takes place when a conductive path is established between the terminals of a source of electrical energy such as a battery or generator. Most of the electrical equipment in the theatre, including lamps, motors etc., is energized by electrical current. It will be the principal subject of the discussion to come.

Atoms in their normal state are electrically balanced, having equal positive and negative charges. The positive charges exist as protons and the negative ones as electrons. In many materials one or more electrons are detachable, if energy is applied. When this happens the atom becomes electrically unbalanced because it has more protons than electrons. This imbalance known as an *electrical potential*, a kind of pressure that causes the detached electrons to want to flow back to the protons deficient in electrons giving up the energy that unbalanced them in the process. Thus energy can be derived from electron flow.

Clearly, energy must be supplied to produce either electricity or electrical current. In a dry cell, for example, this energy comes from chemical reactions that cause a surplus of electrons to build up on the negative terminal and a deficiency to be reflected on the positive. In a generator, mechanical energy is supplied, from a water or steam turbine, for example. Note the semantic difficulty: a *surplus* of electrons (negative charges) results in a charge on the *negative* terminal; a deficiency is reflected at the *positive* terminal. When a circuit is established the flow will be from negative terminal to positive terminal. Ben Franklin's arbitrary decision naming the kinds of electricity still haunts us.

As we shall repeatedly discover, much electrical engineering is devoted to usefully recovering as much of the energy put into an electrical system as possible.

When electrons flow, they usually flow through something, although if under enough pressure, they will pass through a vacuum. Controlling their flow involves the use of conductors, which allow their flow and insulators, which prevent it. As we shall see, "allow" and "prevent" are relative terms which must always be qualified by indicating the pressure (voltage) driving the electrons.

"Flow" of Electrons

Although it is easy to picture a stream of electrons flowing through a wire much as water flows through a pipe, and this analogy is often used, the best information indicates that the actual flow more nearly resembles a row of dominoes toppling one after the other as they fall. A detached electron moves in a way that causes another to be detached and the first to be reattached. The newly detached electron moves still another and so on throughout the circuit. The effect, however, is the same as a constant flow as far as most applications are concerned. Nevertheless we will occasionally need to remind ourselves of the real nature of electron flow when trying to understand what goes on inside of transistors, silicon controlled rectifiers and other solid state devices.

Conductors

These are materials with an electron on the outer part of each atom that is easily detached. Once detached, these electrons can become part of an electrical current. Conductors vary in the ease with which electrons can be detached. Silver, copper and aluminum are among the best conductors. Other materials such as carbon or tungsten which have quite firmly attached electrons are poor conductors. The term resistance refers to the ease or reluctance with which various materials part with electrons. As resistance increases it takes more and more energy to detach the electrons.

Resistance

Choice of type of conductor depends on the purpose in mind. If the goal is to move a maximum electrical current along the conductor with minimum loss, the best conductor that is economically feasible is chosen, usually copper or aluminum. If, on the other hand, the purpose is to convert electrical current into heat, a high resistance conductor such as tungsten or nichrome is used.

The following is a list of good conductors commonly used in theatrical applications and some of those found in nature which influence the safe use of electrical current:

silver	copper
mercury	brass
lead	impure water
aluminum	zinc
iron and steel	most metals
moist concrete	moist earth

Here is a list of poor conductors some of which are much used in electronics applications:

tungsten	carbon
silicon	nickel-chromium alloys (Nichrome)
most nonmetals	

It is important to distinguish between poor conductors and insulators. Poor conductors will carry current and, within limits, will not be harmed by its passage although they will exact a toll in the form of heat converted from the energy of flow of the current. Insulators will not carry current at all up to the point where they break down and are punctured, or char or burn allowing the current to pass.

Insulators compared with poor conductors

Semiconductors

Silicon: the basis of the semiconductor world

A number of materials exhibit the property of conducting current in one direction quite well and almost totally opposing it in the opposite direction. These are known as semiconductors. They are at the very heart of modern solid state electronics, forming the essential parts of dimmers, control circuitry, computers and myriad other devices without which modern technology both within and outside of the theatre could not exist. Although there are a number of elements and alloys that can form semiconductors, by far the majority of those in use are based on the element silicon which has been "doped" with minute amounts of other materials.

In their nonconducting direction semiconductors perform like the insulators described below. They block the flow of current only up to certain voltages. At higher voltages they can break down and conduct, but at the expense of being damaged or destroyed.

Insulators

These are materials which have no detachable electrons. Except under certain rather exotic quantum conditions sometimes called "tunneling," they totally block the flow of current through them up to a point beyond which they are punctured or otherwise damaged and electrons flow. Insulators are used to control the flow of electrons into whatever path the engineer wishes and to provide protection to those who handle current-carrying parts.

Lightning

By far the commonest of all insulators is air, the dryer the better. Mile upon mile of electrical transmission lines depend on the insulating value of air to keep the electrons from straying away from their planned path. Of course, even air has its limits as a lightning bolt clearly demonstrates. Once air has been ionized (electrons have been detached from its atoms, leaving them charged) it becomes a conductor and the lightning bolt carries huge amounts of current until the imbalance created by the storm is eliminated.

Here is a list of insulators commonly found in use in the theatre and in other places where electrical current is in use:

air	glass
almost all plastics	porcelain
rubber	dry paper
dry cloth	dry wood
fiberglass	pure deionized water
silicone rubber	Teflon

Pure water is an insulator

Note that the insulating value of many materials depends on their being dry. Even a slight amount of moisture may change an insulating material into a dangerously conductive one. This is because water, except at its most pure state, is an excellent conductor of current. Remarkably, highly purified and deionized water is used as an insulating coolant for very large xenon lamps where it is circulated through openings in the electrodes to cool them. If this water were conductive, it would short the apparatus and destroy it.

Electron Flow

Electron flow provides a way of transferring energy from one device to another whether that device is a tiny signaling device in a control board or the power supply for a 1000 horsepower motor. Energy put into the system causes the electrons to be detached creating a surplus of electrons at the negative pole of the generating source and a deficiency at the positive pole. If there is a conductive path between the two related poles, electrons will flow until the imbalance is restored. It is very important to understand the rules of this flow. In order for electrons to be attracted and to flow: *There must be a continuous conducting path from the negative pole of the generating device back to the attracting positive pole of that same device*. If there is no such path, no flow will occur and no energy can be transported. For example, connecting the positive pole of one dry cell to the negative pole of another will not result in any flow. Only if the remaining poles of the two batteries, one negative and one positive are connected, thus creating a complete circle, will the flow occur. Put another way the rule is: *Without a return path, no current will flow*.

Each complete path in an electrical device is called a circuit. Many circuits can be interwoven into hugely complicated devices, but ultimately each circuit must be so arranged that it relates its own surplus of electrons to its own deficiency. Note that electrical parts in a complex device may actually serve as parts of several circuits at the same time, the attractions for the electrons sorting themselves out as though each circuit were isolated.

When the electrons flow in such a way that they restore the balance, they give up their extra energy and the system returns to a neutral state. If a continuous flow is needed, energy must be constantly fed into the system to maintain the unbalance. As far as physics is concerned, none of the energy inserted into an electrical system is ever lost. It is converted into various forms, but the total amount remains the same. However practical utilization of the energy is another matter. Much of it may be "lost" by being inadvertently converted into a form not wanted by the users of the system. Usually this comes down to the energy being converted into unwanted heat.

Path of electron flow

A return path is necessary

Circuit

Conservation of energy

The Simple Circuit

Reduced to its most elementary form, a circuit consists of a source of electrical current, conductors to carry the electrons through the complete loop back to the source, insulators to keep the electrons on their path and some device to utilize the energy released as the electrons flow. (Figure 11.1) Usually the circuit also includes a switch to enable the user to turn the flow on or off.

A flashlight is an example of a circuit only slightly more complicated than this. It usually utilizes more than one battery although these act as though they were one.

Note that the order of the parts in a simple circuit makes no difference to its operation. Even if a switch is included it makes no difference where the switch is installed. Also note that the same amount of electrons flows through the entire circuit. Normally it is the current-using device which controls the amount of flow although the capacity of source could also be the limiting device.

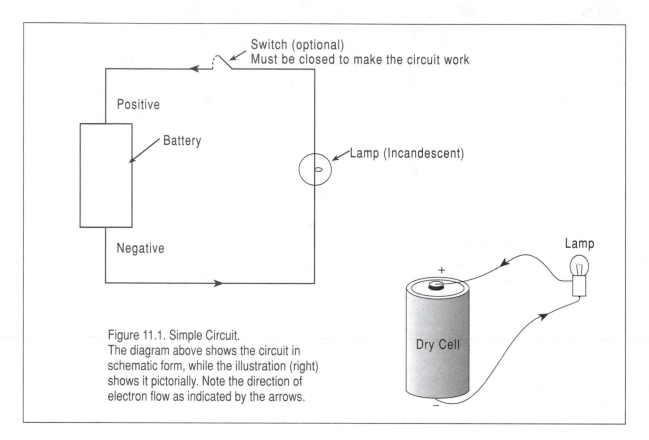

Figure 11.1. Simple Circuit.
The diagram above shows the circuit in schematic form, while the illustration (right) shows it pictorially. Note the direction of electron flow as indicated by the arrows.

Series and Parallel Circuits

Although the variations in electrical circuitry are almost infinite, two general categories must be noted here: the series circuit and the parallel circuit. A series circuit is simply a variation on the simple circuit wherein a number of devices are inserted into the circuit to utilize or control the flow (Figure 11.2). Like the simple circuit, the same number of electrons will flow throughout the entire circuit and a break anywhere in the circle will shut down the whole circuit. The resistances of the parts of the circuit add up to form the total resistance of the circuit (see below for details of electrical mathematics).

Series circuit

A good example of a series circuit is a low-cost string of Christmas tree lights in which there is only one conductor looped from light to light. If one light fails by burning out, the entire string goes dead unless special lamps have been installed that jump over the break when a lamp fails. Series circuits are often used in safety control circuitry in the theatre where the purpose is to be sure that all of the various elements in the circuit are in their proper condition before allowing the action to proceed.

A parallel circuit is one in which there are a number of paths the electrons can follow to make their return to the positive pole (Figure 11.2). This circuit is the most common of all, being used in almost every lighting circuit on stage and in homes and businesses. Opening any one path in a parallel circuit will not shut off the remaining paths. Note that parallel circuits require more wire.

Perhaps the most important part of this study of series and parallel circuitry is to develop a clear understanding of the phrases, "in parallel with…" and "in series with…" These describe the relationship between two or more parts of a circuit. When a device is "in series with" another piece or pieces of equipment this means that the device that is in series can exert control over the others. If, for example, a switch is in series with a string of lighting fixtures, that switch can turn the entire string on or off.

When a device is said to be in parallel with other equipment it has no direct influence over the other things included in the circuit. The lamps in a set of borderlights, for instance, are "in parallel" with each other, and if one lamp burns out, the others remain on.

Sometimes circuits are described as "series-parallel." This means that parts of the circuit may be in series but that other parts are in parallel or that there are several series circuits which are in parallel with each other. Even more complicated patterns may exist.

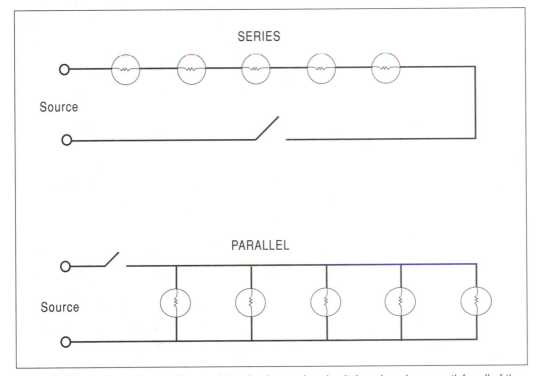

Figure 11.2. Series and Parallel Circuits. Note that in a series circuit there is *only one path* for all of the electrons. Any break in the loop stops the flow completely. The same number of electrons must flow through the entire circuit, giving rise to the phrase "in series with…" which describes the situation where the current in a given piece of equipment is dependent on that flowing through the rest of the circuit.

In parallel circuitry there can be as m any paths as desired. Breaking any one of them merely causes the load in that path to cut off without disturbing the remainder. Thus the phrase "in parallel with…" refers to a situation where each piece of equipment that is part of the circuit is independent of the current flowing through the others.

Modern electronic dimmers are a typical example of the way these terms are applied: The main current-carrying part of the dimmer is *in series* with the load (the lamps). This makes it possible for the dimmer to control all of the lamps attached to it. However, the dimmer control circuitry requires its own supply of power, albeit small. This control power is *in parallel* with the lamp load and remains on whether the lamps are dimmed out or remain on.

Electrical Mathematics

The terms that appear in electrical formulae and in descriptions of electrical apparatus are:

Resistance (Ohm): The opposition that a conductor applies to a stream of electrons flowing through it. All conductors have resistance except a few esoteric substances which have zero or near-zero resistance when cooled to very low temperatures. Resistance appears in electrical formulas as "R." Its unit of quantity is the Ohm, named for Georg Simon Ohm, an early experimenter with electricity.

Impedance: This is a resistance-like opposition to flow encountered only when alternating current is flowing. It is measured in Ohms and functions like resistance in most, but not all cases. It is explained below.

Voltage: Voltage is also named after an early experimenter, Alessandro Volta. It is the pressure that causes the detached electrons to flow and is also known as Electromotive Force (EMF). Voltage appears in formulas as "E" for EMF. Note that "V" is also sometimes used but not in any context of physics, where "V" has long been reserved for "velocity."

Ampere: This is the unit of quantity. It refers to the number of electrons flowing through a conductor. It is an absolutely measurable quantity described as the number of electrons needed to deposit 0.001118 grams of silver per second when the current is flowing through a neutral silver nitrate solution. This could be translated into an actual, but incredibly large, number of electrons. The ampere is abbreviated "I" because the letter "A" is already used in an even more basic formula in physics": F = MA (force equals mass times acceleration). "Ampere" is almost always shortened to "amp." Current carrying capacity is often labeled "ampacity."

Ohm's Law

The most basic of all electrical formulae is Ohm's law:

$$E = I \times R$$

i.e., *voltage equals amperage times resistance*.

Every student of electrical phenomena should memorize this formula which describes the relationship between the elements of a simple circuit. Note that if one knows any two of these elements, the third can be easily calculated. Simple algebraic variations on Ohm's law are as follows:

$$I = \frac{E}{R} \quad \text{or} \quad R = \frac{E}{I}$$

The lighting technician may occasionally need to determine the resistance of parallel or series circuits. The formulae are as follows:

For series circuits: $R = r + r + r + r \ldots$

For parallel circuits: $\frac{1}{R} = \frac{1}{r} + \frac{1}{r} + \frac{1}{r} \ldots$

In which R = total resistance of the circuit and r = the individual resistance of the components

The Power Formula

Ironically, although Ohm's law is the basic formula for all electrical circuits, the theatre lighting technician will seldom use it directly. Instead he or she will use the power formula. This happens because manufacturers and suppliers of equipment for the theatre have already made the most basic calculations using Ohm's law and have labeled their products in watts or amperes.

Power formula

The Watt: All of the electrical units so far defined deal with elements of the flow of electrons in a circuit. However none of them deal directly with the amount of power being carried by that circuit and delivered to whatever device is utilizing it. The watt is the unit that does this. Simple logic indicates that the amount of energy carried by a stream of electrons will be the product of the number of electrons times the force that causes them to move. This is analogous to the energy carried by a stream of water in a pipe, which would be the product of the amount of water and the pressure driving it.

Energy transfer is described in watts.

The mathematical definition of a watt is: 1 amp x 1 volt = 1 Watt. The formula is:

$$W = E \times I$$

In which W = the energy carried, i.e., watts; E the voltage driving the electrons and I the number of electrons moving stated in amperes. It is common for this equation to be written W = V x A using the first letters of the names of the quantities instead of the scientific notation. Either is correct as long as the users know that V = voltage, not velocity and A = amperes, not acceleration.

The Kilowatt and the Kilowatt Hour

Kilowatt

A watt represents a very small amount of energy—even a small night-light lamp is rated at four watts. Therefore the common way of counting watts is by thousands, termed *kilowatts*. Both watt and kilowatt express the amount of energy being transferred at any given moment, not the total amount over a period of time. Since multiplying the quantity per second by time is a more practical way of measuring energy, the term *kilowatt hour* (kWh) has been devised. It represents any sum of wattage that adds up to 1000 and flows for one hour. For example a 100 watt lamp running for 10 hours would use a kilowatt hour of electrical current as would a 2000 watt lamp operating for one half hour.

Kilowatt hour (kWh)

Cost of operation

Electrical current is sold by the kWh. The hourly cost of operating any electrical device can be calculated once the wattage is known and the kWh rate being charged. If, for example, a spotlight draws 2000 watts and the cost of power is 12¢ per kWh, each hour of operation of the spotlight will cost 24¢. If a number of luminaires or other equipment are being operated at the same time, the cost of operation will equal the sum of the individual devices times the cost per kWh. Note that actual calculations of cost of operation can become much more complicated because of dimming. Although electrically dimming a lamp reduces the amount of current it draws, the dimmers themselves and any auxiliary equipment such as ballasts may also draw current. The result is a complex computation.

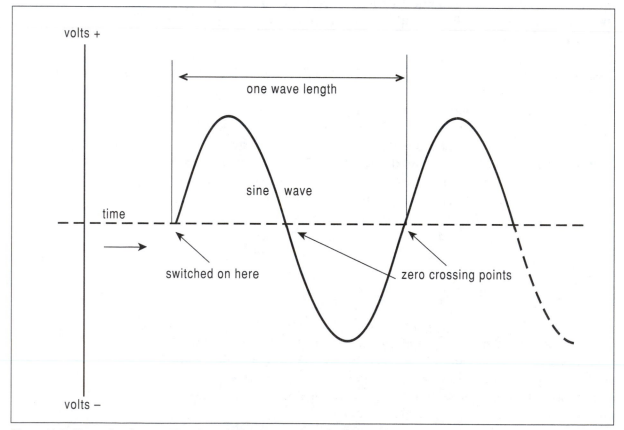

Figure 11.3. Alternating Current. This diagram illustrates the standard alternating current produced by power generators throughout the world. The sine waveform is the natural result of the rotating coil(s) in the generator (See Figure 11.4). This constantly changing voltage will induce voltages in any conductor within its magnetic field.

The Heat Formula

Whenever current flows through a conductor, with the exception of rare superconductor situations, some of the energy being transmitted is converted into heat. Unless heat is being sought, such as inside an incandescent lamp, this heat represents wasted energy and also may prove hazardous. The formula which describes how electrical current is converted into heat is:

Electrically generated heat

$$H \text{ (in calories per second)} = 0.24 \, I^2R$$

Note that voltage does not appear directly in the formula although it has figured into the determination of the amperage. The factor, 0.24 is simply a constant that causes the product to come out in calories. *It is particularly important to note the I^2 part of this formula.* It figures prominently in electrical safety.

Generation and Distribution of Electrical Current

The generation and distribution of electrical current are interlocked because large generating equipment must often be located in remote locations for the reasons mentioned below. The conditions imposed by long-distance transmission of power directly influence the way electrical current is used in the theatre and everywhere else. Long distance transmission of power has, until quite recently, required that the power be in the form of *alternating current* (AC) i.e., current that swings regularly in the manner shown in Figure 11.3. Although high voltage direct current (DC) is now used to transmit huge amounts of energy over long distances with greater efficiency than AC, most distribution of current still utilizes AC circuitry.

Alternating current

We begin with an examination of the alternating current generator. This device can be as small as the alternator in your car or as huge as those at Boulder Dam. It works on a very basic principle of physics: *When a conductor is placed in a moving or changing magnetic field an electrical potential is developed in that conductor. If a path is provided, current will flow and energy may be derived from that flow.* It is important to note that the energy comes from energy of movement imparted to the generator, not from the magnetic field which merely provides the condition for the conversion. Therefore all generators must be provided with a source of energy of motion (a prime mover). The larger the generator, the larger the prime mover must be. Typical prime movers are water power created by a huge hydraulic dam or the energy developed by a huge steam turbine which must, in turn, be driven by a boiler fueled by coal, oil or even atomic energy.

Prime movers

The demand for power in our mechanized society is far larger than the output of even the largest single generating station. Therefore generating plants across the country are interconnected so that many power sources can function as one. Such power grids are able to accommodate mammoth changes in the amount of energy demanded as large cities turn on all of their street lights at once or large plants start or stop, many at the same moment. Normally these grids can also pick up the load if a part of the system is suddenly destroyed, such as in a major earthquake. However, the sensitive and precise electrical control apparatus of these grids have their limits. Under certain rare but possible conditions, an entire grid can sequentially become overloaded and go out of service creating a widespread blackout. This can create one of the many kinds of emergencies that a theatrical lighting system must be equipped to handle. Emergency lighting will be further discussed later in this chapter and in the next.

Parts of Generators

All generators must fulfill the basic requirement above: they must subject one or more conductors to a moving or changing magnetic field. This means, in the case of generators, that either the conductors or the magnet must move, but not necessarily both. In small generators such as those in automobiles, the magnet(s) remain fixed and coils of insulated wire attached to the driven shaft rotate. This moving portion is called an *armature*. The current induced in the armature is transferred to the fixed part of the generator by a series of brass or copper rings mounted around

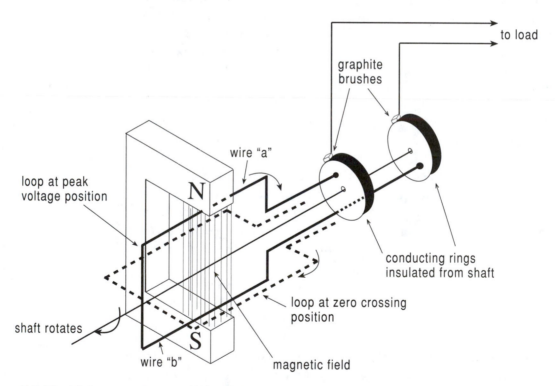

Figure 11.4. The AC Generator. Generation is based on the fact that any conductor exposed to a moving or changing magnetic field will have voltage induced into it. In this simple generator, the conductor is the moving part. Note the wire loop which moves with the rotating shaft. The dotted outline denotes the position of the loop at a zero crossing when no voltage is being generated. As the loop rotates to the point where wire "a" passes the "N" pole of the magnet (the heavily outlined position), the voltage rises to its positive maximum. As the loop continues to rotate, voltage drops again toward zero and reverses. Then, as "wire "b" rotates toward the "N" pole, the voltage reaches a negative peak. Finally, as the rotation continues, the negative voltage dwindles toward zero as the loop moves into its original position.

The electrical energy is removed from the moving part of the generator by the slip-ring arrangement diagrammed. The graphite brushes slide over the moving surface of the rings transferring the current to the fixed wiring supplying the load.

the shaft which contact "brushes." These are blocks of graphite that slide over the surface of the moving rings and collect the current. Graphite is used because it is slippery and a conductor of electrical current. This arrangement is known as the *commutator*. In large generators the magnets are moved and the coils of wire in which the current is induced remain stationary.

While actual generators in power plants are much more complicated, one can visualize how alternating current is produced by imagining a single loop of insulated wire being rotated between the poles of a simple horseshoe magnet, its current commutated by a simple slip ring arrangement. See Figure 11.4. If one begins with the loop of wire exactly at a neutral position with reference to the magnetic field between the poles of the magnet and imagines the coil rotating clockwise, the following sequence of voltages will be generated: (Note that we must keep track of the two halves of the loop labeled "a" and "b.") As "a" moves toward the "N" pole a positive voltage will be generated in the loop (Figure 11.4). This voltage will increase as the conductor approaches the point of maximum magnetic field peaking as it passes the "N" pole and declining as it continues to rotate toward the next neutral position. Continuing the rotation, the voltage in the loop reverses because "b" is now approaching the "N" pole. This reversal point is known as the *zero crossing* and is vital to the operation of most modern theatrical dimmers. As it passes the pole the voltage reaches a negative peak. Then the loop continues rotating, again passing the point where it started.

A single complete pattern of voltages containing one positive and one negative peak is known as a *cycle* (Figure 11.3). The frequency with which these cycles occur will depend on the speed of rotation of the shaft carrying the wire loop. In the real world of power generation the speed of rotation of the generator is carefully controlled to maintain 60 Hertz (cycles per second) alternating current. (60 Hz. AC) which is the standard in the USA. Some European countries utilize 50 Hertz current which means that their generators rotate slower than ours. The name *Hertz* has been substituted for *cycle* to honor an early experimenter in electrical phenomena.

If one could see the electrons moving in a conductor carrying alternating current, one would see electrons rushing first in one direction then the other changing direction each 1/120th of a second. While this may seem fast, electrons are capable of changing direction billions of times per second making 60 Hertz seem slow.

If nothing distorts the pattern of voltage produced by the generator, its graph (Figure 11.3) will display a sine wave. This is a geometrical form that may be created by plotting the values of the sines of all of the angles the coil passes through as it rotates, measured from the zero-crossing point. The sine wave is a fundamental reference to which many other wave forms are compared.

When it is necessary to describe how two waves relate to each other it is common to refer to their *phase* (ø), a term which refers to the point in the cycle under discussion. For example, two voltages might be referred to as "180 degrees out of phase." This

Armature

Commutator

Zero-crossing point

Cycle

The rotating coil produces the fluctuating voltage.

60 Hz current

Hertz

Phase

means that the positive pulse of one wave lines up exactly in time with the negative pulse of the other causing them to cancel each other. Note how the number of degrees relates to the position of the generating coil. Other phase relationships are common and often significant when they occur in dimming apparatus.

Also, in the real world, power generators normally have three coils moving with relationship to the magnetic field. This results in greater efficiency and produces what is known as three phase 60 Hertz alternating current (3ø 60Hz AC). It is standard throughout the USA, Canada and in many other locations. 50 Hz current is standard in much of Europe and also in other countries. The phase relationship between the three voltages is 120° reflecting the fact that the three generating coils are located at 120° intervals around the generator shaft (or multiple coils are arranged to produce the same effect.)

Figure 11.5. Steady Direct Current. Note that, once turned on, this current has no further changes in voltage until turned off. This means that it produces an unchanging magnetic field that cannot induce voltage in any nearby conductors except at the moment of turning on or off. This type of DC is produced by batteries and perfectly filtered DC power supplies.

Other Kinds of Current

Continuous DC: The current, typically derived from a battery, consists of a steady flow of electrons moving in the same direction. (See Figure 11.5) When the current is turned on, it immediately jumps to its full value and remains at that level until turned off or otherwise altered. Since it is unchanging, except for the brief moment when it is turned on or off, continuous DC cannot produce any of the effects arising from the actions of changing or moving magnetic fields. Since most modern electrical apparatus depends on the fluctuations of alternating current for its operation, including most modern dimmers, direct current can be a threat to this equipment.

The theatre utilizes direct current from batteries as a supply for lanterns, torches and the like where supply wiring would be inappropriate and for emergency lighting unless a special generator is provided. Also, continuous DC is necessary to the operation of a wide variety of electronic apparatus. This is usually supplied by a "*power supply," a device which converts AC into DC and filters to remove any pulsations. Power supplies are often built into electronic gear although they are also available as separate units. They can be built to supply voltages ranging from a few volts needed for most transistor-operated devices to high and potentially deadly voltages such as those used in the picture tubes of televisions and computers.

Power supplies are also needed to control the current flow and operate some types of discharge lamps used in the theatre. For example, xenon lamps, some of which draw as much as 10,000 watts, require a very smooth DC supply for their operation plus a "spike" of high-voltage DC to start them. Other HID lamps have similar requirements. It is important to note that the starting pulses are particularly dangerous.

Pulsing DC: This kind of current is produced by DC generators such as automotive generators, and by devices called rectifiers, which convert AC into DC. It consists of a series of positive-only (or negative-only) pulses whose shape may resemble that of one half of an AC wave. (See Figure 11.6) Pulsing DC is used unfiltered in some types of electrical welders and battery chargers but it is usually filtered to smooth it into continuous DC.

It is vitally important for the theatre technician to know what kind of current is being supplied and to determine whether it meets the needs of equipment about to be attached to it. For example, attaching a transformer-operated device to a DC supply might destroy it.

Other Electrical Wave Forms: Electronic equipment can be devised to shape the wave to almost any specification. For instance, certain kinds of equipment utilize square waves. Digital data sent to dimmers from control consoles is in the form of a stream of square wave pulses of varying length.

Square waves

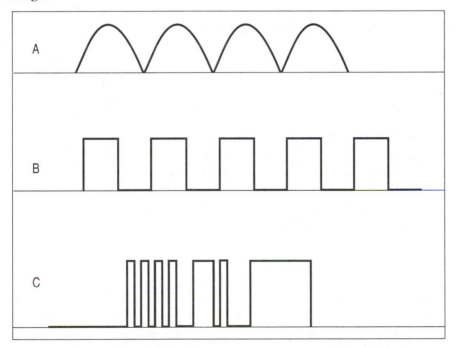

Figure 11.6. Pulsing Direct Current. Diagram A shows the kind of DC produced by a generator such as might be found in an older auto. Note that this particular wave form is basically a sine wave but with the negative pulses reversed in polarity; the reverse is also possible. Pulsating DC is used mainly for charging batteries which will smooth out the pulses when current is drawn from them. Diagram B illustrates the kind of pulsating DC produced by a square wave generator of high quality. Such DC serves many purposes in electronic circuitry. Diagram C shows the kind of irregular but very carefully designed string of pulses that make up the data stream of a computer. A piece of DMX512 data might look something like this.

Calculating AC Power

RMS voltage

The amount of energy transferred by an alternating current circuit can be determined by the power formula, but with this qualification: The voltage figure used in the calculation cannot be the peak voltage because this is reached for only a fraction of a second twice in each cycle. Instead, the peak voltage must be averaged by dividing it by the square root of 2, i.e., 1.41. This results in a figure known as the RMS (root mean square) voltage. Once this calculation has been done, the rest of the mathematics can proceed as though the current were DC. This problem is simplified by the fact that most meters designed for use with AC are built to make the RMS calculation automatically and display the voltage or amperage equivalent of DC. However it is important to remember that the maximum voltage found in AC circuits is the peak voltage, not the RMS voltage. This can make a significant difference when determining the amount of insulation needed to safely operate the circuit. The difference between RMS and peak voltage for a 120-volt circuit is only the difference between 120 volts and about 170 volts which is easily covered by the standard requirement that all insulation for lighting circuits be tested to 600-volt AC. However if the RMS voltage is 5000 volts, as it might be in the power supply for a strobe light, the peak voltage will be 7050 volts. This is enough to significantly change the design of the insulation in the strobe.

Peak voltage determines insulation needed.

Transformers

Power distribution

The invention of the transformer made possible long-distance transmission of electrical energy. Transformers make it possible to raise the voltage of a transmission circuit to a very high number while reducing the amperage proportionately, or the reverse. The total wattage remains unchanged except for a tiny loss in the transformer. Consider the effect of raising the voltage and reducing the amperage on the task of transferring 1,000,000 watts of power over a long line, say from Boulder Dam to Los Angeles. We will assume that the line has a resistance of 500 ohms.

Avoiding heat losses

If the power is transferred at ordinary household line voltage of 120 volts (which we will round off to 100 volts for easy figuring):

1,000,000 watts @ 100 volts = 10,000 amperes

Heat losses figuring according to the heat formula $c = .24 \times I^2 R$:

$c = 0.24 \times 10,000^2 \times 500 = .24 \times 100,000,000 \times 500 =$
1,200,000,000 calories per second

Most of this heat would be generated in the Mojave desert which scarcely needs it and the power to Los Angeles would be reduced to a trickle. This would make the cost of transmission prohibitive. This calculation explains why power from early DC power plants never got distributed far from the source.

However using transformers to boost the power at the generating station to a high voltage, say 1,000,000 volts, and then reducing it back down to the 100 volts needed in the city would result in the following savings:

1,000,000 watts @ 1,000,000 volts = 1 ampere
Losses are: $0.24 \times 1 \times 500 = 120$ calories per second
(a very tolerable loss)

This is the almost incredible mathematics of high-voltage transmission of AC power. In the real world, power is usually generated at about 18,000 volts and stepped up by a huge transformer capable of handling large amounts of power and putting out, say 500,000 volts. This change is accomplished with only a tiny heat loss and a bit of hum from the transformer. Then the power is sent over the long transmission line which is heavily insulated and carefully protected from lightning. While this line is hugely expensive, it has a long life and very low operating cost. At the other end voltage is stepped down to a less dangerous but still efficient for short-distance distribution 6.000-8.000 volts. At the transformer behind your house, or in the transformer vault of the theatre building, the voltage is further reduced to the range used inside. Transformers are the key device is each of these voltage changes.

High voltage DC lines

Some modern long distance transmission lines designed to handle very large amounts of power are now often operated as DC lines because at very high voltages, 500,000 and upwards, losses caused by radiation from the AC lines become significant. Modern converters make it possible to efficiently step up the voltage as AC, convert it to DC for transmission and reconvert to AC at the receiving end of the line enjoying substantial savings along the way.

Early transformer-based dimmers

Transformer action not only determines the availability of power for the theatre, but has also figures repeatedly in the development of lighting control devices within the theatre. In the recent past, much of theatre lighting control depended on direct-control autotransformer dimmers. During this same time, remote control dimmers known as saturable core reactors were installed in a few locations. These too, operated on transformer action. Somewhat later another transformer-like device called the magnetic amplifier came into use. Although all of these dimmers are now obsolete, some of them are still in use. Transformers are also found in the circuitry of a number of control devices and remotely controlled equipment in the theatre and are sometimes used to create special voltages, for example for some types of HID lamps. Thus we need to understand something about their operation.

Magnetic amplifier

How Transformers Work

Two fundamental facts about the relationship between magnetism and electrical current must be clarified:

1. Whenever current flows through a conductor, a magnetic field will exist surrounding that conductor. This field varies in strength with the current and will change as the current changes, therefore AC produces a constantly changing field around conductors carrying it. The field also varies in strength inversely with the distance from the conductor.
2. If a conductor is placed within a moving or changing magnetic field, a voltage will be *induced* in that conductor and, if a circuit is present, current will flow making it possible to derive energy from that current. Note that movement and change of strength have an identical effect on any conductors in the field.

This effect is known as *inductance.*

Inductance

Back EMF

If a length of insulated conductor is stretched out into a line and its resistance to both AC and DC is measured, these figures will be the same. If that same conductor is made into a coil its "resistance" to AC will increase dramatically while its DC resistance remains as first measured. Coiling the wire has concentrated the AC-induced changing magnetic field surrounding the conductor. This field affects the coil itself inducing a voltage that is opposite to and, if there are sufficient coils, nearly equal the voltage being fed into the wire from the outside source. The opposing voltage is called *back EMF* and its resistance-like effect on AC current flow is known as *impedance*. This is the arrangement inside of a transformer where the input coil is known as the *primary*. Its impedance is adjusted so that only a minuscule current will flow through it when no current is being taken from the other coil(s) as described below.

If another coil of insulated wire, known as a *secondary*, is placed within the concentrated and changing field produced by the primary, a voltage will be induced into it. If a circuit is attached to the ends of the coil, current will flow and energy can be taken from it. This energy will come from the primary which will draw current from its source in proportion to the energy withdrawn. More than one secondary coil may be operated simultaneously from the same primary.

A very important effect of this arrangement is that the voltage relationship between the primary and the secondary will be proportional to the number of turns of wire in each coil. If there are more turns in the secondary than in the primary, the voltage will be increased making the transformer a *step-up* transformer. If the turns ratio is reversed, the transformer will become a *step-down* device. Note that within limits, such as quantity of insulation, the same transformer may be operated as either a step-up or a step-down device by reversing the roles of the primary and secondary.

While this transfer and transformation of energy will take place if the two coils of wire are simply placed next to each other, this arrangement is very inefficient. In practical transformers, the coils are carefully wrapped and sometimes even interlaced, around a core made up of soft iron plates. This core concentrates the magnetic field and increases efficiency many times over.

Stepping up or down cannot increase the amount of energy available, indeed there are slight losses, but it can rearrange the relationship between voltage and amperage and effect the changes discussed below.

Another very important effect of using transformers is that they convert the electrical energy coming into them into magnetic energy and then, like a generator, create a new electrical voltage and current which must, however, have the same frequency as the original current. Otherwise, the only connection with the supply current is the energy itself. Not only can the voltage-amperage relationship be completely changed, but also any other conditions such as grounding or phase relationships.

An example of this capability is the *isolation transformer*. This is a transformer with a 1:1 ratio between its primary and secondary. Therefore it does not change voltage at all. However if the primary is grounded as it will be when fed from a standard utility supply, the secondary will remain totally ungrounded ("floating"). This floating secondary is advantageous when powering equipment that must be handled "live," while repairs are effected or, worse, whose outer framework may be live. Supplying the equipment through an isolation transformer will afford the repair person extra safety from shock if he or she becomes inadvertently grounded while working on the equipment. Note that the test bench area should be insulated, including the floor even when an isolation transformer is in use.

Multiple Coil Transformers

Transformers are often built with multiple secondary coils, each producing a different voltage and/or circuit pattern. Obviously, the total power transferred through such a transformer will be the sum of that used in each secondary and should not exceed the capacity of the primary.

Given these facts about electrical current and the equipment required to handle it, we will now follow the course of electrical energy from the power plant to the stage.

Chapter 12

POWER DISTRIBUTION AND THEATRE LIGHTING

This chapter traces the path of electrical current from the generator, which is often far from the theatre, to the stage lighting system. The fact that electrical transmission lines must often extend for hundreds of miles exposes them to nature's powerful electrical generator—lightning. Lightning bolts are huge charges of static electricity that may pass from cloud to cloud or from earth to a cloud. The latter can easily destroy a transmission line if it is in their path, possibly taking the generator out as well. Since transmission lines cost millions of dollars to build and many thousands of people depend on them for electrical energy, such destruction must be avoided. The steps taken to do this affect every user of electrical current, including theatre workers.

Lightning, which passes between a cloud and the earth (actually moving upward from the earth first), seeks the path of least resistance. If that path includes a transmission line, it will be destroyed. Therefore engineers take pains to provide a harmless very low resistance path for the lightning by installing a grounded conductor above the power-carrying lines and also by relating the entire distribution system to the earth. This later step is done by interconnecting one end of each of the three coils of wire in the generator (or their equivalents in more complicated systems) and then attaching these to the earth via an extensive array of conductors buried in the earth. This creates grounded *three-phase AC current*, the standard distribution pattern in the USA. To provide even more protection for the generating station, special traps are installed on the lines leading from it to the transmission system which prevent lightning from backing up into the plant. On the transmission lines themselves, lightning rods and special spark gaps that pass lightning to the earth but block the regular current being transmitted are installed at almost every pole or tower in areas apt to experience lightning.

All of these precautions not only protect the system from lightning, they also influence the way every user of the current must install and handle equipment. The fundamental condition which everyone must deal with is the fact that the entire earth and every conductor connected to it are made part of the distribution system. In effect, everyone who is electrically attached to the earth, by standing on damp ground, for example, is already attached to the common conductor from the generator. Only one more connection is needed to be electrocuted!

The earth is part of every power system.

Grounding the three phases not only affects the conditions likely to cause shock, it also effectively interconnects electrical apparatus in a way that can allow stray currents to pass from one part of the system to another via the ground. This may cause a variety of glitches and even total failure of digital equipment. Obviously grounding exacts a heavy price but its protection is essential in all situations except for systems on ships. Since the hull of a ship is itself firmly grounded by the water, there is little change for lightning to damage the internal electrical system. Furthermore, associating the metal hull with the circuits within the ship is very apt to set up electrolytic reactions between the metal parts of the ship and the water surrounding it that can etch away metal even to the point of destroying the rivets in the hull! Clearly, grounding a ship's electrical system is not a good idea.

Grounding can cause problems.

Many of the following safety precautions are motivated by the necessities of grounding but are designed to make grounding into a safety advantage instead of a hazard.

Terminology

Any conductor intentionally attached to the earth and therefore operating at earth potential, is known as a *grounded conductor*. If it is attached to the conductor representing the combined three wires from the generator and thus serves as the return conductor for the circuits, it is known as the *grounded common neutral*. If it is only connected to the ground of the electrical system via the earth and is installed as a safety precaution to make sure that exposed conductive parts are held at earth potential, it is known as an *equipment ground*.

Grounded conductor

Grounded common neutral

Equipment ground

All conductors carrying current at a voltage other than earth potential, are known as *live* (or "hot") wires. These are potentially dangerous if the voltage in them exceeds about 30 volts.

"Live" or "hot" wires

The current utilized by electrical equipment and any additional current lost along the way is collectively termed the *load*. Note also that the term, load and its companion, line, are also used to refer to connectors. The load connector is attached to the wires running to the load (usually lamps in the theatre) and the line connector is attached to the power supply. This means that the line connector is always live whenever its supply is on but that the load connector is hot only when plugged in.

Load

Line and load connectors

Distribution Systems

To the power company, a "service" is a set of conductors that operate as a unit feeding a building. Note that it is quite possible for a facility to have more than one service, for example, it is required of theatres in some lo-

A "service"

calities that there be a separate service feeding the emergency lighting.

As noted, the basic distribution pattern in the USA consists of three phases, each represented by a live wire and a common neutral making up a four-wire system. Note that for wiring inside structures, a fifth wire is often included which is a safety ground, the *equipment ground*, which will be discussed later. It caries no current under normal circumstances. The four-wire pattern may exist at the common 120-volt household and theatrical voltage or at a variety of much higher and more dangerous voltages.

The grounded common neutral is not always physically present over the entire distance from the generating station to the users. Transformers make it easy to reintroduce this neutral whenever the voltage is changed (see "delta" and "wye" below). Therefore one often sees high voltage transmission lines consisting of just three conductors suspended from large, high voltage insulators, representing the three phases coming from the three coils in the generator.

The grounded common neutral serves as a "return" conductor for all three live wires in the three-phase system. Its current-carrying capacity must be sufficient to handle the load created when all three live conductors are working at capacity. However this current will be less than the sum of the load on the three live wires because of the lag in the current waves. If the load is composed only of devices which alter the amplitude of the 60 Hz wave, such as lamps, motors and early dimmers, the neutral will never need to carry more than the full load of one of the phases and thus need be no larger than the live wires. If the load consists of modern dimmers or other devices which "chop" the waveform, the neutral will need to be larger. This is discussed later in this chapter.

Sizing the neutral

As power is distributed to an area, all three phases, two, or only one may appear at any given user's location. Large theatres, being heavy users of energy, are almost always served by all three phases. Nevertheless it is important for the theatre technician to recognize the following simpler systems because touring to "found locations" (where theatre is performed in whatever space is available) may lead to an encounter with either of these lesser systems.

The two-wire service

This is the simplest and smallest capacity service available. It is normally found only in older homes and small buildings built long before modern heavy-demand electrical appliances were common. It consists of only a single live wire, representing one phase, and a grounded neutral. Total current capacity may be only 30 amperes. Ironically, the wire in these old systems was usually sized for even lower capacity, perhaps 15-20 amperes, and has been illegally upgraded to handle 30 amperes. Fortunately for the many buildings still served by two-wire systems, the original specifications for safe wiring were conservative and the additional 10 amperes usually does not cause a fire or burnout. The old two-wire service will almost certainly not include any provisions for an equipment ground—something almost always required for theatrical lighting.

Theatre workers encountering such a system must either choose to make do with what minuscule wattage is available or (much better) seek to have another service temporarily added to the site.

The three-wire 120–240 volt service

The power company will consider the three-wire service a single phase system because it is normally derived from just one of the company's live high voltage distribution lines plus the common neutral. The supply for a three-wire service comes from a transformer that converts the power from distribution voltage (6000–8000 volts in most localities) to 120–240 volts for the user. The high voltage primary of this transformer is the same as that of any other distribution transformer designed for the voltage in use. The secondary consists of a coil of wire with three connections, one at each end and in the middle of the coil with exactly half of the turns on either side. The number of turns in the entire secondary coil is set to make the voltage from end to end 220-240 volts, depending on the locality. The midpoint of this secondary is grounded making the voltage to ground 110-120 volts on either side. The phase relationship between the two secondary live wires is 180° which means that at the moment one side is at +120 volts, the other is exactly at -120 volts. This arrangement makes the neutral current zero if the loads on the two sides are equal. In the worst condition, the neutral load can only equal the load on one side. Normally, with both sides drawing current, the current in the neutral will equal the difference between the two loads. This arrangement saves wire by making the grounded neutral conductor serve as return conductor for both live wires although it need be no larger than either of the live conductors.

Three-wire services are common in localities where the complete three-phase primary is not available, usually because the power distributor does not deem the potential load in the area worth extending the additional wiring. These services can have large capacity but ordinarily they are used for mid-to-small loads, including small theatres. If the amperage available is enough to satisfy the needs of a traveling lighting technician, a three-wire service will serve as well as the four-wire service (below). However it is necessary that the technician understand the pattern of live and neutral conductors and how the phase relationship is designed to make the neutral serve two live conductors.

Four-wire three-phase services

These services are found in the largest installations and may also be used in many smaller ones. They carry the entire three-phase pattern through to the stage or any other load needing this much power. The phase relationship is reflected in the voltage pattern: any live wire measures 110-120 volts to ground and the voltage between any two live wires measures 208 volts RMS. This voltage reading is the result of the 120° out-of-phase relationship between any two phases.

High voltage supplies for these installations must provide all three phases and may include the neutral. There are two possible arrangements of the primary coils:

Delta: In this arrangement there is no connection for the neutral. Instead the three live wires are connected to the intersections between three primary coils, each with the impedance necessary to handle the primary voltage between phases. (Figure 12.1A)

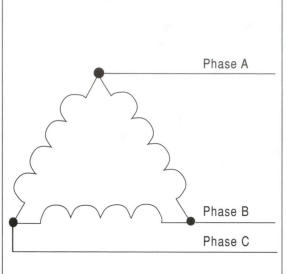

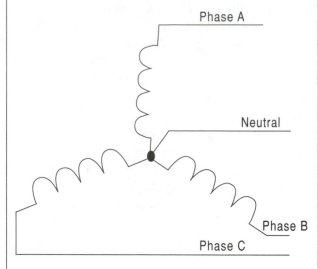

Figure 12.1A. Delta Connection. This arrangement of transformer coils is commonly used in primaries. Note that there is no neutral, however the neutral can be restored by using a transformer with a delta primary and a wye secondary wired as shown in Figure 12.1B.

Figure 12.1B. Wye Connection. This connection is commonly used in secondary hookups of power transformers to supply three-phase, four wire systems. Note that it restores the neutral which is grounded.

Wye: One end of each of the three primary coils is connected together and to the grounded neutral. The other ends are connected to the live high voltage lines. (Figure 12.1B)

For lighting services the secondary coils are always connected in the wye pattern, the three-way interconnection being securely grounded. Note how this reintroduces the grounded neutral even if it is not carried along with the primaries.

Three-phase supply offers economic advantages, particularly where large motors are in use. Therefore theatre structures were, until recently, usually equipped with huge transformer banks supplying three-phase current to the entire facility including the theatre lighting system. However, stage lighting loads have increased dramatically and, in addition modern solid state dimmers have introduced a heretofore unknown problem: harmonics.

Harmonics and the Stage Lighting Service

Until recently, electrical loads in theatres were made up of such things as lamps and motors which simply switch off and on and do not change the waveform the 60 Hz sine wave supplied by the power companies' generators. Dimmers, including resistance types, autotransformers, magamps and saturable core reactors operated by changing the amplitude of the sine wave but did not distort its form. Such loads are known as *linear loads*.

Linear loads

Now things have changed. The "standard" dimmer used in theatres today is a solid state device often called a *phase control dimmer*. Such dimmers constitute a *nonlinear load*. Similar nonlinear loads are also

Nonlinear loads

created by banks of computers and other solid state equipment. These devices do not regulate power by controlling the amplitude of the sine wave; instead, they chop it. Note in Figure 14.2 how the current flow remains at zero until the switching point is reached and the current jumps from zero to a value determined by the supply current wave is at that precise moment and the load. This jump is almost instantaneous. Once the current is turned on, it continues to flow through the remainder of the half-wave and is turned off at the zero-crossing point. Then the same thing happens to the negative half of the sine wave, no flow until the switching point and then flow through the remainder of the half-wave. The result is a chopped wave, no longer a smooth sine wave. The dimming action is controlled by moving the switching point, the earlier in the half-cycle it occurs, the greater the intensity of the light being controlled. The inability of the lamp filaments to respond to these rapid changes assures a smooth light output despite the rapid sequence of on/off periods in the supply current. Note that this description of the chopping action refers to theatrical dimmers only, other kinds of solid state power controls may chop the wave differently.

Chopped wave forms

This chopping effect produces wave forms such as those in Figure 14.2 and, more important to the use of the system, a range of harmonics (unwanted electrical currents) which reflect back through the supply system. The most troublesome harmonics encountered in theatre supplies are known as triplen harmonics. This means that they occur in multiples of three times the original frequency (180, 360 Hz, etc.). They cause current to flow throughout the system and particularly in the neutral, which they may load well beyond the current to be expected from imbalances between the three phases. Such currents can cause overheating, trip breakers even when their regular connected load is well below their capacity, generate noise in sound systems, and cause computer crashes if computers are operated from the same supply. These problems are so severe that the National Electric Code has been revised in a way that strongly encourages the use of a separate and specially designed power service transformer and makes it mandatory that the neutral be either increased in size or downrated and special circuit breakers installed to allow for these often unnoticed currents.

Triplen harmonics

Problems caused by harmonics

Technicians should be aware that their trusty clamp-on ammeter cannot measure these harmonics. A true RMS meter is required. In fact, a comparison between the reading taken with the clamp-on ammeter and one taken with a true RMS meter will give the technician an idea of what proportion of the current flowing through a neutral is normal load unbalance (read by the clamp-on meter) and what load is harmonic-related (the RMS reading minus the regular ammeter reading).

Solving Harmonic Problems

Sizing the Neutral: In permanent installations an engineer familiar with harmonics problems should be employed to evaluate the extent of the harmonics problem and to determine the conductor sizes necessary to operate the system safely over a long period of time. This specialist should note that the theatre is unique with regards this problem because of the possibility of an almost infinite number of variations in the chopping action of the dimmers. Every new setting of any dimmer will alter the calculations. Therefore a rule-of-thumb approach is needed. Typically an increase of about 25% in the size of the neutral will be adequate.

The Power Transformer: Standard power transformers are designed to handle linear loads. Feeding a phase control dimmer system with them can subject them to heating they are not designed to withstand. Therefore K-rated transformers are recommended for this service. This, obviously requires that there be a dedicated transformer for the theatre lighting supply.

The NEC requires that the flow of harmonics into the general building system be limited. A separate K-rated transformer, if hooked up with a delta primary will block circulation of the harmonics back into other supplies operating from the same primary supply. This helps the total system comply with Electrical Code requirements and, just as important, protects the remainder of the building from the hazards of computer failure and other harmonic-induced problems.

Circuit Breakers: The engineer seeking to solve harmonics problems is likely to specify 100% main breakers with electronic trip mechanisms. These breakers are much less likely to trip under false overloads generated by harmonics.

Previously Installed Systems

Obviously there are many lighting systems throughout the country which do not satisfy these standards. Many were installed before harmonics came to light as a problem or were upgraded from linear dimmers to phase control dimmers with no changes in the supply arrangements. Such systems should be carefully inspected for unnoticed damage caused by harmonics. Symptoms such as crashing computers, noisy sound systems and parts operating at higher-than-normal temperatures are likely. The facility's main breaker may be occasionally tripping although the connected load is under its capacity. Such systems may have to be operated at reduced maximum capacity until an upgrade is possible.

Installing new
dimmers in an old
system may cause
problems.

Harmonics are at their greatest power when the dimmers are operated at less-than-full settings although some are present even at full. Therefore operating the system with most of the dimmers at reduced settings, say 80 percent, for long periods will tend to cause the most overheating from harmonics. Those operators with harmonics problems and an inadequate budget for power transformer replacement should get warm lighting on the stage or in the studio by using filters, not by setting all of the dimmers at, say, eight.

Temporary hookups

Although the long-term hazards of heat-induced deterioration may not be a problem, traveling shows are just as susceptible to the remaining problems caused by harmonics as are permanent installations. Heating of the neutral needs to be considered. If the portable dimmer banks are being supplied by separate conductors (now a very common practice), the neutral should be sized at 130 percent of the live feeders. If a "hose" or cable (multiple conductors in the same covering) is being used, its neutral must be considered a current carrying conductor and must be derated to 80 percent of the capacity specified for current-carrying wires to meet NEC standards.

Sizing feeds for portable hookups

Service Entrance Equipment

The term service entrance equipment designates the electrical equipment which brings the power into the building, meters it, and makes the primary distribution to the various parts of the facility. Normally, the power company brings the wiring to the building and attaches it to fittings supplied by the owner. The owner is responsible for wiring from this point on but is usually required to provide metering arrangements immediately after the power is brought into the building. The power company provides and installs the meter. Note that in a large installation, such as a large theatre building, the service entrance equipment may include a transformer or transformers and extensive equipment such as high voltage circuit breakers or switches. Metering will be complicated by the use of current transformers that enable the meter(s) to measure the power indirectly instead of as it flows through the meter itself. However the principle of dividing the responsibility for installation and maintenance remains essentially the same.

High capacity service entrance equipment

Given the power needs of the theatre lighting system and the complications produced by the harmonics-generating dimmers, the lighting system in most modern theatres will likely have its own entirely separate service.

The main switch

Each service must have a main switch or breaker that cuts off the entire supply of current. If it is a switch, the main fuses that protect the entire system will be installed immediately below the switch mechanism. If it is a breaker, it will be large, often motor operated. In either case, it is the last resort cutoff protection in case of major shorts. Although the theatre technician will seldom need to operate this switch, he or she should know where it is and have access to it in emergencies. If the building has multiple services, a common situation in buildings containing theatres plus other major power-using facilities, users should be aware that shutting off only one of the main switches may leave large parts of the building wiring still live. It is even possible that the building will have service entrance equipment in more than one location. Therefore workers should take precautions before touching any internal parts or bare wires by checking each conductor or piece of equipment to be sure that it is not live even after turning off the main.

The last-resort cutoff

Users should note that if fuses are used at the main, the failure of a single fuse only turns off that part of the system served by that fuse, the remainder remains live. If a multipole breaker is in use, and this is the most common type, it will shut down all lines passing through it.

Mains are sized when the building is built or during major renovations. They should be designed to allow for future expansion of the electrical load. Since theatres are very apt to acquire additional lighting equipment over the years, there is a tendency for the lighting load to increase, eventually using up the capacity allowed for expansion. This can lead to a very expensive wiring project because new service entrance equipment and its installation are hugely expensive and time consuming.

General building supplies

Although the trend toward separate services for theatre lighting make it less likely, many theatrical services will also include supplies for the remainder of the building, including such heavy power users as air conditioning, heating and ventilation, shop equipment and the like. These supplies will branch off directly from the main. Normally the theatre technician need only know what these supplies are and recognize that they should not be inadvertently shut off.

Emergency lighting

Power for emergency lighting

Emergency lighting will be discussed in detail later. However it relates to the mains because almost every electrical code requires, at minimum, that there be a separate supply dedicated to the emergency system. In some localities the requirement is even more stringent: There must be a separate service independent of all other supplies from the power company lines inward. Some even require that the power company provide separate high voltage feed for this service, a very expensive arrangement.

House lighting supply

House lighting must be independent of stage lighting.

The law usually requires that the house lighting be arranged so that it will continue to work even if the stage lighting system fails completely. Note that this is not part of the emergency lighting which may be battery or generator operated, but a requirement for the normal house lighting. This requirement can usually be met by providing a separate branch-off for house lighting immediately after the main. This system may contain dimmers for the house lights if they can be overridden in an emergency.

Stage Lighting Supply

As noted, in modern facilities this supply will come from its own transformer and therefore have its own power lead into the building and its own meter. On older buildings that have not been updated, the stage supply will be one of the larger branch-offs coming just after the building main. In either case, the switch or breaker serving the stage is the last resort overcurrent protection for the entire stage lighting facility. It is also the shutoff to be used when servicing the stage main switch or breaker. Again a caution is necessary: Shutting off this stage main will not necessarily render the total stage lighting setup dead. Emergency circuits, house lighting circuits and control wiring for assorted electrically operated switches (relays) may remain live. Always test before touching.

Heavy-current wiring

A cardinal rule of electrical wiring is that an overcurrent protector must be installed at each point where wire size is reduced. This fuse or breaker must be sized to protect the wiring beyond the overcurrent device. It cannot protect that which comes before it. In the case of the wiring leading to the stage lighting system this works out as follows: If there is a special transformer and service for the stage lighting, a main overcurrent device will be installed in the service entrance area just beyond the meter sized to protect the wiring going to the theatre itself. If the theatre supply comes from a larger, but not separate building service, its main will be a branch-off from the general building supply sized to protect the wiring leading to the theatre. At the theatre end of this wiring another main is installed which is sized to protect the wiring from that point forward to the dimmer bank and other stage lighting equipment. Note that this means that there are two main breakers, one at the service entrance and one at the theatre. To prevent random failure in case of heavy loads or shorts, the breaker at the theatre end should have a smaller ampere rating than the service entrance breaker.

> Overcurrent devices protect only those elements beyond them in the system.

Note that the breaker at the theatre end is *not* the main blackout switch—it should only rarely need to be thrown, particularly while loaded. Switches or breakers used for protection of wiring and equipment are not designed to be used frequently to control lighting and will fail prematurely if so used. Modern electronic control affords myriad ways of setting up a blackout when one is needed, all of which use dimmers and dimmer-like off-on devices to control the current, not the main.

> The main is not the blackout switch.

From the stage main, the current will be conducted within the cabinets and the dimmer rack by means of bus bars. These are copper bars mounted on insulators inside the enclosures. They are arranged to allow ends of wires and the input ends of breakers or dimmers themselves to be attached to them. If the theatre has three-phase feeds, there will be four bus bars, one for each phase and one, much larger, for the neutral. The arrangement of these bus bars and the heavy wiring going to and from them is a matter of much consideration for the equipment designer who must take into account the very strong magnetic field that will surround these conductors when they are in use. If a loop is inadvertently created, the entire enclosure may be turned into a "coil" of a transformer creating stray but heavy current in the frame itself.

> Bus bars

Temporary hookups

Well equipped theatres will have a *company switch* installed on stage that solves the problem of the touring stage electrician who needs to power up a portable lighting system. It will be properly protected by a breaker or fuses, will have special bus bars to which the portable system may be attached and will be labeled as to capacity, voltage and phases

> Company switch

present. There will be no other theatre equipment fed from this switch. Regrettably, many older stages have company switches (sometimes called "bull switches") that have been "pirated" to supply stage equipment or have mysterious (and unlabeled) arrangements of bus bars or hookup points. In other cases there will be no company switch at all. In this case, the touring lighting technician, the building engineer or even an outside electrician hired for the job must make attachments to whatever service offers enough amperage to run the show, obviously after gaining the proper permission. Therefore it is necessary for theatre lighting technicians to understand the intricacies of general building supplies and to be able to make the proper safety tests before attaching any wiring or concluding that a professional electrician must do the job.

Jury-rigged hookups

Older systems which lack a company switch will probably have a "stage main" somewhere on or near the stage which serves as the last-resort protection for the stage system short of whatever is installed at the service entrance point. If this "main" is not already loaded to capacity (or if a substantial part of the load can be turned off when the portable system is in use) it can serve as a good substitute for a company switch. It should be carefully tested for its phase arrangement before any connections are made. Also proper permission should be acquired before making any connections.

The stage main can sometimes serve as a company switch.

If such a main is not usable, it may be necessary to use the building supply equipment at the service entrance point. Such connections tend to be more complicated than those made at the stage main. It may even be necessary to do the work "hot." Unless the traveling technician is a licensed electrician, familiar with building wiring practices and quirks, and with the dangerous art of working on live wires, it is advisable that such an electrician be hired to make the connections.

Study the System, Then Make the Connections

The first step in making a connection at the company switch or the stage main should be to open the enclosure and examine the wiring, being careful not to touch any parts that could conceivably be live. A modern main for a stage supply or company switch will normally include all three phases plus the grounded neutral. The neutral will be the large bus bar to which one or more large white insulated wires are attached and which may also have a number of small white wires attached. Note that the neutral will not be opened by the switch or breaker that controls the three hot wires. It must remain continuous according to the NEC.

If the switch under consideration is part of the service entrance equipment, it is likely that a bare copper wire (or a wire with green insulation) of considerable size will be attached directly to the steel switch enclosure and perhaps, depending on local practices, to the grounded neutral. This wire is an equipment or "safety" ground. Its other end will be attached to a nearby cold water pipe or to a special grounding rod driven into the earth. This connection is unlikely to appear in a company switch. Its enclosure is grounded by the metal conduits attached to it.

CHAPTER **12**

If the switch is a stage main, it may be mechanically attached directly to a distribution panel that includes rows of breakers that fed the stage dimmers, non-dim circuits and any utility circuits served by this main. The usual configuration will be a set of three long bus bars arranged so that the feed side of the breakers can be attached directly to them. The loads will be attached to the output end of the breakers. Old fuse-controlled systems follow much the same pattern. It is absolutely necessary to discover from local authorities what these loads are and what part of them can be turned off to release capacity for the temporary equipment. The mechanical attachment of the portable feeds will have to be made by means of clamps attached to the bus bars wherever there is space to make the connection without shorting anything out. However this connection should not be made until after it has been determined that the system can handle the load and proper permission has been received.

If the switch is a company switch there should be no wiring attached to the output of the breaker or switch, instead the live conductors should terminate in bus bars to which the feeds for the portable equipment can be clamped. If other circuitry has been "pirated" from the company switch, the local electrician will have to be queried to find out how much of that switch's original capacity has been taken away and whether any of the pirated loads can be temporarily turned off.

If other conductors are found in the main switch enclosure or if it contains relays, these should be treated with caution and avoided when the hookup is made. Note that in some large installations, the main breaker itself will be a motor-driven or magnetic device which may include small conductors as part of its inner workings. These small conductors may remain live when the main breaker is in "off" position.

In either a company switch or stage main the three phases will be supplied by conductors which are normally colored, black and red, and blue, one color for each phase. Note that some old systems may not follow this color coding. Test before handling following the instructions below. Unlike the neutral, these conductors will pass through both the meter and the main breaker or switch and fuses. They will definitely be live as long as the main is on. Also note that the lines feeding the main will be live and will remain live even when the breaker or switch itself is turned off. If there is another breaker or set of fuses that protects these lines, it will be a large capacity device found immediately following the meter. From the meter outward, there is seldom any more overcurrent protection short of the fuses in the high voltage feeds for the supply transformer. These are not apt to open for any short circuit less than catastrophic. All of this wiring should be carefully avoided while working.

After surveying the service entrance setup, the technician should be ready to make the tests below to be sure of the voltage and phase of any connections being considered and to also be sure that whatever equipment is to be handled is not live. Note that many professional electricians make connections to live equipment and do so with safety. The theatre technician is advised not to try this unless he or she is a professional electrician and has complete confidence in his or her ability to do the job.

Note that these same precautions and procedures for investigating the supply wiring apply if a failure occurs in the main power supply system and theatre technician must try to repair it. The most important rule: *Do not touch any potentially live part without first testing to be sure that it is dead and making certain that it cannot suddenly come on.*

Testing for hot and neutral connections

Test equipment: Any standard volt-ohm-milliammeter (VOM) will serve. Actually only its voltage function will be needed for this test but VOMs are often cheaper than simple voltmeters and offer other features that the technician will find useful. These devices are available at any electronics supply house for very reasonable prices and should be part of the tool kit of every theatrical technician. One or more lengths of insulated wire equipped with insulated pinch clamps at either end will aid in extending connections from the inside of the equipment to the meter and to a ground connection.

The following tests should be made on any equipment before touching potentially live parts, labeled or not. It is wise to make two sets of tests, the first with the main switch in off position and the second with it on. This should give a clear picture of which parts are continuously live and those controlled by the switch or breaker. During all of these steps, the technician should be absolutely certain that he or she is not grounded.

1. *Test for hot and grounded conductors.* As these tests are made, the operator should be sure to handle only insulated parts of the VOM. Set the scale of the meter on about 300 volts and be sure that it is set to read AC voltage.

    A. *Locate a known ground connection* such as a cold water pipe (*not* gas or hot water), or the frame of the electrical equipment if the system is reasonably modern. If there is any doubt about the ground, locate a known hot connection such as the live side of a convenience outlet and attach one lead of the VOM to this and the other to the probable ground. The meter should read 110-120 volts; never more than 130 volts.

    B. *Test the various parts to determine if they are "live."* Attach one lead from the VOM to the now-known ground. Use the other lead as a test probe to evaluate various parts of the equipment. If the part is live, the meter should read 110-120 volts. If any part tested causes the meter to read 130 volts or more, there is either major trouble with the system or the panel being examined is designed to use higher voltages than the theatre can use. The connection should be avoided.

    C. *Test for grounds and open connections.* Parts that produce no voltage reading at all or only a tiny waver of the VOM needle, must be treated with suspicion. They may be totally disconnected or they may be part of a circuit that will come on unexpectedly, such as a yard lighting system designed to come on at dusk. Such conductors should be rare in main service panels, but they can turn up just often enough to trip up the unwary. Avoid them.

        When testing old systems it is also a good idea to test for voltage between the system's grounded neutral at the main and a good earth ground such as a cold water pipe while the resident system is in operation. There should be little, if any voltage between these two points. If more than a few volts difference is found when the system's dimmers are all at full on, an electrician should check the entire system for faults. Such voltage can cause noisy sound systems and numerous other troubles.

2. Determine the type of service. This should be evident from the number and color coding of the live wires present, but should still be carefully checked. Odd voltages and strange phase relationships can occasionally occur. For instance, two hot lines and a neutral would normally be assumed to be a three-wire 120-240V service. However, changes made to adapt the system to increased loads may lead to other possibilities: The two hot wires may be two thirds of a three-phase supply or they may both be the same hot feed from a single-phase 120-240V supply.

Refer to the table below, Voltage Test Using a Voltmeter, for the range of proper voltages readings to be expected. Readings above or below these figures indicate either special circuitry or that the equipment is faulty. In either case, avoid any conductors that produce such readings.

3. *Determine the amount of power that can be drawn from the supply for the traveling production.* If the hookup point is at a company switch which is properly labeled its capacity will be evident. If not, check fuse sizes or the ampere rating of the breaker. Such figures should not be trusted without noting the size of the breaker or main switch feeding the company switch. If the system is old and the resident stage equipment inventory has grown, this may already be loaded to capacity without taking into account any load from the company switch. The best source of information on this subject is the local stage electrician, if one is available. If such a person is not available or is unable to supply the information, the traveling technician will have to add up the wattage of all loads on

VOLTAGE TEST USING VOLTMETER	
CONDITION TESTED	METER READING
Both conductors from same phase	zero
Two live busses from single phase 120-240V feed	240 volts
Both busses from one side of above feed	zero
Any two live busses from 120-208V three-phase system	208 volts
Hot bus to ground	100-120 volts

The above voltage readings may vary several volts in either direction without cause for alarm. However higher than normal voltages will shorten lamp life

the resident system that must remain on, calculate the amps and subtract that from the amp rating of the main supply. The difference will be the maximum load available. It is advisable to leave at least a ten percent safety factor when making the actual hookup particularly if the voltage of the supply is subject to variation.

4. *Hook up the portable equipment.* Proceed as follows:
   A. Hook up the equipment ground of the portable system to a known and secure ground such as a cold water pipe. *Do not use the local system grounded neutral as the equipment ground.*
   B. Attach the grounded neutral conductor(s) from the portable system to the grounded neutral connection at the company switch (or the main, if that is being used).
   C. Hook up the live feeds matching the feeds to the portable system to the available phases in the resident system. This may involve making internal adjustments in the portable dimmer racks to adjust for various phase situations. Make these adjustments and carefully test before activating the system.

Note that it is of the utmost importance to hook up the grounded neutral before hooking up any live conductors. This guarantees that no voltage over 110–120 volts AC will be imposed on any part of the portable system as long as its internal connections match the phase arrangement of the supply.

ELECTRICAL SAFETY IN THE THEATRE

Electrical current is dangerous. Every year people are killed or seriously injured by electrical accidents. There are two kinds of danger: that from electrical shock and that caused indirectly by electrical fires. The danger of electrocution is often ignored because of our familiarity with electrical equipment. Even in our homes, there is enough electrical energy at any socket or outlet to kill several people at once. In the theatre, although the voltage is the same as that at home, the amount of current can be many times that available in a home outlet. This increases both the danger from shock and the danger of electrical fire.

Even home current is dangerous.

How Much Current Is Fatal?

Electrical shock kills by overwhelming the body's own electrical system—minute electrical impulses which convey many of the signals that pass constantly through our nervous system. Heat can also play a part. The amount of damage done when current flows through the body depends on the part of the body involved and the amperage that flows. Voltage, per se, is relatively harmless without appreciable current. Therefore the body can withstand, with only minor annoyance, the effect of several thousand volts of static electricity passing through it as the result of scuffing across a dry carpet. On the other hand, a fraction of an ampere at "only" 120 volts passing through vital parts of the body can be fatal. Worse, under certain conditions a much smaller amount of electrical energy can kill. Fortunately it is not likely to happen on stage or at home, but even a few thousandths of an ampere at as low as 40 volts can kill if this current passes through the most vital parts, while say, on an operating table. Thus electrical danger varies with the part of the body included in the circuit—not a matter to be studied by trial and error!

Very small amounts of current can be deadly.

Legal Aspects

The basic hazards in the use of electrical current are based in the laws of physics, how electrical current flows, its affect on the human body and on the equipment that uses it. Since human beings do not always act in a way that conforms with the laws of physics, man-made laws are devised to control their folly. These can be state, county or city ordinances or codes that the theatrical technician must be aware of and obey if he or she is to work safely and avoid legal difficulties. Many of these laws have their origin in the *National Electrical Code* (NEC), a model safety code produced by the National Fire Protection Association, a nongovernmental body supported by the fire insurance companies. This document, generally known as "the Code," is revised every three years. Revisions have the benefit of input from theatre specialists by way of representatives to the Code revision body from the United States Institute for Theatre Technology (USITT) and from Entertainment Services and Technology Association (ESTA). Additionally, as revisions are being worked out, input is solicited from a wide variety of sources, including theatre technicians in addition to those who sit on the committee. The final version is then published and is widely available including copies in public libraries and on sale at many bookstores. It may also be purchased directly from the National Fire Protection Association, 60 Batterymarch Street, Boston, Massachusetts 02110. Every theatre technician should have a current copy in his or her library.

It is important to know that "The Code" has no legal status of its own; it is merely a set of recommendations. However, it is almost universally written into local law either by being accepted wholesale or as a backup to local law. This practice gives the code the power of law. Generally in large municipalities such as New York City or Los Angeles, an extensive locally-written code is enforced which is more stringent than the National Code. In such places, there is nearly always a "cover-all" stipulation that says that any areas not specifically covered by local ordinance must conform with the NEC.

Clearly every lighting technician must be very sure that he or she understands the safety laws. This includes not only a familiarity with the NEC, but specific understanding of local ordinances. This is important for everyday lighting activities but comes to the forefront when the lighting technician is making recommendations for renovation or construction of theatre lighting systems. Often this knowledge will work to the advantage of the technician. Local ordinances that cover general construction often impose wiring practices that are not only inappropriate to the theatre, but are excessively costly. With the exception of very large cities, few local laws involve themselves with the specifics of the theatre. Referring to the NEC will provide the technician with details specifically related to the theatre and moreover, these regulations will be better suited to the needs of the theatre.

The UL Label

The National Fire Protection Association also supports another safety-related activity, the Underwriters' Laboratories, Incorporated. This is an

National Electrical Code (NEC)

Who has input into the code?

The Code is the basis for most local laws.

Local codes are often inappropriate to the theatre.

equipment-testing group which, for a fee, tests electrical equipment for safety and grants the use of the "UL label" to equipment that meets its standards. It is very important to note that the UL label relates only to the safety of the equipment, not to its durability or effectiveness. Testing is voluntary, although having a UL label can be a great advantage, particularly when local laws require UL-approved equipment and/or specifications for new facilities insist on it.

UL label

The cost of testing, which may be considerable, is borne by the manufacturer who submits the equipment to the laboratory for testing. Each model change requires a new test at additional cost. Therefore lighting equipment manufacturers tend to limit testing to those items in their inventory that are planned to be in their catalogues for long periods of time. Thus the absence of the label, particularly from rare or newly released equipment, should not be interpreted to mean that the equipment is unsafe. It will be up to the theatre technician to study the equipment and make a judgment as to its safety as well as its efficiency and durability. If a large purchase is being considered, it may be worthwhile to have a testing laboratory examine the equipment. Additionally, some municipalities require testing of equipment being purchased, sometimes even in addition to the UL test, if this has been done. This can add a great deal to the cost of the equipment.

Special Legal Obligations of the Lighting Artist or Technician

The lighting specialist's first obligation is to the audience. They are his or her guests and there is a legal obligation to protect them from injury. The second obligation is to protect the life and limb of the theatre personnel and, finally, to protect the theatre, its equipment, and the production onstage from damage.

Since the audience is the first priority, the theatre worker will find that there are usually extra-stringent laws concerning their surroundings, particularly what hangs over their heads. For example, a falling color frame is a menace anywhere, but laws usually require that frames be prevented from falling on the audience by special mesh barriers at the openings of any lighting positions over the house. Backstage however, luminaires with color frames may hang in the open on battens although many localities require that they be restrained by safety lines.

Overhead safety

In addition to the moral obligation that each member of the theatre troupe has toward the audience, there is the very real risk of personal liability suits if someone is killed or injured. When an accident happens and a suit is filed, the usual procedure is to sue everyone who might conceivably share the blame. This can include anyone working on or in the production. If the suit is successful, the damages may be apportioned among all of those sued. A judgement can cloud one's financial future for years making credit difficult to get and taking away earnings. Obviously, the best defense against this threat is to abide by safety laws in every detail and make every effort to care for the audience and one's fellow workers.

Personal liability

Lighting Equipment for Safety: Exit Lights

Backup power for exit lights

Special signs reading "EXIT" are illuminated so that they can be seen even if all other lighting is off. This means that they must operate on special electrical circuits that are guaranteed to remain on during a power outage. The extent of this guarantee depends on local law—there are even instances where the local code requires that the exit lights be baked up by gaslights on the theory that these will continue to operate for a useful period of time on the gas in the lines when all else fails. A more reasonable approach is to provide each exit sign with two lamps, one operated on its own special supply taken off at the service entrance and the other supplied by the emergency lighting batteries or an emergency generator circuited to come on if the first goes out.

Exit lights must remain on with the brightness established when they were installed. No orders from a director should be allowed to cause them to be turned off or obstructed in the theatrical interest of a complete blackout or because they distract from a dark scene. If the lighting technician cannot enforce this rule himself or herself and the remainder of the theatrical hierarchy cannot or will not enforce this rule, the fire marshal should be notified and asked to inspect the premises and explain the rule on the operation of exit lights. A reminder of the risks of personal liability suits may also help.

It is illegal to tamper with the exit lights.

Maintenance of exit lights will not ordinarily fall to the theatre technician but that person should be supplied with a stock of the proper lamps for replacing those which go out when the regular staff is not available and there is to be an audience in the theatre. It is both illegal and dangerous to go through a performance with a non-operating exit light.

Panic Lighting

Any space occupied by an audience should be equipped with special lighting to enable the audience to leave safely in case of an emergency which causes the regular lighting to fail. Even if the space is so small that the law does not require such equipment, prudence dictates that it should be present.

Panic lights operate when other power is off

Panic lighting is normally off. A special transfer switch turns it on automatically when the regular power fails. The supply is either a special bank of batteries or a special generator equipped to start up when the panic system calls for energy. The evidence of the panic system will often be the presence of a mysterious second lamp in each house lighting fixture and exit light case. It is reassuring to observe these lamps come on when there is a power outage and remain on until the power is restored even when no audience is present.

Although maintenance and testing of this system is not a normal task for the theatre electrician, that person should be familiar with the panic system and know how to operate it in an emergency. This system is subject to inspection by the fire marshal without notice. It is also required to be inspected at regular intervals by designated member of the building staff. A prudent theatre technician will accompany some of these inspections to be assured that the inspections are being properly done and that the equipment is in good working order. For example, it is not enough for a staff "inspector" to open the door to the battery room, determine that the batteries are still there close the door and move on. The batteries should be checked for proper charge and for any signs of impending trouble such as sludge in the bottoms of the containers or low electrolyte.

Inspecting the panic system

"Package" Panic Lighting

Small theatres and other locations where panic lighting is required because the laws have changed since the facility was built or where such lighting is a good idea although not legally required, can often make use of package units that can be installed with a minimum of wiring. These units contain a battery, a trickle charger to keep the battery at full charge, one or two low voltage lamps similar to automobile spotlight lamps, and a system to turn on the battery operated lamps if the AC power fails. AC is supplied for the battery charger and the sensor by a regular AC cord plugged into a convenience outlet or the unit may be hard wired to a normally-on AC line.

Clearly, these units do not provide the reliability provided by a complete panic lighting system; for example, they respond to failures in the circuit feeding them even if the remainder of the building is still powered. They too, should be checked regularly for proper operation and to determine the state of the battery. If the battery is allowed to deteriorate, the unit may come on in a crisis and almost immediately dim out—a very dangerous event.

Package units must also be inspected.

Preventing Electrical Shock

Most electrical shocks are technically grounds. That is, they are caused by the victim making a connection between a live part and something electrically connected with the earth. Of course, it is equally or even more deadly to become part of a connection between two live wires on differing phases, but this is less likely. Since the earth is a part of almost every electrical distribution system in use, one must remember that being connected to the earth is the equivalent of holding one of the wires from the generator. Only one more connection is needed. The best policy is to assume that you are grounded unless you are certain that you are not. Structural steel, stage pipe battens, concrete floors, plumbing, electrical conduit and enclosures are all grounded as are external metal parts of luminaires, microphones, sound equipment, stage floor pockets and almost any other conducting material that encloses electrical apparatus. This grounding is required by law so that, if a fault occurs and the part becomes live, this will immediately constitute a short circuit which will open the fuse or circuit breaker eliminating the danger and signaling that there is trouble.

Electricians who must work with live equipment take precautions to avoid being grounded and try to work with only one hand, keeping the other in a pocket. It should rarely be necessary for stage technicians to work "hot." However, as discussed below, there may be situations where

Assume you are grounded.

Equipment is grounded for safety.

the technician finds that he or she has inadvertently encountered a live piece of equipment.

Common Backstage Hazards

Perhaps the most common hazard occurs when a luminaire goes dead and a crew member is sent to find out why and, if possible, get it back in service. The failure could be simply a burned out lamp, it could be caused by the leads burning off at the socket, or a number of other faults in the wiring. If the luminaire is properly wired with an equipment ground (below) and the burned-off lead touches its frame there should be a short circuit which trips the breaker or burns out the fuse. However equipment is not always properly wired and burned off wires do not automatically contact the frame. If an unsuspecting crew member handles the equipment without disconnecting it and the supply remains on, as it often does if another luminaire still in use is also on the same circuit, that crew member is in danger of shock if he or she contacts anything grounded. The proper practice is to unplug the equipment at the connection nearest to the luminaire before handling it. This is the reason that luminaires are equipped with short leads; there is always a connection within easy reach. Note that it is not safe to merely shut off the circuit at the console before working on it. Someone may accidentally turn it on. Even if the equipment only requires relamping, technicians should remember that many types of lamps have current-carrying parts that extend some distance from the base of the lamp and thus can be contacted as the lamp is being inserted. *Always disconnect the equipment before working on it.*

Another hazard, frayed leads where they enter the equipment, has been somewhat diminished by the use of modern materials. Until recently all luminaires were wired with asbestos-insulated leads because these could withstand the high heat inside. Asbestos, while resistant to heat, was subject to abrasion and often wore through at the point where the wires entered the housing. However asbestos is now outlawed and all lighting equipment should have heat-resistant leads of fiberglass or high-temperature plastic. Both resist abrasion better than asbestos did but both will eventually fail. The solution is proper maintenance of equipment and the use of a proper equipment ground. Note that if an old theatre still has asbestos leads in service, these should immediately be replaced observing the proper procedures for handling the asbestos.

An equipment ground is a separate conductive path from the frame or enclosure of any piece of electrical equipment to the earth. Although this path may be connected to the grounded neutral at one point, usually at the service entrance, it must be continuous without depending on the grounded neutral. In permanently installed gear, the equipment ground is usually the metal framework of the equipment itself which is firmly connected to the earth. Where a wire is used to maintain the continuity of the equipment ground, it may be either bare copper or insulated with *green* insulation. (Note that the grounded neutral is required to be *white*.)

Portable equipment presents a special problem. It cannot be perma-

Asbestos insulated leads are outlawed.

The equipment ground should be either bare copper or have green insulation.

nently wired to the earth. Therefore it must be so wired that it becomes grounded before it is connected to any electrical supply. A third conductor, colored green, is carried along in all supply cables and connected by means of special prongs on the connectors that are longer than the current-carrying connections so they will make contact first. Inside the equipment itself the green wire is firmly attached to the conductive frame or enclosure. This makes certain that the outer parts of equipment remain at ground potential and that any contact between a live wire and the frame or enclosure will cause a fuse to blow or a breaker to open. *It is legally required that all portable equipment in new or largely renovated theatres have an equipment ground.* All old installations should be converted to the equipment ground system as soon as possible.

Modern wiring codes require that the grounded neutral contain no interruptions that might break its continuity. This is why it bypasses any fuses or breakers in the service panel. However a problem may arise in temporary installations where the power wiring is reconnected at each location. Proper procedure requires that the equipment ground be the first connection made, the neutral second, and then the live conductors. If this procedure is not followed and two or more phases are hooked up first and accidentally turned on, more than 120 volts may be applied to the equipment, including dimmers and lamps. Older dimmers may burn out (modern ones are usually capable of protecting themselves). Lamps will burn out rapidly creating a costly lamp replacement bill and the equipment will display higher and more deadly voltages where these should not be. *Always connect the equipment ground and the neutral before connecting any live conductors.*

Connect the equipment ground first and disconnect it last.

Avoiding the Dangers of Electrically Generated Heat

Electrical current is not only dangerous because shock can maim or kill, heat from an uncontrolled electrical flow can cause fire or explosion destroying equipment and buildings and very possibly taking lives. Therefore special equipment is used to be very certain that a flow of current is either under control or is cut off almost instantly.

We have already examined the way electrical current almost inevitably generates heat and the way that the heat generated increases geometrically with the current (the heat formula). Except for the phenomenon of superconductivity, which is not found on stage, every flow of current involves the production of heat. The greater the amperage and/or the resistance, the greater the heat. Fuses and circuit breakers are designed to protect against unwanted increases in amperage. However they cannot protect against unwanted increases in resistance. Although heat only increases linearly with resistance, it can have an insidious effect. If, for example, a loose connection develops in a stage connector while it is in use thereby increasing its resistance, more than normal heat will develop at the connection. This heat will cause oxidation of the brass or copper parts of the connector and wire. Oxides of these metals have greater resistance than the pure metals, increasing the resistance at the loose connection still more. The greater heat hastens more oxidation and the vicious circle spins to a fiery conclusion: Parts of

Electrically caused heat can cause fire or explosion.

Fuses or breakers will not protect against the effects of loose connections until they short out.

the connector break down and a short circuit or fire may result. Ironically, all of this can happen without any increase in the amperage (until a short occurs) and thus will not be controlled by the fuse or circuit breaker.

This sneaky heating of loose connections is often the cause of "mysterious" nighttime residential fires. A loose connection smouldering away in the attic is not a pleasant thing to contemplate. Fortunately for the theatre, this nighttime hazard seldom happens there. Theatre equipment is routinely shut down after the show and no current is available at any loose connections until the equipment is turned back on in the morning. However, when the current is on, the failure and destruction of equipment from loose connections remains a hazard. It can interrupt a production or even set the theatre on fire.

Careful maintenance and vigilance are the best protection against loose connections. Every technician should develop the habit of occasionally feeling any connectors within reach to see if they are warm or worse, hot. If any are found, they should be repaired or replaced as soon as possible.

Overloads and Short Circuits

Overload

An *overload* is defined as any flow of current greater than the equipment, or the weakest part of an array of equipment is designed to handle. This can be as little as a fraction of an ampere or it can be so massive that it has the same effect as a short circuit.

Short circuit

A *short circuit* is an essentially uncontrolled flow of current. Resistance has dropped to near zero and all of the current available will attempt to flow through the short circuit. The only limiting factor is the amount of current available in the system and the resistance of the lines leading to the short circuit. The effect of a short circuit can be fire and violent explosion if not immediately controlled by an overcurrent device. Long runs of wire can be turned into red hot copper, their insulation set afire or even vaporized almost instantly. Fire, often extended over the entire run of wiring leading to the short, is almost immediate. Even if the short circuit clears itself in moments by burning off the conductors, it can leave a fire smoldering and dangerous.

Short circuits are dangerous.

Note that there is little difference in the effect of a massive overload and a short circuit. Both impose a huge increase in current on the equipment and can have the same effect. It is academic to note that the massive overload is "controlled" by whatever low resistance exists in the circuit as compared to the totally uncontrolled flow in a short circuit.

There are two ways a short circuit can happen:

Phase-to-phase short circuit

- Two current carrying conductors fed from different phases come into direct contact with each other with no current-limiting device such as a lamp or motor between them. For example, two wires fed from different phases bared because their insulation has worn off touch and create a short circuit.

Live-to-ground short circuit

- A live conductor leading to a load comes into contact with a conductor electrically attached to the earth. Since the earth is part of the electrical system, a very low resistance circuit is completed back to the generator and all of the current available in the live conductor flows through the contact point. Again, the result is sparks, fire and explosion.

The conditions for a short or ground may occur while the current is off and the actual damage appear when the current is turned on.

If the return conductor (the grounded common neutral) from a load contacts a grounded part, a *ground fault* will occur instead of a short. Current will continue to flow normally through the load but will return through the regular return path *and through the ground*, in proportion to the resistance of each path. Although such a ground will not usually cause immediate trouble, it should be found (see ground fault circuit interrupter below) and corrected to avoid trouble with sound or other equipment that depends on a "clean" ground connection (one through which no current is flowing). Also, heat may be released at the point of contact with the ground causing a fire.

Ground fault

Control of Short Circuits and Grounds

Obviously the first defenses against shorts and grounds are the use of good quality equipment and the practice of preventative maintenance. Portable equipment, particularly cables should be checked frequently, connectors replaced when they show signs of wear and the entire cable inspected for evidence of crushing or tears. Any cable which runs hot while in use should be checked for overload and the load reduced or the cable replaced with one of higher current carrying capacity.

Good maintenance is vital.

Given good equipment and maintenance, the backup protection lies in overcurrent protection devices—in a theatre this means fuses or circuit breakers. Overcurrent devices are designed to cut off the current if trouble develops. While this will avoid a disastrous electrical fire or explosion, it will also interrupt all or part of the lighting for a show, a situation that must be avoided if at all possible.

Fuses and circuit breakers

Fuses

These are the earliest and simplest of overcurrent devices. The working part of a fuse is a piece of soft alloy (somewhat like solder) usually in the form of a ribbon sized to heat up, melt and break the circuit at the current rating of the fuse. This piece of metal, known as the *fuse link*, is located in the circuit so that all current that passes through the circuit must pass through the fuse, i.e., it is in series with the load. If too much flows, the link melts (or explodes in the case of a heavy short), breaking the circuit. Fuses up to about 60 amperes are throwaway devices. Once they have blown, they are discarded. Larger sizes are often made with replaceable links as described below.

The fuse link

Fuses are sized when the electrical installation is made following the stipulations of the NEC and/or local ordinances. Sizing is either based on the size of the wire that leads away from the fuse toward the load or on the rated amperage of the equipment to be protected by the fuse, whichever is smaller. Once established by a qualified electrician, the size should not be altered except by another qualified person who is following the latest code information.

Sizing fuses

Although there is a huge variety of fuses, only a few are normally found in theatrical lighting situations. The two most common are cartridge fuses and plug fuses (Figure 13.1). Although the working part of both is much the same, their appearance is quite different. Cartridge fuses are usually used for heavy current situations such as mains or sub-mains. Their sturdy outer enclosure can withstand the considerable explosive effect of a blowout under a massive short circuit. The larger amperage types have blade connections to handle the large amount of current they must carry. These fuses are often made so that they can be disassembled and a new fuse link installed. This allows for capacity changes within limits determined by the size of the housing and also for replacement in case of burnout. Small cartridge fuses are usually not made to be disassembled. Although small cartridge fuses rated at 30 amperes or less were common in early stage lighting installations, they are rare now. They were replaced first by plug fuses and more recently by circuit breakers.

Plug fuses are still quite common; they are still in use in old household power boxes and in some old theatres. They come in a variety of amperages, from 5 to 30 amps, all the same size and shape. Any of these amperages will fit into the standard fuse socket designed for plug fuses. This interchangeability is their weakness. It makes it far too easy for an unknowing or careless person to increase the amperage limitation on a circuit by simply replacing a low-amperage fuse with one of greater am-

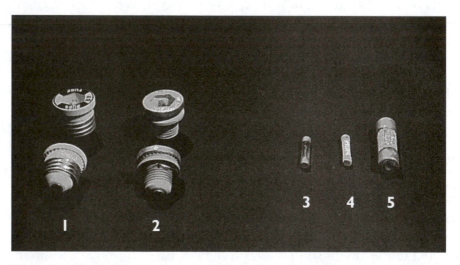

Figure 13.1. Fuses. This picture shows some of the types of fuses still found in older theatres, and in many older homes. (1) the "standard" plug fuse. This is still common in many old installations. The same mechanical size comes in amperages from 5 to 30 making up-rating very easy. (2) shows a set of Fusestats. A different thread size for each amperage makes them non-interchangeable. A special insert (not shown) must be installed in the fuse holder to accept the Fusestat.

(3), (4) and (5) show some of the many types and sizes of cartridge fuses available. The smaller ones, (3) and (4), are commonly found in low current devices such as consoles, moving light power supplies and may also be used to protect some small wattage dimmers. The larger ones such as (5) may still be found as master and submaster fuses for very outdated switchboards. Cartridge fuses come in sizes running into the hundreds on amperes. Photo by Herbst.

perage. Indeed, this practice is so common that traveling theatre technicians almost automatically expect it in old installations. Nevertheless, it is dangerous and illegal. A little reflection on the heat formula will reveal that increasing the amperage from 15 to 30 amps (the most common substitution) will result in making it possible for the system wiring to become four times as hot before a fuse blows. Fortunately most old wiring was conservatively rated when installed and will survive this treatment for a long time although not without heat damage to insulation.

Plug fuses do offer one advantage over other types. When one opens, observation will often indicate whether it opened because of a slight overload or as the result of a short circuit or very heavy overload. The top of a plug fuse contains a window through which the fuse wire itself can be seen. If the window of the blown fuse is covered with blackened or spattered metal, the fuse opened from a short circuit or a very heavy overload. If the window is still transparent and the melted-off ends of the fuse wire can be observed, the fuse opened because of a slight overload.

Overload and short blowouts

Fuse response time (lag)

Fuses can be designed to respond almost instantly to an overload or to delay cutting off the current for a predetermined amount of time. Fuses designed for use with incandescent lamp loads must be built with a sufficient delay to allow their normal inrush current to pass without opening the fuse. Therefore the fuses normally found in theatrical installations will respond relatively slowly to very slight overloads but their response time will decrease rapidly as the size of an overload increases. They will respond to a short or heavy overload almost instantly.

Lag varies inversely with the size of the overload.

This delayed response to minor overloads when combined with circuits controlled by dimmers can lead to an insidious situation: A slightly overloaded circuit may continue to operate for most of a production during which the load is dimmed, only to open at the worst possible moment—the climax. The fuse has been heating for the entire time at near-capacity and reaches overload when the cue at the climax calls for bringing the dimmer to full. Therefore:

Delayed opening on dimmed circuits

1) carefully check loads when installing equipment and avoid even the slightest overload.
2) After the luminaires are all installed and circuited, allow them a "burn-in" period of an hour or so *with all dimmers at full up*. This will not only catch any slight overloads, but may also catch any newly installed lamps about to fail because they are faulty.

Burn-in is good practice.

Fusestats

The Fusestat was developed to defeat the efforts of those who would up-rate plug fuses. It is really a system, consisting of special socket inserts, one for each fuse size from 5 to 30 amps, and appropriate fuses that fit only into the proper insert. Once an insert has been placed in a fusé socket, it cannot be removed without destroying it—an arrangement intended to permanently prevent substitution of the wrong size fuse. Unfortunately this system is rather easily defeated because the inserts are not very difficult to remove, after which a standard plug fuse can be again inserted in the socket and the amperage increased.

Both regular plug fuses and Fusestats are susceptible to heating if they become loose in their sockets. This can occur from the inevitable 120 Hz vibration induced by the AC current passing through them. Therefore it is good practice to tighten fuses on a regular schedule. This will also give the technician a chance to check the temperature of each working fuse. If the fuse is tight in its socket but running very warm, it is loaded to near capacity and may open if the voltage increases slightly causing more current to flow. Such loads should be reduced.

Changing fuses

With the exception of plug fuses that may blow because they become loose in their sockets and overheat and fuses improperly operated in an overheated enclosure, all blown fuses are a sign of trouble. Either an overload or a short circuit caused the fuse to blow. There is no such thing as fuses "wearing out." There is nothing in them that can wear out, only the inert piece of fuse wire. Therefore the first action after a fuse blows should be to discover the cause and remedy it. In the theatre this is often known from the very moment the fuse blew— someone inadvertently plugged an extra load into an already loaded circuit, or a short occurred in a connector as it was being plugged in. However, there will be times when the technician will have to hunt down the cause by tracing the path of the current from the fuse to the load looking for evidence of trouble along the way. Often it will be necessary to disconnect everything from the load circuit served by the fuse, replace the fuse and reconnect things one by one until the fuse blows again indicating that the last item connected, perhaps a luminaire with bad wiring, was the cause of the trouble. If an overload is the problem, individual luminaires should be checked for correct wattage and the entire load recalculated. Occasionally overloads can be spotted by the use of a clamp-on ammeter and a special adapter that makes it possible to clamp the ammeter around only one conductor at a time. However this will not catch very small overloads that may take hours to heat up a fuse to the point of failure.

The physical act of changing the fuse is relatively simple for plug fuses; the only caution is to handle only the insulated parts of the fuse and to tighten it securely into its socket. Cartridge fuses are somewhat more risky. If possible, turn off the feed to the fuse holder before removing the blown fuse and inserting the new one. If this is not possible, disconnect or turn off the load. A fuse puller is the safest way to remove or insert cartridge fuses. This is an insulated pliers-like tool that can grasp the fuse so it can be pulled out. If a fuse puller is not available and it is necessary to pry the fuse out of its clips with a dry piece of wood or other insulating material, pry the live end out first so that the fuse will move away from the live parts as it comes loose. The new fuse can be placed in the clips and shoved firmly into place. Insulating gloves are recommended.

A blown fuse is a sign of trouble.

Tracing down the cause of a blown fuse

Changing fuses

Figure 13.2. Circuit Breaker. This breaker is typical of many installed in lighting circuitry. It is a combination heat and magnetic sensing breaker. When installed, only the top, which resembles an ordinary electrical switch, is visible. When it opens, the switch handle moves to a center position between "on" and "off." To restore power, turn to "off" then to "on." *Breakers should not be used for day-to-day control of loads.* Photo by Herbst.

Circuit Breakers

These are devices that serve the same purpose as fuses while avoiding many of their problems. Breakers may work on several principles, including heat-sensitive elements which trip a switch-like spring-loaded pair of contacts, magnetic coils which also trip the switch arrangement and electronic circuitry which can cut off the current in case of overload or short circuit. Some combine the heat sensitive mechanism with the magnetic coil. Since circuit breakers are sized when installed and need no replacement when they open, there is much less chance that they will be up-rated.

Circuit breakers come in an almost infinite variety of amperage ratings ranging from tiny breakers used to protect sensitive electronic gear to monstrous units that can protect an entire power plant by cutting off megawatts of power almost instantly. Those most often found in the theatre and in home service panels resemble switches. (Figure 13.2). Despite this appearance, they should not be used as a substitute for switches; their contacts are not made to handle repeated on-off action under load and they may fail. Unlike fuses, breakers which are used to control more than one live line at a time are usually mechanically linked so that the entire set of lines will be cut off if any one is overloaded or shorted. Main breakers are normally this type.

Circuit breakers are made so that it is impossible to hold the mechanism in an "on" position when a short or overload is present. The handle becomes detached from the inner parts of the breaker and will not move the contacts back into their "on" position. This same action also causes the handle to move to a middle position between "off" and "on" when the breaker trips. After the short or overload is cleared, the breaker must be switched all the way to "off" and then to "on" to restore power.

Move to "off" then to "on" to restore power.

Circuit breakers have two ratings: 1) the amperage at which they will trip, opening the circuit, and 2) the interrupting capacity, a large number indicating how large a short circuit they will handle. Breakers for ordinary service are rated at 10,000 amperes interrupting capacity. This apparently huge number may not be enough for some theatrical applications where the system is supplied by its own transformer, the wiring is conservatively rated, and there are short wiring runs between the transformer and the lighting equipment. Those designing theatrical control equipment must

Current rating

Interrupting capacity

use caution in specifying breakers because a short circuit that fails to be interrupted by the breaker(s) can quickly become a major catastrophe. Breakers installed must be capable of interrupting the largest current the system can supply plus an adequate safety margin. Obviously, if the theatre technician is faced with the task of replacing breakers in a system, he or she must make sure that the new breakers have the same as or greater interrupting capacity than the old ones.

For theatrical purposes, breakers are much more desirable than fuses. Not only do they avoid the problem of wrong-size replacement, they also make it easy to restore a circuit the moment the fault is eliminated, a great advantage when the fault happens during a production or rehearsal.

Breakers are preferred.

Breaker response time

Breaker lag time

Circuit breakers, to an even greater degree than fuses, can be made to respond to an overload almost instantly or to delay breaking the circuit (lag) by whatever period of time the engineer considers appropriate. Whatever the response time, it is designed to decrease rapidly as the overload increases and to be nearly instantaneous when a short circuit occurs. This can create the same insidious delay of cutoff mentioned above in connection with fuses. The solution is also the same: careful control of loading and a "burn-in" time to catch any errors.

Choice of breakers for theatrical use

Heat responsive breakers are the cheapest to manufacture and are often quite satisfactory for locations where the ambient heat will always be low. However theatrical breakers are often installed in dimmer racks or in "magazines," cabinets enclosing many breakers fed from the same source. Such locations tend to trap the natural heat caused by the flow of current. This can cause heat-sensitive breakers to trip even when the load is less than their rating. Magnetically operated breakers are a better choice. If there is a problem with harmonics created by the chopping action of the dimmers on the 60 Hz current, electronic breakers are recommended, particularly on mains.

Heat sensitive breakers may open falsely.

Ground fault circuit interrupters (GFCI)

As noted above, a ground fault is a situation where some or all of the current in the return line from a load becomes detoured through the earth because the return line has made contact with a conductor that is attached electrically to the earth. This causes an imbalance between the current flowing into a load and that returning via the grounded neutral. That portion of the current straying from the normal path to the connection with the earth may cause noise in sound systems or even sparking at joints in conduit.

Much more serious, it is possible that a person can become the ground fault by making a connection between a live source and the earth. Such a connection can be deadly. Therefore ground fault interrupters are required by modern codes to be installed where there is a danger that people will be well grounded and that they will be handling equipment fed by live lines, for example, operating an electric drill in a shop with a concrete floor.

There are three principal types of GFCIs commonly available: The first combines the function of a GFCI with that of a circuit breaker and is installed in breaker panels and other permanent locations. These GFCIs normally have a small colored test button that enables the technician to test the unit for proper operation. Such GFCIs are the most sensitive of all which can cause nuisance outages if the wiring in the system is old and leaks small, harmless amounts of current. Such nuisance outages also rule against the installation of such GFCIs in theatre lighting systems. Nuisance outages cannot be tolerated during a show.

Another kind of GFCI is made to be installed in place of a standard household outlet or convenience receptacle. It has no circuit breaker function but does have a test button. It includes the normal two receptacles of a standard household outlet, both of which are protected as are any circuits wired "downstream" of the GFCI. Note that outlets between the GFCI and its supply are not protected.

Outlet box GFCIs

A third type of GFCI is often installed at the plug-end of cords attached to portable appliances, such as hair dryers, which are often used in wet, grounded locations. It protects only the appliance to which it is attached. These GFCIs are normally equipped with a test button to assure the user the device is working properly. When this test button is pressed, the appliance won't work until the button is restored to its operating mode.

Although local codes may vary, most require that GFCIs be installed wherever there is a likelihood that personnel will be grounded, say, working on a concrete floor, and will be handling electrical apparatus. In some cases this installation will be required only at new construction or at major renovations. In other localities, retrofitting may be required immediately.

Regular commercial GFCIs are considered too apt to react to minor, harmless ground faults and shut down vital circuits to be installed in theatre lighting systems. However, there are now highly reliable GFCIs built into special dimmers that are sensitive enough to protect swimmers in underwater acts. The shops are another matter, particularly the scene and paint shops where workers are often handling power tools while standing on a frequently damp concrete floor. Not only law, but prudence should require that GFCIs be installed on all circuits.

GFCIs may be too sensitive for theatrical circuits.

They should be installed in all shops.

Sizing Overcurrent Devices

In an ordinary lighting circuit in a home or building, the wire is the part that must be protected against overloads and shorts. Incandescent lamps, by their nature as resistance devices, are self protecting as long as the voltage does not rise above that for which the lamp was built. Because the wire has little resistance (the less the better), it will strive to carry whatever current is allowed to pass through it heating up rapidly according to the power formula. Thus it must be protected. However many circuits, including those containing theatrical dimmers, contain equipment that may need protection from smaller currents than the rating of the wire. In these cases, the size of the overcurrent device is determined by the "weakest link" in the circuit, i.e., that part with the lowest load capacity. In most theatrical lighting circuits, this is the dimmer. If modern dimmers are in use, this problem is automatically solved as far as the dimmer is concerned because electronic overcurrent protection is built into the dimmer. Its electronics will automatically turn it off if it is overloaded or subjected to the wrong voltage. In addition, a circuit breaker may be included in the dimmer to protect wiring. In modern systems that use modular dimmer racks, non-dim circuits are controlled by devices similar to dimmers that simply turn on and off. These too contain built in overcurrent protection. In older lighting installations there will be a bank of fuses or breakers, one for each dimmer, sized to protect it. Non-dim circuits will be sized to protect the wiring or to meet code requirements.

Avoiding line drop

Electrical code regulations are stringent on the matter of wire size and current limitations. For instance, the NEC defines a standard branch circuit, such as the run from a dimmer to a luminaire as a 20 ampere circuit. This would, according to allowed wire sizes in the code, require No. 12 wire. Even if the dimmer in the branch circuit is rated at 1000 watts and is protected by a 10 ampere fuse, the wiring must be at least No 12. Moreover, if the wire run is long, say to a position in the ceiling of the house, good wiring practice will require that the wire size be No. 10 to reduce line drop from the resistance of the wire. Thus the circuit will consist of No. 10 wire, rated at 30 amperes, carrying less than 10 amperes from the 1000-watt dimmer. This also meets the requirement that the branch circuit be rated at no more than 20 amperes.

Chapter 14

ELECTRONIC DIMMERS

As we have noted, modern dimmers tend to be "invisible" to the console operator and the designer. Except for checking the load on the dimmers as the show is mounted (and even this is largely automatic with modern dimmers which sense an overload and shut down to alert the technician), these complicated devices do their job so reliably that they seldom call any attention to themselves. Of course, if there are not enough dimmers, the designer or technician will try to rent or purchase more and/or will set up a re-circuiting procedure to make dimmers do double duty. However, this is becoming an unknown problem as more and more theatres are equipped with dimmer-per-circuit systems.

The design and engineering of electronic dimmers is beyond the scope of this text. Indeed, this is a specialty that requires the services of professionals who not only understand the engineering concepts involved but also the application of dimmers to theatrical lighting. The fraternity of dimmer specialists is an exclusive group indeed!

Nevertheless an understanding of the general principles which control the operation of these vital units and facts concerning their operation should be part of every technician's knowledge. He or she may be called upon to make recommendations concerning the purchase of new dimming equipment or may have to service the dimmers if they fail.

Basic Operating Principles

Early dimmers all worked by reducing the amplitude of the AC wave as shown in Figure 14.1. In the earliest dimmers this reduction was effected by inserting resistance into the circuit in addition to that provided by the lamp(s). If the added resistance was sufficient, the lamps could be dimmed out. However, the dimmer resistance had to be proportional to the resistance of the lamp(s) making the dimmer "load sensitive." To work properly, the resistance of the dimmer had to be 3-4 times that of

Modern dimmers

Amplitude control

Load sensitivity

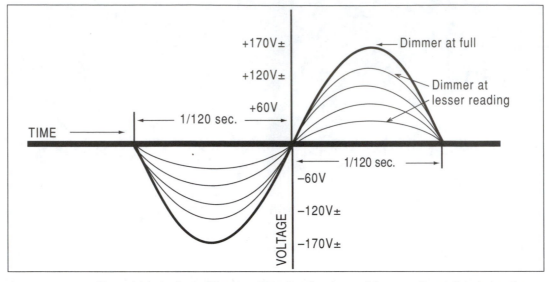

Figure 14.1. Analogue Dimming. Note that the shape of the curve is not distorted as the dimmer operates. Its amplitude is merely reduced. This avoids generation of harmonics. (Voltage indications are approximate.)

the lamp(s). Adding insult to injury, these dimmers converted a substantial share of the load current into heat when they were at any setting except "full" or "blackout." Operating a bank of resistance dimmers had a lot in common with fueling a boiler!

Variable autotransformers

Later, variable autotransformers were used to control the amplitude of the AC wave. These changed the voltage without respect to load making them non-load sensitive, a feature much valued at the time. They also produced very little heat.

Control board location

Up until the late 1930s, almost all control boards were located backstage, often in a position where their operators could see little or nothing of the results of their efforts. This was necessitated by the fact that all of the available control devices were direct control, i.e., the handle on the device was directly connected to the parts which carried and adjusted the current. To avoid long runs of wire which required a pair of wires for each dimmer circuit, the dimmer banks were located as close to the load as possible. This meant backstage operation.

Direct control

Some attempts were made to operate the early dimmers remotely by means of motor drives. "Tracker wires," a system of wires and pulleys that enabled the operator(s) to work the dimmers from a remote location were perfected and much used in Europe but did not catch on in the USA.

Saturable core reactor

The first genuine remotely operated dimmers were transformer devices, the saturable core reactor and the magnetic amplifier. These were voltage-setting devices akin to the autotransformer but designed for remote operation. But both were heavy, unwieldy devices and the saturable core reactor had an almost intolerable lag in its response. Only a few reactors were installed. Magnetic amplifiers, on the other hand, were rather widely used until they were replaced by phase-control dimmers (below).

Magnetic amplifier

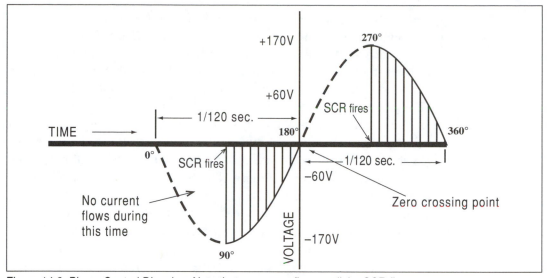

Figure 14.2. Phase Control Dimming. Note that no current flows until the SCR fires at whatever point in the cycle is determined by the controller. Then it rises very rapidly to the value determined by the voltage curve and continues to flow until the voltage reduces to zero at the zero crossing point. This "chopping" action effectively controls the lamp output but also creates harmonics.

As these early developments were taking place, designers were chafing under the limitations of manual control and, particularly under the lack of subtlety that these unwieldy, direct control dimmers imposed on the cue taking process. Lighting artists from Adolphe Appia forward, dreamed of being able to control patterns of lighting of any degree of complexity with utter flexibility from a position in the theatre where the operator/designer could see the show as the audience did and could "play" the lighting much as an organist plays music. The beginnings of realization of this dream had to await the invention of phase- control dimming and computer-assisted control.

Phase Control

Unlike amplitude control of current, *phase control adjusts the amount of power passing to the load by clipping parts of each pulse* (Figure 14.2). This results in pulses of current with zero-current spaces between them. The thermal inertia of the lamp filaments levels out the effect of the pulses into a smooth output proportional to the size of the pulses.

The operative heart of early phase control dimmers was the *thyratron*, a device similar to the vacuum tube which was the basis of all early radio and electronics equipment. We can best understand thyratrons by examining how vacuum tubes work. In vacuum tubes there are at least three elements, cathode, anode and grid. The cathode may be simply a heated wire (termed the "filament") or it may be a separate element heated by a resistance wire that is electrically separate from it. In either case, heating makes it capable of emitting electrons. The grid is a screen-like device placed between the anode and the filament. The anode, also called the plate, is unheated and cannot emit electrons. It is literally a flat piece of metal designed to receive electrons. These parts are insulated from each other and surrounded by a vacuum. If a negative voltage is

Thyratron tube

Cathode, anode and grid

Anode (plate)

applied to the cathode and a positive voltage to the plate, electrons will pass through the vacuum from the filament to the anode. Note that there can be no flow in the reverse direction because the cold anode cannot emit electrons even if it is given a negative charge. The cathode-anode flow can be regulated by a very small signal voltage applied to the grid which is physically located between them. This produces a magnified replica of the original signal. Vacuum tubes can exercise complete control over filament-to-plate flow. However the amount of current that these tubes can handle is limited to current far below that needed for the control of theatrical lighting equipment. The solution was to utilize an electronic relative of the vacuum tube, the thyratron tube.

Two thyratrons are needed to make a practical dimmer, one for each half of the sine wave. A thyratron is a large tube with an anode, grid and cathode similar to those in a vacuum tube but with one very important difference: instead of being evacuated, the tube is filled with a gas such as mercury vapor or xenon. This changes its control characteristics. The point during the AC cycle at which the cathode-plate flow begins is determined by voltage applied to the grid. When thyratrons are used for theatrical dimmers, this voltage is derived from the AC line voltage via a special circuit that moves the sine wave backward or forward in time, i.e., *phase shifting* it (hence the name of the circuit). Once the grid voltage causes the cathode-plate current to flow, i.e., "fire," the grid loses control over that flow. No matter what voltage is applied to the grid, electrons will continue to flow from filament to plate, limited only by the circuit in series with the tube. This current continues until the voltage between plate and filament is reduced to zero which occurs at the zero-crossing point in the AC sine wave at the end of the half-wave. Once in the off state, the tube conducts no current until the cathode again swings negative, the anode positive and the grid is again raised to the critical voltage. Meanwhile, the other tube in the dimmer is being fired to control the other half of the AC sine wave. The result is a chopped current flow similar to that diagrammed in Figure 14.2. Note that it consists of a series of pulses, each with a very steep rise at the firing point. When fed to an incandescent lamp larger than a few watts, the heat inertia of the filament smooths out this chopped wave and produces an even light output proportional to the amount of the original sine wave allowed to pass. The advantage in using thyratrons is that a pair of these tubes can control much greater current flows than vacuum tubes, easily enough to handle theatrical loads and, in fact industrial loads many times larger still.

The phase shift circuit that determines when the tubes will fire is a voltage-setting circuit which draws very little current. This characteristic makes possible the design of elaborate mastering and submastering arrangements on the console discussed in Chapter 4. Its development accelerated the design of consoles independent of the engineering demands of the heavy, bulky dimmers and current-carrying devices which had begun with the develop of magnetic amplifiers and saturable-core reactors.

Thyratrons are filled with gas.

Thyratrons can carry heavy currents.

Control of phase shift is essentially voltage.

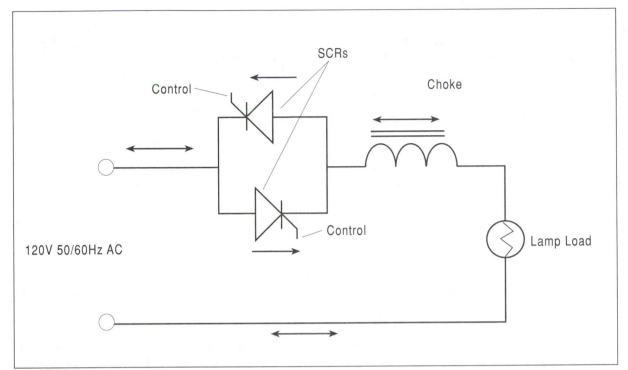

Figure 14.3. SCR Dimmer. This schematic shows in simplified form the basic circuit of all SCR dimmers. The output of the control circuitry (phase shift or digital) is fed to the SCRs through the points marked "control." The current flows through the load in both directions, depending on the 60 Hz alternations of the supply. However note the arrows indicating the direction of current flow in the SCRs. One carries the current in one direction for a half wave, then the other carries the reverse flow for the other half wave. The choke, which is in series with the load, slows the rise time and limits current flow to short circuits and heavy overloads.

The Silicon Controlled Rectifier (SCR)

Early remote control dimming systems, which became available around 1950, used thyratron tubes which, while they dimmed the lighting effectively, required heavy filament current and produced considerable waste heat. Within a few years a solid state device, the *silicon controlled rectifier* (SCR), was developed. It quickly put the thyratrons out of business. The development of SCRs parallels that of the thyratron. First the transistor was developed. This is a device analogous to the vacuum tube in which two electrically charged parts are separated from each other by a "gate," a layer of material capable of controlling the flow of electrons through it to the collector and out to whatever the device is feeding. Transistors, like early tubes, could handle only tiny currents and thus were incapable of serving as dimmers. SCRs were made so that their gate operated like the grid in a thyratron, determining when current flow will start but having no control over it, once started. Indeed, their operating characteristics were in some cases, so near the same as those of thyratrons, that they could actually be substituted into the same circuitry with only minor changes.

SCR has parts analogous to those in a vacuum tube.

SCR gate works like the grid in a thyratron.

Problems Inherent in SCR Dimmers

The most important problem encountered in the engineering of an SCR dimmer is the steep wave front created when the SCR fires. These devices

Steep wave front

can turn on so fast that they create radiated electronic noise well into the radio frequency range. This is known as *radio frequency interference* (RFI). It can invade sound systems by induction making them intolerably noisy. In television studios, RFI can also disturb the video signals. The solution to this problem lies in including devices called *chokes* in series with the SCRs. These are transformer-like devices consisting of a single coil of insulated wire wrapped around a laminated iron core. They have the effect of slowing down the rise time. Chokes used in SCR dimmers are rated by their current carrying capacity in amperes and by their effect on the rise time of the wave front in milliseconds (1/1000ths of a second). Useful rise times run from about 300 ms to over 600 ms. The longer the rise time, the quieter the dimmer but the slower its response to cues. Iron core chokes are also heavy; those producing the longer rise times are the heaviest. They can also generate mechanical noise making a dimmer rack a source of noise wherever it is installed. Electronic chokes are also available which are lighter in weight but more costly. Either type of choke adds to the cost of the dimmer, increases its size and reduces its efficiency because chokes use energy.

The same steep wave fronts that generate electronic noise can also cause the dimmers, and some lamp filaments, to buzz. This problem is particularly serious in film and television studios where sensitive microphones may be operated close to luminaires. Dimmers equipped with high millisecond rated chokes may alleviate the problem but the ultimate solution is the direct current (DC) dimmer discussed below

Thousands of console/dimmer setups using SCRs were made and many are still in use. Dimmer banks were removed from the stage and placed in secure, well-cooled rooms strategically located to keep wire runs reasonably short. The control console ("desk") was normally located at the back of the house or even in the house, its location designed to give the operators a good view of the stage, Wiring to the console consisted of small gauge multiconductor cable plus a small 120-volt feed for operating the console.

Digital Dimmers

Meanwhile computer control was being perfected and computer memory becoming abundant and cheap enough to make the storage of hundreds of lighting cues feasible. Since the computer-operated console from its inception was and is a digital device and the phase shift principle which controlled the SCR dimmers was analogue, each dimmer required a digital-to-analogue converter to mate the console with the dimmers. This added cost, extra complication, and, occasionally, poor operation.

Actually, the signal needed to turn on an SCR needn't be derived from the AC supply. This approach was simply the most convenient when phase shift control was first developed. A spike from a computer would do just as well, if not better. As long as this firing spike could be timed to occur at any point in the half-wave of the power supplied to the SCR, control could be effected. Thus the all-digital dimming system evolved. Dimmers respond to a digital signal directly and in the bargain, return information about the dimmers to the console via the control lines. Such

Radio frequency interference (RFI)

Chokes

Lamp buzz

A digital spike can fire an SCR.

data as load, operating temperature, voltage output are continuously available to the technician. The result is that most modern dimmers are all-digital. Computer-based consoles create complex digital signals for controlling dimmers and other lighting equipment such as scrollers, store vast numbers of cues digitally, and even offer the designer the opportunity of taking the complete set of lighting cues home to review and revise on his or her home computer. Wiring between the console and dimmers is also simplified because the entire string of digital commands for the dimmers can be transmitted on one coaxial cable. Two may be installed for security.

Modern all-digital dimmers

Dimmer Racks

The traditional place for dimmers has been mounted in a rack located at some back- or below-stage position convenient for short wiring runs and near enough to the stage itself for emergency maintenance. This has often meant the allocation of a special vault-like room, equipped with air conditioning and sound insulation, usually under the side stage or tucked in beside the orchestra pit.

A dimmer rack designed for modern dimmers (Figure 14.4A) is a complicated device in itself. It contains the power distribution equipment to supply the dimmers including overcurrent protection, and the digital processing equipment that receives the cue data from the console and distributes it to the dimmers. The power distribution system is, in itself, an engineering challenge. Huge amounts of current must be controlled and delivered to the dimmers while avoiding any physical arrangements of the conductors that might induce unwanted currents into the frame of the rack or into other electrical parts. Since these power carrying conductors may also carry harmonics (see below), they must also be engineered to handle and help to control these unwanted but often unavoidable flows. If the dimmers are the type that sends back data to the console, as most modern dimmers are, this digital processing unit will also handle that data. These processors may also have the capability of memorizing and making available to the dimmers a number of light settings that can be used in case of failure of the console. These may be activated at the rack and/or from a special emergency control panel.

Power distribution

Data feedback to the console

Modern dimmer racks are also available as traveling units (Figure 14.4B) equipped with wheels and the necessary connections for power supply. These units are the mainstay of the traveling concert industry and of touring professional theatre companies. They are "portable" only in the sense that they can be moved by a team of stage hands into a location and then wired to run the show. After the show they must be disconnected and readied for shipping.

Each of these racks may contain as many as 90-100 dimmers and several racks may be needed to operate a large show. Obviously such setups require large power mains and special heavy feeders. The consoles that control their operation are as complex and flexible as any found in fixed locations.

Travelling consoles

Figure 14.4. Dimmer Racks. Dimmer racks are no longer a simple framework to hold dimmers. They not only distribute huge quantities of power to the dimmers, providing overcurrent protection and avoiding stray induced currents, they also serve as a vital part of the digital control apparatus by receiving digital signals from the console and distributing them to the dimmers. Many racks also contain digital control circuitry making it possible for them to operate the lighting in a limited emergency manner without the console. This can cover in case of console failure and also facilitates in maintenance and trouble shooting.

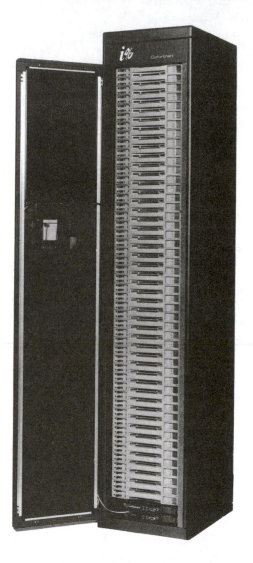

Figure 14.4A. The "i96" Dimmer Rack. This rack is designed for fixed installation. Its capacity is 96 dimmer modules each of which can accept a variety of dimmers ranging from dual 1.8 kW to double-high (takes up two module spaces) 12.0 kW dimmers. Dimmer parameters such as line voltage regulation speed, control response speed, and user-programmable output curves can be programmed from a hand-held terminal or from a computer. Individual dimmer status can be monitored from an on line PC or a special remote video station. The dimmers are cooled by a fan which adjusts its speed to the temperature of the dimmers. 96 looks may be stored in the module's memory for operation independently of the console. Courtesy Colortran.

Figure 14.4B. The Sensor Touring Rack by ETC. This rack, can accommodate 24, 36 or 48 dimmer modules (48 module version shown) each of which may consist of 2 1.8kW or 2.4kW dimmers or a single 6kW or 12kW dimmer. The dimmers are cooled by a low-noise fan. An electronics control module handles data and emergency programming including programmable 32 backup looks. In and out power connections on rear including main breaker and hot pockets and convenience outlets. Courtesy ETC.

Package Dimmers

Package dimmers have a relatively long history, going back to portable piano boards and a bit later portable autotransformer packages, neither of which were very portable. The piano boards, so called because their shape resembled a crated upright piano, contained resistance dimmers equipped with mechanical mastering. These were the standard of the touring theatre industry for a long time, even after autotransformer dimmers were the standard for new installations. They weighed hundreds of pounds and were portable only for a team of beefy stagehands.

Package autotransformer units offered the first application of electrical mastering available to most theatres. A much-used package unit consisted of six 1000-watt ATDs and one 6000-watt unit complete with the necessary overcurrent protection. Transfer switches made it possible to feed any or all of the 1000-watt units from the 6000-watt unit or directly from the main. These packages, only slightly more portable than piano boards, became the standard for many community and school theatres because of their flexibility and relatively modest cost.

Package ATD boards

Both piano boards and ATD boards were installed backstage wherever that always-crowded space would allow, and fed either from a company switch or from the bus bars of the existing lighting equipment. They were also installed, often for only the duration of the show, in school auditoriums, churches and community theatres borrowing space.

Electronic Package Units

SCR based dimmers are, by their very nature, much lighter in weight than autotransformer dimmers. Thus electronic dimmers finally brought the theatre its first really portable control equipment. A package containing six or twelve 2000-watt dimmers can be easily carried by one person—the six 1000-watt ATD unit was a very heavy load for two sturdy stage hands.

Electronic dimmers also brought the concept of remote control to package control boards. The dimmers are built into one unit to be installed backstage and the controllers into a separate console to be installed wherever the operator(s) could see the stage and operate without disturbing the audience. The two parts are interconnected by means of a low-voltage, low-current-carrying cable. Even the most economical package systems now usually include at least the possibility of two-scene presetting and most include a modest amount of memory and the capability of running memorized cues.

Remote control package units

15

DESIGNING AND ADAPTING PROJECTION TO THE STAGE

The term, "scenic projection," encompasses the various processes by which images in light are created on the stage. It includes shadow projection, lens projection including motion pictures, holographic images, and images produced by laser scanning. Scenic projection offers the designer a variety of methods for producing images that are far more flexible and vivid than the time-honored way of painting an image on a surface. Because they are not attached to a surface, projected images can appear or disappear, blend, flow, change color, change size, move in or out of focus, and even exist in space with no apparent surface to "hold" them. This flexibility offers the designer the intriguing possibility of using changing images as a major element in his or her treatment of the rhythm of the production.

The designer who adds scenic projections to his or her array of specialties almost inevitably enters the realm of scenography—that concept of theatrical design wherein there is one master designer who approaches the design of the setting, lighting and other elements as a four-dimensional expression in space and time. The single-designer concept need not be necessary to all production organizations using scenic projection. However, if the artistic potential and technical needs of projection are to be met, it will be advantageous that the setting, lighting and projections be designed by the same artist.

A single artist for lighting, projections and scene design

Projections heavily influence both art and technology of staging.

Projection and the Unity of the Production

With the exception of "convenience projections"—such as a background scene viewed through a window,—projections tend to be a major artistic element in a stage design. Both their artistic power and their technical requirements will strongly influence every element of the staging.

A decision to use projections should motivate the director and designers to focus on the unity of the production. Without special attention, the risk of disunity is high indeed. Uncontrolled scenic projection is one of the most overpowering means of upstaging actors yet invented: imagine an ordinary-sized actor attempting to get and hold the audience' attention against a 50' x 30' background of high intensity, vividly colored, moving projections. However, given artistic control, scenic projection can be a powerful artistic addition to a production and can solve many design problems that might otherwise require extensive staging yet result in inferior artistic results.

Projections can be powerful attention-getters.

Styles of Projection

Projections may range from naturalistic clouds, sunsets, storms, and actual photographs of items related to the play to abstractions fitting the most nonrealistic staging. They may be intentionally didactic and obvious (as in many Brechtian productions) or they may exist as subtle textures and patterns that engulf the entire stage including the actors or dancers, or they may be so completely blended into the total visual production that the audience will not know which images are projected and which are painted. Fluidity of the stage image may be the only clue that projections are in use.

A "screen" Is not an essential part of scenic projection.

The first step in understanding how scenic projection blends artistically into a production is to put aside the notion that projections will exist on a "screen." While it is often technically essential for there to be a surface on which or through which the images will appear, the audience

Figure 15.1. *Orféo*. This photo illustrates the close integration of projection techniques into a production—an adaptation of the Orpheus legend into a one-hour music/dance/multi media presentation. Scenic projection and video techniques are used to present the audience with scenes such as this photo and Plate XI show. (Note that these photos are not trick photography—they show what the audience views.) The images are produced on stage in a way that allows the actors to appear to interact with them, not merely playing in front or behind them. *Orféo*: Creative concept/theatrical direction Michael Lemieux and Victor Pilon; Associate Director, Ginette Prévost; Music, Michael Lemieux; Costume Designers, Gabriel Tsampalieros and Carole Courtois; Stage Projections Designers, Victor Pilon with the assistance of Marc Bilodeau. Lemieux Pilon Création Inc., Montréal, Canada.

should only rarely be aware of that surface. Here are some examples of alternatives to using a "screen:"

- Images projected on the bodies of dancers
- Images projected into a haze-filled space
- Images projected on 3-D scenic elements
- Images projected on and through layers of theatrical gauze so that multiple images are seen.

Many more examples can be found and an ingenious designer will devise still more for each production he or she encounters. The important element is artistic control over the total design package: scenery, lighting and projections.

Art and Technology Intersect

Early planning is absolutely essential.

Early planning is as important to the technology of projection as it is to its design. Particularly setting and lighting designs must be devised with the use of projections in mind from the very beginning.

Time and money are essential.

While artistic unity achieved by blending of projections, scenic design, and lighting is aesthetically obvious and easy to articulate, technological problems make its execution difficult. Only productions blessed with a very generous budget of both time and money–perhaps the two scarcest commodities in theatrical planning—are apt to succeed. The most troublesome problems are:

Figures 15.2 and 15.3. *Odysseus* Scenography by Josef Svoboda. Note the extensive use of projections. Both the concave wall at the back of the stage and the underside of the moving platform representing Odysseus' boat were used as projection surfaces. Photos by Josef Svoboda courtesy Jarka Burian.

1. Stage lighting tends to dilute the projected image already weakened by the poor reflectiveness of the projection surface. This problem can be best solved by the use of very high powered projectors, if funds are available to buy or rent them and space can be found to operate these large devices.
2. The space between the projector(s) and the intended projection surface must be kept clear of objects, including actors, that are not intended to cast shadows into the image. This a matter of deep and early concern for the director who must adjust the blocking of the actors and accept significant design limitations in the setting.

Significant compromises may be necessary.

Fortunately compromises are eminently possible if all artists involved are willing to give. Some of these are discussed below. The artistic results, while satisfying, may not reach the peak of perfection possible with the best (and most expensive) projectors properly installed and operated.

Achieving Artistic Unity While Using Projections

The key to artistic success in making projections function as a significant part of the design is *blending*. The issue is not whether the audience is to be aware of the projections as projections or not, but rather that projections should never work at cross purposes with the total design. For instance, the color and brilliance (or lack thereof) of the projections

Use lighting cues to maintain artistic balance.

Figure 15.3. *Odysseus*.

should coordinate with the brightness and colors of the acting area and background lighting. The goal is to use color and intensity to blend the entire stage picture into an artistically satisfying whole. No element, scenery, lighting or projections should predominate more than the script and the director require.

Accenting the rhythm of the production

Many lighting cues will be generated by the need to maintain balance between the artistic parts of the scene. Indeed, many cues will be written and executed that produce no change in the lighting that is consciously perceived by the audience. For example, a shift from a projection of high brilliance to one of lesser brilliance will probably require a lighting cue, timed to match the change in the projection, to subtly reduce the brightness of the stage lighting. Similarly, a change in the color of the projected parts of the setting may require a subtle shift in acting area and set lighting color to maintain the proper blend and balance. These "invisible cues" can make the difference between artistic success and an annoyingly disunited stage picture.

Maintaining the Projection Surface

A projection that only covers part of the cyclorama, either by design or because of limitations in equipment, should be blended into the remaining parts of the cyc by specially angled floodlighting equipment at a color and intensity that vignettes the image into the field of color surrounding it.

If a large part of the setting, such as a cyclorama, is to display projections for most but not all of the show, designed illumination must be provided for that surface when projections are not in use. Particularly when the surface is white, there can never be a time when there is no designed lighting or image on it. Otherwise, the spill light from every luminaire and work light on stage will probably be apparent to the audience.

Exploiting the Artistic Potential of Projection

The greater the artist's experience with projection, the more he or she will marvel at the vast flexibility of the medium. The following are but "teasers" to stimulate the beginner's creativity:

Keeping actors within the stage picture

• *Changeability*: It is technically possible, although not necessarily desirable, for projections to be changing at every moment of the show even when using "still" projectors as opposed to motion picture machines. The designer can develop a counterpoint pattern of projections, lighting and action that accents the rhythmic structure of a production even to the extent of improving upon that rhythm as it exists in the script. Obviously, the director must participate in this kind of design.

Changes may be as drawn out as a sunset or as rapid as the abrupt change brought on by an actor closing a door. They may encompass the entire stage or only a tiny part of the total projected image. Still more complicated but artistically challenging, there may be changes within changes if enough projectors are available.

Clearly changes must evolve from the action of the play and must, in many cases be accompanied by the characters reacting to them or at least using their effect as part of the development of character and plot.

- *Focus of Attention*: A well-designed projection can aid in directing the audience's focus of attention to the actor or actors who are designed by the director to "take the stage" at a particular moment. This can be done by using the traditional elements of line form, color, texture and the like in the design of the projection as it combines with the scenery and lighting. The traditional injunction that the stage picture should appear incomplete without the characters in their places upon it holds, perhaps even more emphatically, when projections are in use. It will be this "empty spot" in the designed image that the actor fills in and that, in turn accents the actor. The ease in changing projections in time with the rhythm of the production makes it possible for that focus may be changed as often as needed.

Turning distortion to an advantage

It is particularly important that the designer of projections and settings take care that the actors do not become reduced to small figures intruding on the bottom of a huge image projected onto the cyclorama behind them. This is especially apt to happen in stages with square proscenium openings. Either the projection design and the lighting must focus attention down toward the actors on stage or, better, the actors must be able to work near the center of the image by utilizing the height offered by a three-dimensional setting. (See Figure 15.4.)

- *Symbolic Values of Projected Images*: This is a limitless challenge. It encompasses all of the potentialities of graphic imagery, i.e., the entire world of painting, sculpture and all manner of graphics that uses images to carry artistic import.

The projection artist will find a unique advantage over the easel artist as he or she creates images. The effect of optical distortion, which must be tediously painted or drawn into ordinary graphics, can be almost instantly created and adjusted by manipulating the arrangement of the image material, the lens and the projection surface. This turns an otherwise annoying technical difficulty into an artistic tool of great potential. The distortions characteristic of expressionistic paintings and set designs come first to mind but the range is much wider. Furthermore, distortion need not be static. Devices exist that can continuously adjust the distortion at whatever pace is needed.

- *Movement*: Most commercial projection systems include rotating drives to move circular image material through the aperture or linear drives to move belts of image material. Such devices can produce anything from a field of drifting clouds to fast moving images that may be far too attention-getting for the designer's taste.

• *Color Intensity and Purity*: Images in light produced by projection have none of the limitations of painted images. They are not dependent on the reflectiveness of frequently impure pigments but instead get their brilliance from the power of the projection light source. Thus the brightness range of projected images far exceeds that of painted images.

The introduction of dichroic filters which are capable of producing spectrally pure colors at high brilliance fills in some heretofore distressing gaps in the designer's palette particularly in the blue range.

Despite the often severely limited amount of time available to the designer of lighting and, by extension, projection, experimentation is strongly encouraged. Lack of experience with new technologies and unfamiliar old ones may lead the artist to miss much that could widen expressiveness and increase his or her artistic satisfaction.

Chapter 16

PROJECTION USING CONVENTIONAL OPTICAL SYSTEMS

When we project a movie or slides, we make every effort to make the conditions ideal: We darken the room, provide a special screen with a surface designed to distribute the reflected light evenly to the entire audience, and we arrange for the projector to be directly on the centerline of the screen in such a way that the slide and screen are exactly parallel. These ideal conditions can seldom be met when using projection on stage. Instead, the screen is apt to be minimally reflective material and the projector and slide will be located somewhere at an odd angle to the screen. Worst of all, the stage will by brightly lit with an array of spotlights, many of which may spill light onto the projection surface. Under these conditions there are only two methods available for making projections on stage functional:

1. *High light output*: This requires special high-efficiency lamps, efficient light collection, fast lens systems and low-density image material which transmits as much of the light to the "screen" as possible. All of these are expensive.

2. *Readjust the stage lighting levels and angles to favor the projections*: This will require careful planning and often compromises the blocking of the actors. The lower the power of the available projection equipment, the more severe the compromises will have to be.

Considerations in Adopting Projection

The decision to use projection must come early in the production planning process. The pros and cons of its use should be clear to all members of the production team from the beginning. As noted in Chapter 15, the artistic advantages of properly used projection can be impressive. Contrariwise, an ill-advised decision to use projections, perhaps to avoid the effort and cost of building settings or to avoid difficult painting techniques can turn out to be a trap. The goal will probably not be reached and the production will be seriously damaged by the lost time, effort and funds squandered on projections that do not work.

Time and monetary savings are elusive.

The following techniques offer practical and artistic solutions to design problems and can, on occasion, even solve problems in a way that saves time and funds. However no production company should count on these savings actually accruing until they have a reserve of experience using projections and know their equipment and their theatre well enough to realistically predict what will happen when projections are used.

Perhaps the first step in understanding the use of projections is to divest oneself of the notion of a "screen." This opens up the artist's thoughts to many challenging and creative alternatives as projection surfaces. The second step is to avoid the "classroom" or "movie theatre" notion of only one or two projectors doing the job—onstage projection may use numerous projectors located in a number of places backstage. This approach can have many advantages:

Multiple projectors can make the job easier.

1. Large areas can be covered with images that could not be handled by a single projector short of a hugely expensive and massive device.
2. Brightness levels of the projection can be high because only a limited area is being illuminated by any individual projector.
3. Multiple projectors make it possible to change parts of the projected image without changing the whole. This opens vast artistic possibilities to the designer.
4. Multiple projectors make it possible for individual projectors to be oriented towards the surface they are designed to cover much more precisely than if one huge and powerful projector had to cover all of the surfaces on the setting. This makes control over distortion much simpler and increases artistic variability.

The simplest of all projection techniques, shadow projection using a small ("point") light source and opaque materials, is an ancient Oriental art form which was reinvented for the theatre in the 19th century by August Linnebach, a German theatre designer and technician. Some Linnebach projectors (also termed square law projectors or direct beam projectors), mostly homemade, are still used today. Linnebach projectors produce very large but often soft, rather dim images at short throw distances. They can be the lowest priced projectors available, but in most situations, one of the modern array of lens projectors, ranging from reasonably priced units upward, will be a better choice.

Square law ("Linnebach") projectors

Lens Projection

All slide and motion picture projectors, ellipsoidal reflector spotlights, and sophisticated automated luminaires work in basically the same way. In modern projectors, a lens, usually much more optically refined than that in an ERS, is used to form an image of a "slide" placed in the strongly illuminated aperture. The source of illumination is a high-powered T-H lamp or, more likely, an HID lamp. Its light is gathered and passed through the aperture in such a way that it converges on the entrance element of the projection

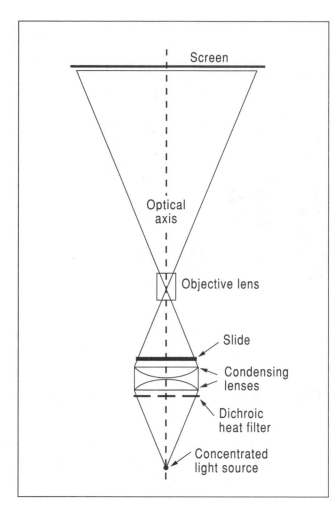

Figure 16.1. Lens Projection. This schematic drawing shows the essential elements arranged on the optical axis. Actual projectors may be more complicated but the principle of gathering the light from the source, passing it through the slide to the objective lens which forms the image on the screen applies to all lens projectors.

lens (Figure 16.1). The slide can be anything from the conventional glass plate with a photographic image bonded to it to a complicated arrangement of moving elements designed to create images of flames, rain or any other effect the designer can devise. The size of the projected image depends on the slide size, the focal length of the projection lens and the distance to the projection surface. Efficiency depends on the light source, the light gathering system, the density and size of the slide and the "speed" (i.e., the efficiency) of the lens. Sharpness of the image depends mainly on the optical quality of the lens.

Theatrical lens projectors have evolved from custom-made units often made in-house by an optical specialist, to modern commercially manufactured units, some of which are masterpieces of the optical engineer's work but very expensive and bulky (Figures 16.2A and 16.2B).

Modern luminaires such as ellipsoidal reflector spotlights and automated luminaires are basically projectors. Ellipsoidal reflector spotlights can be fitted with gobos to produce simple images which can cover about the same area as the pool of light normally produced by the luminaire. Similarly, automated luminaires can be fitted with slides and will produce high quality images covering about the same area as the luminaire would otherwise illuminate. With the exception of situ-

Spotlights as projectors

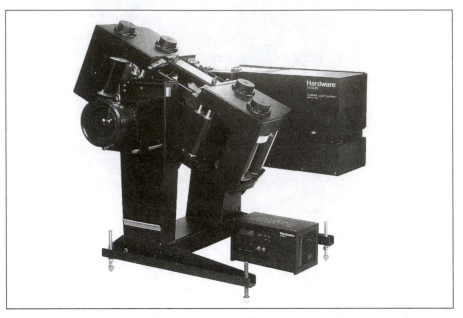

Figure 16.2A. Top-of-the-Line Scenic Projectors. These very expensive and massive machines represent the finest of the projector engineers' work. While usually too expensive for most theatres to own, they can be rented. Rental also usually includes the services of the rental agency's technical staff who can assist in the complicated job of setting up the machine(s) and preparing the image material. Photo courtesy Hardware Xenon, Inc.

ations where exceedingly powerful projections are needed, automated luminaires are rapidly monopolizing the field of scenic projection wherever they are affordable. (See Figure 16.4B.)

The Optical System

The optical axis

All parts of a good projection system are centered on its *optical axis*. This is a line through the center of each optical element and, ideally, extending to the center of the screen (Figure 16.1). Not only should all parts be centered on the optical axis, their optical planes should also be at right angles to it. Under these conditions, there will be no distortion due to misalignment, but optical distortion from lens or reflector faults may still exist.

The lamp house

The lamp house is the enclosure around the light gathering apparatus that contains spill light from the lamp and supports the lamp and its electrical leads. It may also carry the aperture apparatus and the objective lens. A lamp house is much like the housing of a high-powered spotlight; it must withstand heat, contain dangerous radiation, withstand occasional rough handling, and may have to be engineered to contain the violent explosion of a high-pressure lamp. In the case of theatrical projectors, it often fitted with mounting equipment such as a yoke and "C" clamp or a base that allows accurate tilting and panning.

Lamp house must withstand lamp explosion.

Collecting the light

The principle of collecting light in a projector is the same as that discussed in Chapter 7 in connection with the design of spotlights. However

Figure 16.2B. Pigi Projector. This machine combines a powerful lens projector with a sophisticated "moving strip" image apparatus that can move two strips of images accurately in relation to each other. Movement can be in unison, in opposite directions or a still image with a moving one superimposed. The entire lens mount and aperture apparatus rotates via a motor drive making rotating images also possible. Image format is 155 mm x 155 mm.

The light source is either a 4kW or 7kW xenon lamp. Control is remote, including focus, speed and direction of image strip movement, intensity (via mechanical dimming), and rotation. All parameters are controlled by a computer which is compatible with EBU, SMPTE and MIDI protocols. Courtesy Fourth Phase (Production Arts Lighting).

collecting light for projection is more demanding. The object of the system is to gather as much of the light output of the lamp as possible and direct it through the slide and into the rear element of the objective lens. In general, two approaches are to be found:

1. A conventional spherical mirror, plano-convex lens arrangement upgraded by the use of the best quality mirror and one or more high-quality lenses designed to converge the cone of light to a diameter equal to the diagonal of the slide. Furthermore an additional lens, sometimes called a "collector," may be installed just in front of the slide to converge the light passing through the slide into the rear element of the objective lens.

2. Adaptations of the ellipsoidal reflector system may be more efficient overall than the lens system above. These gather and direct the light with greater efficiency than the lens train method. These special mirrors can also be made of dichroic material (see Handling Heat below).

Handling heat

Any incandescent source powerful enough to be useful in scenic projection will produce a large amount of heat, part of it as heated air and the rest as infrared (IR) light. The heated air must be exhausted either by convection or forced ventilation. The infrared is picked up by the collection system and passed along to the slide unless special precautions are taken. A "low tech" solution to this problem is to install a heat filter of IR blocking glass in the optical chain just before the slide. This filter will absorb the IR, converting it to heat which must be removed by air circulation. A better solution is to install a cold mirror (dichroic filter) at the above position. This will pass the visible light and reflect the IR back toward the source (see Figure 16.3). In addition, using a hot mirror (also a dichroic filter) as the light collecting mirror (spherical, ellipsoidal or special geometry) will pass the IR through the back of the lamp house and reflect the visible light toward the lens. If these measures are not sufficient, or if they prove too costly, the slide may have to be cooled by a blast of air from a special fan. This will make additional noise and require extra electrical circuitry.

Dichroic mirrors can filter out IR.

Although HID sources are much more efficient than incandescent, they may still produce enough heat as IR to require the use of dichroic mirrors and filters.

Image Material

Slide shows both on- and off-stage date well back into the nineteenth century. These used painted slides first and later photographs. Moving stage effects such as rain, clouds and fire produced by rotating disks moving through the aperture have an equally long history. Modern moving effects include a wide variety of moving gobos and strips of film accurately controlled and highly sophisticated in their quality of images. (See the Pigi and other projectors in Figure 16.2.) Furthermore, projection specialists even today may devise apparatus as needed for specific shows. In any case, this image material must be accurately placed on the optical axis, carefully located within the depth-of-focus region of the lens and fully illuminated.

Whatever the image material, it must be capable of resisting the effects of the heat in the beam and, if it is a photographic or painted slide, resisting the fading action of the light. With the exception of silhouette-type slides intended to produce shadow images, the lower the density of the image the better. A photographic color slide developed for the lightest density possible while still retaining the image quality needed, can often add more to the brightness of the image than any other single element in the entire optical system.

Low density photographic slides preferred

Objective Lens

The objective lens is the most important part of the optical system. Ideally it should transmit a high percentage of the light striking its rear element, focus every part of a large slide sharply and evenly and distribute the image over the screen without hot spots or dark areas. It should do all of this at very short throw distances and be highly resistant to the effects of high heat from the light beam. Finally, it should be light in weight, small in size, and economical to purchase. Such a lens does not exist.

The ideal objective lens

The objective lens, or better, a set of objective lenses, will usually be one of the most expensive parts of the theatre's projection system. The best lenses are specially made for this service and come as close to the ideal as cost and optical skill will allow. One major difficulty is the optical fact that the shorter the focal length of the lens, the more difficult it is to make it meet the other theatrical requirements. Thus the lenses most needed—those for short throws—are the very lenses that are hardest to make and are therefore the most costly.

Objective lenses are described by their focal length stated in inches or millimeters and their speed (the efficiency with which they handle light) stated as an "f" number (e.g., 4.5 inches, $f=3.0$). Objective lenses may come as part of a system or be purchased separately. Since the outside diameter of objective lenses varies considerably from lens to lens, the projector must be equipped to allow the secure but adjustable mounting of each lens. Worse, projectors designed for a particular set of lenses are not likely to accept lenses of another make without devising special adapters.

Note that camera lenses will not serve as projection lenses for high-powered projectors even though they may have the proper speed and focal length. They cannot handle the heat load and will be destroyed.

Audiovisual Projectors on Stage

There are two types of standard audiovisual equipment that are adaptable to the stage, although with limitations. These are the 35mm slide projector and the overhead projector. In an academic situation these can sometimes be borrowed from the audiovisual department, although it will be far better for the theatre to own this equipment. The wrath of an A-V department receiving its much-abused projector back complete with paint and dye spatters and evidence of overheating is not pleasant to contemplate.

35mm Audiovisual Projectors

If the stage is small and the projected image need be no larger than the usual slide image for classroom projection, a standard Carousel or similar projector may be used. Standard lenses are usually available down to about a three inch focal length and zoom lenses are common. The three-inch lens or a zoom set to its shortest focal length will produce theatrically useful image sizes at backstage throws. Since these projectors are not designed to hold the same slide on the screen for long periods of time, care must be taken to limit the continuous "on" time and to allow time for cooling between uses. Otherwise slides may be destroyed and projector parts overheated. Also, these classroom projectors will not take kindly to dimming unless they are rewired to remove the fan from the lamp circuit which may then be dimmed.

Classroom projectors on stage

Specially adapted 35mm projectors are also available. These have improved light gathering systems, much more powerful lamps, some including xenon, and are equipped with special cooling blowers wired separately from the lamp circuit. They can also be fitted with special, faster projection lenses capable of handling high heat loads. Note that regular slide projector lenses may not survive in these high-powered projectors.

Powerful 35 mm projectors

Overhead Projectors

Overhead projectors are commonly used in situations where the lecturer wants to use overlays to build up an image as the lecture progresses. The image material, usually printed on clear acetate stock, is placed on a glass plate which forms the top of the lamp house. The light collection system directs the light to cover the entire glass top and then converges it into the rear element of the objective lens which is mounted on a post extending over the slide. The lens includes a prism which redirects the light toward the screen.

The open slide area of these projectors makes them useful for all manner of projection devices including some which can provide movement of the image. For example a shallow dish holding colored oil and water can be gently moved or rhythmically tapped to form a constantly varying pattern. This is the principle of the "psychedelic" images common in night clubs of the sixties. Unfortunately the same open construction makes these projectors produce lots of spill light. Attempts to dim these units may cause the fan motor to overheat if it is not separated from the lamp circuit.

Dealing with Distorted Images

Distortion may be controlled to artistic advantage.

Distortion is not always a negative factor. In many cases, such as projecting clouds, it can be an advantage. Likewise in the projection of abstract forms for, say, an expressionistic production, distortion can become a major element of the design. The key is control. The artist must be in control of the distortion and be able to adjust it to his or her wishes. With experience, designers will learn to control distortion by choice and adjustment of lenses, placement of the projector(s), the location and nature of the projection surface, and by the manipulations discussed below.

Although there are many sources of distortion, the most common one on stage is caused by the fact that the slide and the projection surface are not parallel to each other. If the slide cannot be made parallel to the screen, here are some other methods of controlling this type of distortion:

Preparing a distortion correcting grid

1. Develop a distortion grid to be followed as the slide is being painted. (See Figure 16.3.) This method is used by professional projection artists who paint their own slides. It can be a very exact method. Many theatres, particularly European opera houses maintain a complete set of distortion grids developed for various projector locations for projection onto their cyclorama. Note that if either the projector or the projection surface is moved, the grid will become inaccurate and a new one may be needed.

    One of the most accurate and efficient ways of developing a grid is to use a special drop gridded with horizontal and vertical lines every foot. This drop is hung at the plane of the intended projection and illuminated. A camera is placed at the projector location, its film plane parallel to that of the intended projector, and photos taken. Positive prints of these photos may be enlarged or reduced to fit the size of the slides to be painted and used to guide the artist in that painting.

2. Use photography to correct for distortion. The image is painted on a flat surface with the design shown as it is intended to appear on stage. It is then photographed by a camera placed at the same relative angle and position to the image material as the slide will be when used on stage. The lens makes the distortion corrections. This will work as long as the projection surface is essentially a plane.

This method can be expensive because of the need for large-format color transparencies. Such transparencies must be as low in density (transmit as much light) as is feasible. This means that the theatre must either equip and operate its own color laboratory or must find a custom color lab that will understand what is needed and produce consistently useful slides. The slides should be ordered in multiples because they will be subject to bleaching

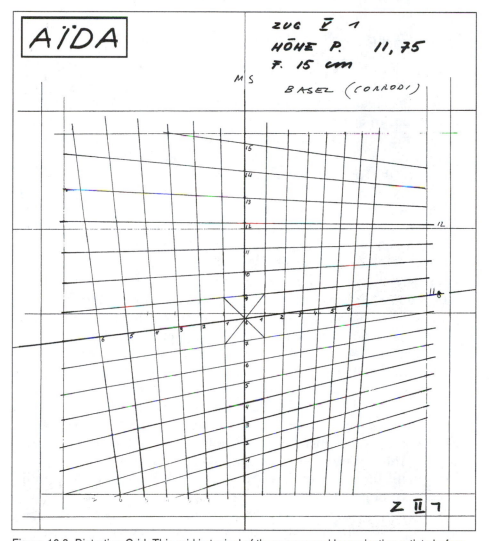

Figure 16.3. Distortion Grid. This grid is typical of those prepared by projection artists before sketching in the outlines of a painted slide. It is for a production of *Aida* designed by Annaliese Corrodi, scenographer, Basel, Switzerland. Note the line marked "M." It defines the middle of the projected area and is one of the key orienting lines followed by the artist. Grids are prepared for specific projector "screen" locations and must be redone whenever either the projector or the projection surface change position.

and warpage from the effects of the light beam.

3. Use computer graphics techniques. This involves scanning the original art work or photographs into a computer with enough memory to handle the large files thus created, and manipulating the images to get the desired image, including distortion correction. Then the digital image is printed on color film to make up the projection slide. The 35mm format is economical for this process, although larger formats may produce sharper images.[1]

This digital technique requires the use of sophisticated and expensive equipment such as high-quality scanners and film printers, plus skilled use of graphics programs such as Adobe Photoshop. If this equipment is available through an academic computer facility, it may be possible to use it with low cost. Another more expensive option is to use the facilities of a computer service bureau.

Front and Rear Projection

Stage projection may be done from either the front or the rear of the projection surface or even a combination of the two. Obviously rear projection (RP) requires surfaces that transmit light and, ideally, disperse it over an angle equal to the widest part of the house. A variety of commercially made RP screen materials is available in assorted "gains" and in both white and black screen types. The "gain" of a screen describes its ability to narrow the spread of the image and thereby increase its brightness to the observers within its effective angle. Gain is described by numbers beginning with 1 which describes a 100% diffusion screen that spreads the light evenly over 180°. Higher numbers describe screens that produce a brighter image but over a narrower viewing angle.

White screens are often slightly more efficient, i.e., they transmit more light, but they are also more apt to pick up spill light on the front which dilutes the image. However, they can also be used for front projection or simultaneous front and rear-projection. Black screens absorb spill light and thus increase the contrast and apparent brightness of a rear-projected image. Both white and black screens will evidence a "hot spot" or flare visible to members of the audience on a line from their point of view to the projector unless their dispersion is great enough to eliminate this effect. This degree of dispersion may make the screen too inefficient for some uses. Yet another way of avoiding "hot spots" is to place the projector so that no member of the audience is on a direct line-of-sight with it. This results in less efficient projection because no light passes through the screen directly toward the audience, but can produce evenly distributed brightness.

A variety of materials other than commercial projection screen material can be used for either front or rear projection. While these will not usually be as optically efficient as the commercial materials, they may blend into the setting much more effectively and can lead the designer

"Gain" of a projection screen

"Hot spot"

---

[1] See "Multi-Image Slides for Everyman" by Barrett Cleveland and David Guard, *Theatre Design & Technology*, vol. 33 no. 5 Fall 1997, p 28 ff, for details on this technique.

to create very unusual and artistically effective stagings. For example, Josef Svoboda, the well-known Czech scenographer, has used multiple layers of theatrical gauze dye-painted with abstract designs as a projection surface for front projections. Each gauze layer was spaced from those near it. The combination of the fixed (painted) images and the much-varied projected images was further enhanced by the fact that the projections were multiplied by passing through several layers of gauze before they became invisible. The projected images were seen as offset from one layer of gauze to the next because the projectors were directed towards the gauze drops at an angle. If the designer is sufficiently skilled at projection, specially designed parts of the projected images can be superimposed over

Projections on multilayered gauze

Figure 16.4A. Projection On Scenic Elements. *Tannhauser*, Venusberg scene. The setting is made up of irregular reflective elements large enough to tower above the actors standing in the openings. Scenography and photo by Josef Svoboda.

Figure 16.4B. "Droplet Gobo." These images are produced by automated luminaires all equipped with the same gobo. Note how the shapes of the setting pieces vary the effect of the images projected. Courtesy High End.

specific parts of the painted image producing designed color changes.

Given a satisfactory RP screen, RP is more desirable for stage use if there is back stage space for the projector(s) at proper throw distance. This is because RP is usually more efficient than front projection and also because actors can play near the front of the RP screen without casting their shadows into the image. However it is still necessary to protect the image from spill light.

Settings As Projection Surfaces

In many cases the designer will plan to use parts of the setting as projection surfaces. (Figures 16.4A and 16.4B) Naturally, the more reflective these are, the better. Since most scene paints dry to diffuse surfaces, they are useful, but low in gain, if the pigments are light enough in color to reflect adequate light. The rules governing the effect of colored light on colored objects will prevail making the effect of the projection dependent on the color of the surface.

Fabrics, either as costumes or as parts of settings or as a sky drop or cyclorama, can also serve as projection surfaces if they are not dark and heavily absorbent. Dark velours, for example, are almost totally non-reflective. Obviously the shape of the set pieces or costumes will determine the way the audience sees the projections. This is a matter to be controlled by the designer who should be able to exercise total control over setting, lighting and costumes for this purpose.

Cycloramas and sky drops provide reasonably good projection surfaces, however age and soil tend to reduce their efficiency. Cycs, in particular, present a problem in both coverage and distortion control. The sheer size of the cyclorama and limits on backstage space almost always rule out rear projection. Front projection will be the only choice and it must deal with the "U" shape of the cyc. This is not a problem for projection of clouds or completely abstract images but rectilinear images will be severely distorted. The grid and photographic methods for correction can be effective but a special problem will be encountered: Covering a full-stage cyclorama with front-projection will almost always take at least two projectors angled from the tormentor positions toward the opposite upstage corners of the cyclorama. This means that the two images will have to lap at the upstage center of the cyc—the most conspicuous part of the image. One possible solution will be for the designer to create slides that avoid linear elements in this area and to plan for the images to overlap and blur somewhat. If a really sharp image is needed stage center, it is best to go to a three-projector setup with the third projector operating on the center line of the stage.

It is instructive to note that many European stages use flat panels of cyclorama material instead of a continuous curved cyc. Distortion is easier to control and the gaps between the panels provide otherwise impossible upstage entrances. The designer must take the corners formed where the panels meet into consideration when slides are being designed.

Chapter 17

LASERS AND HOLOGRAMS

Effects Yet to Be

This chapter deals with the future—with technology not yet ready for routine theatrical use, particularly on the dramatic stage. It deals with the fascinating, spectacular, and sometimes very dangerous light produced by lasers. Although lasers have been used in the theatre, particularly in spectacles and dance productions and have become commonplace in the concert world, they are almost unknown to the legitimate theatre. The reasons are several:

- The effects presently available are seldom subtle.
- Lasers can be dangerous. Therefore specially trained operators are needed. Under some circumstances, these people must be licensed.
- Many of the effects depend on the stage lighting being dimmed to a low reading and the air filled with mist or fog.
- Laser equipment is expensive.
- Legitimate theatre artists and technicians have had little experience with laser applications and have little knowledge of their artistic potentialities.

Lasers produce a special kind of light. This is obvious the moment one observes the special granular quality of a pool of laser light. Scientists call this coherent light. Although its complete scientific explanation is far too complicated for this text, a general description of its characteristics will be useful. We resort to the wave theory of light for our explanation:

> The light emitted from an ordinary incandescent or HID source consists of waves vibrating randomly in all planes. Wave lengths of ordinary light also vary and may include every wavelength visible to the eye. Light from a laser is quite different—it is much more orderly. All of the waves vibrate in the same plane, are in

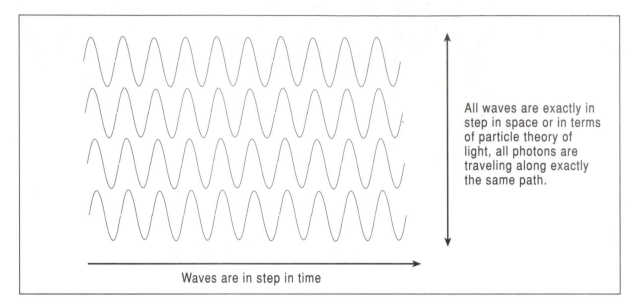

All waves are exactly in step in space or in terms of particle theory of light, all photons are traveling along exactly the same path.

Waves are in step in time

Figure 17.1. Laser Light. This light is termed *coherent*, i.e., the waves are all of the same wavelength—the same color if visible. The waves are exactly in step in time and space, and the beam is almost completely collimated, diverging only very slightly from parallel. This results in the concentration of the energy of the beam into a very small space, a characteristic which makes laser beams both potentially dangerous and very useful.

phase, i.e., in step (Figure 17.1). Note that it is quite possible to have a single laser produce several bands of differing wavelengths at the same time. However each band will be made up entirely of waves of the same length moving in the same plane.

Coherent light is produced in lasers by a very complicated process involving quantum mechanics which results in photons being reflected back and forth inside of the laser tube, gaining more and more photons of their kind as they move. The energy is supplied by a source outside of the tube such as a powerful strobe light or electromagnetic radiation. Ultimately the photons exit from one end of the tube as a tiny but very powerful beam of coherent light. Although this beam is not precisely parallel, it approaches that state and can be brought even closer by optical means.

Incredible amounts of energy can be packed into a laser beam. This makes lasers both dangerous and highly useful. Powerful lasers are used for cutting and welding, for surgery, and have been used in experiments seeking to initiate nuclear fusion. Smaller lasers are used for such applications as stage effects, surveying, "readers" for bar codes in markets and making and reading compact disks.

Dangers from Lasers

Although large lasers can cut and burn, the greatest danger from laser light as used on stage is to the eyes. The power in a laser beam is already concentrated into a very small area and this energy will be further concentrated by the focusing power of the lens in the eye. The result is a tiny, extremely intense point of light that can burn and destroy parts of the retina. Such damage causes a permanent blind spot where the retina was injured.

Because of this danger, OSHA and also the safety authorities of many other countries have developed strict laws governing the use of lasers that apply whenever the laser is powerful enough to be harmful. *These must be followed.* In general, they require that the laser be so arranged and used that it is impossible for anyone's eyes to get in the way of the beam. If the laser is dispersed for effect, as it often is in stage use, the dispersed beam must meet strict standards limiting its power to well below the danger point. Inspections are made using special meters that measure the energy that might enter an observer's eyes.

Even lasers effects that operate well below the danger level can be dangerous on stage. If the dispersed beam strikes an actor or dancer in the eyes, it may form a temporary afterimage that will prevent the person from seeing well for several minutes. This could cause a fall and/or may prevent the actor or dancer from continuing the action of the scene.

Theatrical Applications of Lasers

The spectacular quality of laser light makes it most adaptable to pop concerts, outdoor extravaganzas, light shows, and other events where attention-getting effects, not subtlety, are intended. The powerful effects that can be created by lasers are easily capable of upstaging all but the most commanding arrangements of actors, singers or dancers.

Spectacles

Using the Beams Directly

Like all other light traveling through space or clean air, a laser beam is practically invisible except for the spot where it strikes a surface. If smoke or mist is added to the air, the beam suddenly becomes luminescent creating a line of intensely brilliant light which can cut through almost any other effect on stage. Such beams are often used out doors on hazy or slightly foggy nights to create spectacular effects in the sky. Inside, with the air filled with haze or smoke, these beams can create spectacular effects such as causing the beam to appear to "explode" an object struck by it. This is accomplished by timing the moment the beam strikes the object with the explosion of a flash pot at the point where it hits. (Ironically, a very powerful laser—much too dangerous for stage use—might really cause such an explosion without the need for any theatrical trickery.) Even at stage power, the laser will need to be controlled by a computer that checks the be sure that all performers on the stage are in the exact positions they have been assigned and that all parts of the setting are exactly in position. If anything is out of order, the computer keeps the laser and the flash pot from firing.

Scanning Laser Beams

Since a laser beam has no mass and moves with the speed of light, it can be moved about much faster than the eye can follow. Therefore a dot of rapidly moving laser light will be seen by the eye as a luminous line. If this line is retraced often enough, persistence of vision will cause it to appear

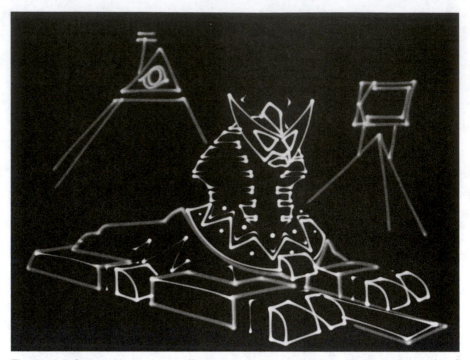

Figure 17.2. Scanned Laser Image. These images are produced by a laser beam moving so rapidly that the visual persistence of the eye makes its path seem to be a luminous line. From Laser Graphics and Animations - a permanent laser show at the Lotte World Theme Park, Seoul, Korea. Courtesy Laser Media Inc. See also Plate VII.

Scanners

as a steady line of light. The process of moving a laser beam to produce such a line of light is known as "scanning" and the device which does this is a "scanner." It consists of a very lightweight mirror which is moved by electromagnetic means, much in the manner of the voice coil of a loudspeaker, to direct the beam as needed. Indeed, early experimenters with scanning actually fastened bits of mirror to the voice coils of loudspeakers to make a moving mirror that would scan in synchronization with music. Since the mirror in a modern scanner can move with great rapidity and accuracy, it is possible to direct a scanner with a computer to "draw" images in laser light.

Scanners controlled by computers can produce wide variety of images useful for spectacles and advertising (Figure 17.2. Powerful lasers can produce these images in brightness capable of cutting through almost any lighting situation. Computer programs are written to direct one or more scanners to create images of considerable detail and in a number of colors. Since the essential information for the effect is stored in computer language, these effects are portable. They can be moved from place to place provided the computer can handle the data and the setup of lasers and scanners is the same as the original. A number of such programs are commercially available.

Generally these computer-drawn images lack subtlety and are only minimally detailed. They are mostly useful in spectacles and as advertising devices. However further refinement of the technique seems likely to provide the dramatic theatre with yet another way of producing images in light.

Interference Patterns

Interference is the phenomenon that takes place when two waves of the same type of wave motion intersect causing the peaks and valleys to either add together or to cancel depending on their relationship to each other. The wave motion can be waves generated in a pond of water, sound waves or, our present topic, light waves.

Reinforcement and cancelation

The effect is that in the space where the overlapping occurs there will be places where the two waves reinforce each other producing amplitude equal to the sum of the two waves (reinforcement) and other places where the waves cancel each other out producing areas of amplitude equal to the difference in the strength of the intersecting waves. Total cancellation is occurs if the two waves are of equal amplitude. Note, however that the energy represented by the wave motion is not destroyed by cancellation, but passes through the interference area and on in the direction of the original waves.

Interference of light waves occurs whenever two waves intersect but produces visible effects only when the waves are of the same wave length and there are no other wavelengths present to mask the effect. When this is the case, an interference pattern will be seen that consists of areas of darkness and areas of light brighter than either of the original waves. The "image" formed by these patterns may be as simple as bars or concentric circles of light and dark or may appear as complex patterns sometimes resembling abstract art.

Unlike images formed by lenses, the interference patterns are in focus at any distance although the pattern of the image varies constantly with distance.

The usual method of producing interference patterns for theatrical use is to pass a dispersed beam of laser light through an irregular piece of glass or plastic that will break the beam into myriad rays which travel on slightly different paths, in effect breaking up the inphase nature of the light. Since these rays are out of phase in varying amounts depending on the optical nature of the mottled glass, they will interfere with each other producing patterns throughout the path of the light. The result is spectacular patterns in light the color of the laser which can be directed onto any surface at any distance (up to the point where the light is dispersed into uselessness). Although at every distance the patterns will be somewhat different, they will seem related and can easily acquire artistic import when inserted into a theatrical situation. It is quite possible to add synchronized movement and change to the patterns by including an electromagnetic means of vibrating the dispersing glass.

Abstract patterns of light

Despite the fact that these patterns are, for all practical purposes, random they are so theatrically stunning that they have often been used as projections for dance productions (Plate VII). In fact, this was one of the earliest applications of lasers to the stage, coming long before means were developed to scan laser beams to form images.

It is practically impossible to create the same interference patterns twice because any change in the distance or angle between the beam and the dispersing glass that exceeds a tiny part of the wavelength of the laser light is enough to alter the image.

Although interference patterns are striking, they are rather dim. The laser light is dispersed over a wide area and some of it lost in the glass. This makes the light safe to use on stage with actors or dancers, but requires that the stage lighting be quite dim. Of course, a more powerful laser will make brighter patterns but this may be dangerous and expensive. *Extreme care must be taken to prevent any possibility of the undisbursed laser beam reaching the stage and possibly striking the eyes of the performers.*

Holography

This is a process by which three-dimensional images of objects can be created in space. These images have the property of changing perspective as the eye of the observer moves, just as moving around a real 3-D object will bring different parts of it into view. The key part of the holographic display is a *hologram*, a piece of photographic film which records interference patterns instead of images formed by a lens.

Coherent light from a laser is necessary to the process of exposing the film which, once exposed, is developed much the same as regular photographic film. Some holograms must also be displayed using coherent light, others can produce images using white light from a point source.

The basic principle of a hologram is that it is a record of interference patterns generated when light coming directly from a laser source is made to interfere with light from the same laser that has been reflected from the object being recorded. This is accomplished by splitting the laser beam into two parts, one of which travels directly to the film. The other part of the beam is used to illuminate the object which is so placed that part of the light reflected from it will also strike the film. When properly exposed and developed, the film becomes a hologram.

Unlike photographic film, the hologram film displays nothing visible to the eye, only a mottled "foggy" blur. However when coherent light (or even white light from a "point" source) illuminates the hologram at the proper angle, an image of the original object appears either reflected from the surface of the hologram or in the light passing through it. This image is three-dimensional and, within limits, changes as the observer moves showing depth just as would a real object. The effect can be so striking that the observer may wish to reach "into" the image and try to grasp the object to be convinced that the object is not really there.

Although holography has progressed considerably in the past few years, it is still not regularly capable of producing stage-size images. Neither is it possible to display a hologram with consistency over a wide audience viewing angle. Thus holography has not yet found a place in the legitimate theatre although it has been used to produce some film effects and has become sufficiently advanced to generate artists' displays of holograms exhibited not for their novelty, but for their artistic import.

Holographically Produced Effects Filters

Diffraction is a process by which light is bent in proportion to its wave length by causing the beam to pass very close to an edge. If a large number of "edges" are created by ruling many lines per inch on a piece of glass a "grating" is created that can produce a spectrum by diffraction. Such gratings have existed for many years in physics and optical laboratories where they are used in spectroscopes. Recently holographic techniques have made it possible to produce gratings very economically. Pieces of plastic with gratings reproduced on them are available as effects devices.

Diffraction gratings

For Experimenters

All of the above techniques and devices invite careful experimentation to devise new ways to adapt these devices to the theatre. Some, for example powerful lasers, are dangerous and must be handled only by those who are trained in their safe use, but many are benign. They represent a challenge to student designers and technologists.

18

LIGHTING DESIGN IN THE CRITICAL REVIEW

A critical review, whether for a dramatic production or another form such as musical comedy, should be based on standards cited by the reviewer and shown to be relevant to the production at hand. Normally, if the subject is a dramatic production, the basis for relevance of the standards is found in the script. In other theatrical forms the basis for the standards may be found in style, in comparison with other similar productions or even in tradition.

Most reviewers choose to include the visual production in their reviews, although this is not always necessary. When they do, they may find themselves in a realm where they have little competence. Retreating into such glib comments as. "The lighting added brilliance to the production," does nothing to enhance the review and may even reduce its credibility. Therefore the following general criteria for dramatic and spectacle lighting are offered to give the would-be critical reviewer some basis for developing specific standards.

A good choice of standards for evaluating the lighting will be rooted in the reviewer's analysis of the production as a whole and therefore should interrelate with the reviewer's evaluation of such things as the interpretation of the script, the clarity of the artistic import, or the consistency of its style.

Although the following criteria are listed in their most likely order of importance, another order may sometimes be appropriate. However, ignoring any of them should only be done after very careful consideration.

Criteria for Lighting Dramatic Productions

- *Plasticity*. Actors' faces should be lit in a way that makes it easy for the audience to read their expressions and thus perceive the characterization they are developing. Acting, directing, and lighting form a trilogy that develops plot and characters and communicates them to the audience.

Plasticity can be a powerful interpretive element; a designer can manipulate key/fill ratios, angles of key light, ratio of facial lighting to the background, and color to make a major contribution to the development of character and/or to build a scene. Clearly, this must be done in harmony with the work of the actor(s) and the director.

- *Focus.* The lighting should assist in guiding the audience' attention toward the focal point of the action. The audience' focus on a scene is a function of the blocking, usually controlled by the director; the arrangement of the setting; the costumes, particularly their color; and in a major way by the lighting, without which none of the other factors can function. Control of focus by lighting involves subtly changing the focal point (the brightest area) in coordination with the director's changes in the blocking. Multiple focal points created by the director call for multiple foci in the lighting. Another approach involves the lighting designer, in cooperation with the director, creating a variety of focal points on the stage into which the director moves the actors as needed. These may be subtly increased in brightness when they are in use and dimmed back into the overall lighting when empty. The degree of importance of the various focal points should be clearly established through brightness and contrast and carefully altered as the dramatic action shifts.

Control of focus is most effective when timing of cues is so synchronized with the movements of the actors that the light seems "attached" to them making the cues imperceptible to the audience unless there is good dramatic reason for them to be obvious.

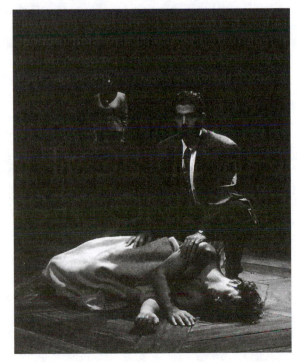

Figure 18.1. *Equus.* Final scene after reenactment of blinding the horses with the spike. This is an example of good modeling lighting applied to a scene that depends heavily on audience perception of facial expression. Produced at Constans Theatre, University of Florida, Gainsville. Director, Dr. Judith Williams; scene design, William Jacobsen; costumes, Pamela Crevcoure; lighting, Ellen Jones. Photo courtesy Ellen Jones.

- *Rhythm.* A well-written, well-staged production will have a very definite rhythmical pattern, primarily controlled by the writing and the directing. Good dramatic lighting should supplement that rhythm. Therefore the pacing of cues should parallel the pacing of the action. Rhythm and degree of change in the lighting should normally harmonize with the dramatic action, making a powerful contribution to the rhythm of the production.
- *Atmosphere.* Good dramatic lighting adds to the development of an environment for the action that has unity and relevance to the dramatic import of the production. Atmosphere is the result of careful manipulation of light and shade, color, and intensity in such a way that these harmonize with the other elements of visual production such as setting, costume and makeup design. Moreover, the total atmosphere should appear to emanate from the style and import of the script as interpreted by the director.

Criteria for Spectacles

Spectacles range in type from plotless pageants, light shows, revues, and concerts to musical productions. Instead of emphasizing plot or dramatic import, spectacles seek to dazzle and impress by presenting a rich assortment of stimuli designed to please the eye and the ear.

Unity in spectacles derives, not from a central core of dramatic import, but from style. This is often imposed on the material by the producer, the director and/or designers and may be subject to major changes as the production is developed. Indeed, such forms as revues, often have interchangeable parts ("numbers") which can be rearranged, added or deleted, altering but not destroying the unity of the whole.

The following criteria are suggested for reviewing lighting of spectacles, unlike those for dramatic productions, these criteria have no particular order. Any combination of them may be relevant to the production at hand:

- *Focus.* The stage picture in a spectacle should never be more than momentarily without a focal point. Creation of focus is a function of the blocking or choreography, the costumes, particularly their color, the setting, and, most powerfully, the lighting.

    In some cases the focal point may be quite arbitrary, in others it naturally evolves from the presence of a soloist or lead dancer, or from the "plot" of the number being performed. Whatever its motivation, a focus must be established by the various means available and particularly the lighting. Almost always, this focus will be the brightest lighted area on the stage.

    The simplest, and often the most effective way of creating focus with lighting is the high powered follow spotlight or "light cannon." This overriding source not only creates a focal point by providing a brilliant pool of light wherever it

Figure 18.2. *Nicholas Nickleby*. See also Figure 1.1. This drama depends heavily interaction between sets of characters. Note how the lighting is arranged to make varying degrees of emphasis on the people surrounding the central figure easy to adjust. Scene lit by Cindy Limauro.

Carnegie Mellon Kresge Theatre; directors, Gregory Lehane and Jed Allen Harris; set design, Tony Mileto; costume design, Cletus Anderson; lighting design, Lauren Crasco (Part I) and Cindy Limauro (Part II). Photo by Harold Corsini, courtesy Cindy Limauro.

Figure 18.3. *Hamlet* (Gertrude's chamber just after stabbing of Polonius). Staged at Stephen Foster Memorial Theatre, Pittsburgh. Director, Stephan Coleman; lighting, Ellen Jones. Photo courtesy Ellen Jones.

is directed but also may create a visible beam of light extending from the luminaire to the stage to serve as a "pointer" directing the audience' attention. Obviously, it lacks subtlety but subtlety is not the name of the game in spectacles.

- *Plasticity.* Although the faces of the individual actors may not be at the center of the theatrical significance of the scene, flat, poorly delineated faces and figures are uninteresting. Key/fill ratios must be great enough to emphasize the shapes of the actors (and also the scenery when it is also three dimensional).

- *Color rendering*. Color of set and costumes is often one of the major attractions of a spectacle. Lighting colors should be carefully chosen to heighten these colors and add to the total color scheme. Additionally, it is quite possible that the lighting will itself provide bright patches of color or even sweeping changes in color (see below.)
- *Lighting as spectacle*. Unlike the dramatic style where lighting is a dependent art beholden to the acting and directing, "spectacle" may include "light shows" wherein lighting itself is the center of attention. A complete technology has developed around this concept in the pop concert and *son et lumiere* world. Moving luminaires casting beams through haze-filled air have become a standard technique which is often supplemented by such attention-grabbing elements as vivid scenic projection, strobe lights, laser effects and even fireworks.

  When the style is "light show," all pretence of subtlety vanishes and the designer moves into a world of fantasy, masses of color, banks of moving lights, stages filled with haze or smoke to accent light beams and cues that follow one another to the beat of the drum. If the performers or musicians are intended to be at the focus of the scene, powerful follow spotlights, often in multiples, may be needed to center attention on them.

Obviously, the theatrical intent of the production as determined by the reviewer forms the starting point of a critical review. From that, the reviewer moves toward consideration of the production's dramatic intent, if it is a dramatic production, or towards its style if it is a spectacle. This often requires some development of plot and characterization and may include comparison with other productions of the same work or with similar works. Through this process the reviewer develops his or her standards for reviewing the production, supporting their appropriateness by reference to the dramatic import of the drama or by citing the style evident in the spectacle. Application of these standards, usually supported by examples, rounds out the review. Lighting may well be one of the production elements evaluated in such a review.

The author of a critical review of a production which includes an evaluation of the lighting may take satisfaction in the probability that the lighting designer is as apt to read the review as are the actors or the director. Recognition of the art of lighting, even if qualified, can have a significant effect on the future work of the designer who usually suffers more from lack of recognition than lack of praise. In particular, a knowledgeable critique of the lighting can make a contribution to the artistic growth of a lighting designer, not only through recognition but may also encourage that person to develop his or her creative abilities, to dare to reach for the freedom to dream, to entertain the artistically impossible.

Figure 18.4. Dance. Group Motion Dance Company, Philadelphia. Note the use of highly directional light to emphasize the dancers figures. Lighting by Richard Devin. Photo Richard Devin.

Figure 18.5. *Richard II* (Shakespeare). Staged at the Colorado Shakespeare Festival. Director, James Symons; scenery, David Barber; costumes, Jannice Benning; lighting Richard Devin. Photo Richard Devin.

Figure 18.6. *Orestes* (entrance of Menelaus after the sacking of Troy). Staged at the Constans Theatre, University of Florida, Gainsville. Director, Mickel Pinckney; scene design, William Jacobsen; costume, Tim Dial; lighting, Ellen Jones. Photo courtesy Ellen Jones.

INDEX

St. Louis Community College
at Meramec
LIBRARY